Aspects of Playwork

Play and Culture Studies

Edited by Fraser Brown and Bob Hughes
Introduction by Bob Hughes
Foreword by Jim Johnson

HAMILTON BOOKS
an imprint of
ROWMAN & LITTLEFIELD
Lanham • Boulder • New York • London

4501 Forbes Boulevard
Suite 200
Lanham, Maryland 20706
Hamilton Acquisitions Department (301) 459-3366

Unit A, Whitacre Mews, 26-34 Stannary Street,
London SE11 4AB, United Kingdom

Printed in the United States of America
British Library Cataloging in Publication Information Available

Library of Congress Control Number: 2018951183

ISBN: 978-0-7618-7060-9 (pbk : alk paper)
ISBN: 978-0-7618-7061-6 (electronic)

∞™ The paper used in this publication meets the minimum requirements of American National Standard for Information Sciences—Permanence of Paper for Printed Library Materials, ANSI/NISO Z39.48-1992.

Printed in the United States of America

This book is dedicated to the memory of Stuart Lester,
a great playworker. 1951–2017

All royalties from this book go to UNICEF

Contents

List of Tables and Figures

TABLES

FIGURES

Foreword

Jim Johnson

Devoting this fourteenth volume of the *Play & Culture Studies* to Playwork is timely given this field's increasing presence and value in countless practical settings of a growing number of countries (including recently the USA, e.g., Imagination Playground in New York City), and because of the significance of this specialization within play studies. The term Playwork was coined in the 1970s as an alternative to other labels such as "play leadership" from the late nineteenth century, hoping to distance itself from adult-centric connotations of such designations for their field. Playwork puts in sharp relief the role of the adult in children's play, both in theory and in practice.

Playwork is about space, time, energy, objects, children and adults and other ingredients (i.e., there are indeed many aspects of playwork as the title of this book announces); these are coming together always in new and unique ways, and always in a way that is saying, most assuredly, that *this* play and *this* play setting is to be taken seriously.

Playing is perhaps the most important way one has, starting as a baby, to saying YES to freedom, and to being who one is (think of the satiated baby's tongue playing with mom's tit, beginning to get a glimmer of self and agency). In play one wants time and space (as one is experiencing it in a particular situation at a given moment) NOT to be bothered by being directed by another. So what responsibilities do we as adults have with respect to the play of children?

So many of us have wrong answers to this question. We have been accused, probably rightfully so, that we are rearing a "nation of wimps," that we have turned childhood into a project of "concerted cultivation," with our kids not allowed to be and grow naturally, instead to be over-scheduled and hyper-parented. All too often child-initiated play is altered or squelched by grownups. In a very real sense, then, Playwork is for these adults as much as playwork is for children. We need to try to learn more how to think and act like playworkers performing their craft, doing their thing as they say to the children, "shall we go."

As series editor it is my pleasure to write this brief foreword to *Aspects of Playwork,* a book that is an excellent addition to The Association for the Study of Play's *Play & Culture Studies* series. I urge you to accept the invitation that these chapters provide for becoming more educated about playwork's many splendored things, gaining the insights and the knowledge contained herein; an intellectual treat awaits. Enjoy, suck it up, but please don't bite.

Acknowledgments

The editors would like to place on record their thanks to all the contributors to this volume.

Bob would like to say thank you to Annie, and Fraser would like to say thank you to Anne. It takes great patience to be the partner of someone who is trying to produce a book.

Introduction

Bob Hughes

This book is about different aspects of playwork or, to be more specific, it is about different aspects of playwork practice and the thinking and ideas that practice generates and which generate practice. For like play itself, playwork is not a fixed point.

It can be partially defined, I have done it in the past, but like play, any attempt to gather up its infinite manifestations, renders the product, the definition, sterile and unsatisfying. That all children play, or would if they could, is undoubtedly true. Although observation and description of what any one child does when playing—capturing, recording and analysing the myriad interactions—is highly problematic; the principal difficulty being the sheer speed of action. And we all know, as players or ex-players, that what is happening in the child's imagination, in its head, perhaps manifested in fine motor movements of fingers and eyes, is even more profoundly complex.

So, whilst some of what is printed here is complete and informative practice, some other offerings are reflective of playwork's enormous and multifaceted nature and its impact on space and time, while others again are just beginning what might be a long journey, as works in progress. Rough guides rather than complete maps.

What is so wonderful, is that because of this diversity of approaches to writing, *Aspects*, which is what it is bound to be labelled by supporters and critics alike, does reflect our current understanding of play and the position of play in the evolution of playwork.

I will not attempt to summarize here what the following chapters contain, their various approaches, perceptions and angles—I could not even if I wanted to—because play pervades every sentence, influences every paragraph and colours every word chosen, and like an observed electron, how each chapter's content is apprehended, is highly dependent on the individual journey and appreciation of the reader. It is all a matter of perception, so I leave it for you to decide. Better perhaps that you come on our journey by reading from chapter to chapter, and then, like any other fantastical story, see how you feel about each distinct narrative and the road travelled.

Although I have tried many times, for me, play continues to defy description: perhaps encapsulation is a better term, because like all complex processes, there is always another layer waiting to reveal itself. You can only imagine both the awe and the fear experienced by the early playwork pioneer writers when they came to that realisation.

And because of our inability to "nail" play itself, playwork suffers much the same fate. It is unique and ubiquitous, complex and simple and mysterious and obvious. It is the subtle application of values whose genesis, evolution and manifestations, can only be viewed and understood by observing children playing and recalling your own. As play reveals itself, often only briefly, as a realm, more intuited than inhabited, more dreamed than actualised.

Playwork, like the play it supports, is an applied forecaster, an extrapolator, a reader of trajectories. It attempts to isolate the cypher that enables the two-way communication between the child and the Cosmos that bore it, and so facilitate a playful "*conversation*" between the child and the playworker—at once a negotiation, a dialectic, and an acknowledgement.

Above all though, Aspects is a collection of pieces by people who have been there and done it; who in most cases still are practicing playworkers. However it may seem, what is in the following Chapters is a genuine reflection of what working with children in play situations makes you do, think, reflect on and wonder. To be a playworker, engaged in all aspects of playwork is a truly powerful and humbling experience and one that informs every chapter of *Aspects of Playwork*.

Chapter One

Three Reflective Tools for Playwork Practice

Sarah Wilson

Playwork, unlike some other practices of working with children and young people, asks practitioners to bring a lot of themselves to their work. There is no rigid code of practice; instead the Playwork Principles (PPSG 2005) outline the ethos for the work without being specific about how this work is done. Playwork practice draws on the playworker's knowledge of subtle habits, meanings, cues and ways of being that are situated deeply in a particular space at a particular time (Lester et al., 2013). The purpose of this chapter is to highlight some of the forms this "situated" knowledge may take by pausing to reflect on the importance of stories, sounds and an understanding of how emotions may relate to the physical environment. Any interventions made by playworkers will be based on their situated knowledge. Playworkers often get the sense that they are working things out as they go. The playworkers' and the children and young people's expectations of the possibilities within the playwork setting are always in the process of being shaped by what happens and what the responses of the children, young people and playworkers are.

Reflective practice is central to the playworker's ability to recognise and begin to read some of the complexities within the play space. Playworkers reflect on children's play to try to deepen their understanding; they reflect on themselves, their reasons for being a playworker and what they find challenging. They also reflect on particular incidents, moments, children and dynamics in an attempt to challenge assumptions and come at things from different perspectives: reflections are sometimes made alone and sometimes with colleagues.

This chapter is primarily about three playwork tools that may be used to capture something of what goes on within play sessions, in order to support reflection. Each of the tools has proponents in other fields and I will touch on some of their work in order to highlight why and in what ways they might be useful in playwork. We cannot hope to truly represent or know all of the complexities of play spaces. Lorimer (2005) highlighted the need for research to be more than representational and to aim to "make sense of the ecologies of place created by action and processes, rather than the place portrayed by the end product." (Lorimer, 2005: 85) With each of the tools highlighted in this chapter their value is in the reflective process they spark, not in the gathered material itself. This material could never capture all of the complexities which collide and play out within the play space, but reflection on what has been captured may highlight aspects of that which may have been overlooked.

TOOL ONE: STORY TELLING

Every playworker tells stories on a daily basis. How often have you or a colleague said something like, "Did you see what Khadeja did with that bucket of sand?" Story telling is much more crucial to our practice than one might realise. I do not mean observations that claim to give an objective truth about what happened when I say telling stories. Rather we need to recognise that any story we tell is always told from our own perspective. In the telling of the story we share all sorts of information about how we feel, what judgements we made and how we responded. Focusing only on looking for "what I could have done better" restricts what more could be said (Lester et al., 2013).

Here is a story from the playground I currently work on:

> It was a cold and dark Autumn evening. We had a fire burning outside. There was a group of children in, who knew each other well and went to the same school. They were playing a zombie hunting game where one of them was the zombie. They ran around the outside space and through the building. The boy who was the zombie stopped off to pick up items of fancy dress each time he passed through the building, creating a terrifying costume piece by piece. He had a big fur coat and a hat. He used face paints to paint blood on his face. He stayed in character the whole time. Some younger children came in and wanted to play but were scared of the zombie. The zombie let out the secret that he was scared of shiny things. We made sure those who were feeling scared had a shiny thing to protect them and sure enough the zombie ran away from them. It didn't take long before one of the children found the ultimate weapon against the zombie; glitter. They picked up a pot, ran outside and threw some over him. The zombie ran into the building and picked up the other pot, ran to the fire and poured all of it into the flames, disposing of the weapon.

Some interesting points of reflection about children's play can be drawn out from this story. For example, how play makes use of the resources available. Not just the dressing up clothes, the face paint, the glitter and the fire but also the darkness of the night in creating a scary scenario. There is something in this story about how play can change, evolve and shift to include new objects and new people. In terms of what this story might have to say about playwork, we could reflect on the importance of resourcing spaces with wide varieties of easily accessible things.

You can tell from this story what role I had in the narrative. Firstly I witnessed what was happening. I also helped to find shiny items for younger children. But neither I nor the other playworker on site stopped the children from taking the glitter outside where it was thrown and burnt. Some might say that the glitter had been wasted. The telling of the story has drawn out a potential area of tension between preserving and maintaining resources and their sometimes unusual uses required by children's play. The tension offered an interesting point of discussion for our staff team and meant that we were able to come to a shared understanding of the importance of waiting for scenarios to unfold. It is in the telling of stories such as this that we come to understand what it means to be a playworker within the day to day interactions of play spaces. It is in these moments that the ethos set out in the Playwork Principles (PSGG 2005) is given form, shape and colour. The fourth point in the Playwork Principles, for example, states that for the Playworker the play process takes precedence, and here that process was given precedence over what might be considered the "proper" use of resources.

It has been said that playwork *is* a network of everyday stories (Lester et al., 2013). What constitutes playwork practice is constructed on a daily basis by our role in interactions and by our telling and retelling of stories. Play spaces are constructed by the interactions that take place in them and the stories that are told. Armitage (2005) collected stories while researching about how physical features supported particular types of play in school playgrounds. He spoke to former pupils of one primary school and discovered that a particular black guttering down-pipe had been used by children to play the same game for nearly 80 years (a familiar game that is a mixture of "hide and seek" and "tag"). The game was passed down through its practice and the stories that were told about it. The stories that are told about spaces go on to shape how those spaces are used.

Massey (2005) argued that space consists of many different trajectories, or stories-so-far that have both a past and a future. There is not just the story of the play that is happening right now, but of all of the elements in that play that are on their own trajectories with their own stories-so-far. The interaction and negotiation of these different trajectories adds to the stories-in-the-making.

For playworkers the sharing of stories becomes an opportunity to explore the possibilities of the play space and their role within it. Some stories become legendary—this one is about the zip-line:

> One evening a boy decided he was going to make a zip-line. He found a long rope and tied one end to the top of one of the wooden structures. He slid on a short length of plastic pipe and then secured the other end to the ground. After thoroughly testing his knots and working out a way to get the plastic pipe to the top, he gathered the courage, went to the top of the structure, took hold of the black pipe and tried it out. It worked, but it was very slow. With the support of staff he found a way to increase the tension of the rope. He tried again and this time it was faster. Everyone else in the playground had stopped what they were doing to watch him. He was the only person brave enough to go on the zip-line, although a couple of others climbed the structure to try before changing their minds. The zip-line stayed up for about a week before staff decided that it had to be taken down in anticipation of the busy school holidays where there would be more young children and it might become a safety hazard.

The story of the zip-line is retold regularly, and different children have been trying to rebuild zip-lines ever since. This is not just a story of something that happened in the past. It is alive and well and being played out within the perceived possibilities of the play space. The sharing of the story helps those hearing it to read the space, but it also shapes and creates it at the same time. Like all legends the story itself evolves over time with exaggerated accounts of the speed and safety of the zip-line, all of which feed into the perceived possibilities of the space.

TOOL TWO: SOUND RECORDING

In the past we have used video recording in play settings to capture something of what happens in order to support reflection, but recently I have been experimenting with sound recordings. In playwork we rely heavily on different aspects of sound, whether consciously or not. We pick up on the subtle tones that suggest someone is playing and we sense changes in the atmosphere of the play space through changes in what we are hearing, as well as seeing. However, when thinking about our settings we often focus disproportionately on how they look. Because of this unintentional bias sound recording offers a different opportunity for reflection than does video recording.

It is important to remember that before making either video or sound recordings playworkers should seek permission from their organisation and refer to any policies and procedures they have about recording and storing data. At this playground our registration forms state that we sometimes make recordings for the purpose of training and professional development, so provided what has been captured is not made public, no further permissions are required. There are also ethical issues to take into account. One major issue is the question of if, when and how you introduce the children to the recording device and how you explain the purpose of the recordings. Undoubtedly informing the children will have an impact on what is captured. Recording is intrusive in a setting that children may consider to be their space. Before undertaking any recording one must give this issue serious consideration. When I was making sound recordings it was decided that the children need not be informed since the recordings were not going to be made public. If we were to make further recordings I would revisit this depending on the purpose for making them and what they were going to be used for. For regardless of whether the children have been explicitly informed or not, it is important to think carefully about respecting their privacy. To make this easier, I put the recording device on my belt rather than in a static location to make sure that those being recorded were aware that I might be able to hear their conversations and so were unlikely to say anything they would not be happy to be repeated. Many children and most young people carry recording devices on their mobile phones and there is an assumption that there are CCTV recording devices covering large areas of towns and cities (including some schools). Although these factors have positive as well as negative potential, they do form the background to children and young people's views about being recorded. It is also important to find out how colleagues feel about being recorded, and one should work together with one's organisation to come up with an arrangement that everyone is happy with. One crucial tip is to put the recording device in bubble wrap before putting it into your pocket or onto your belt, as it reduces the sound of walking.

Sound recordings have gained increased attention from researchers in the field of human geography. This is because this technique "is particularly useful for highlighting hidden or marginal aspects of places and their inhabitants." (Gallagher and Prior, 2014: 268) This is certainly what I found as I listened to what I had recorded, but it is important to also listen beyond what is said to hear the "affective, precognitive, ephemeral aspects" (Gallagher and Prior, 2014: 271). Sound is deeply involved in the construction of environments. According to the Playwork Principles (PPSG, 2005) playworkers are involved in supporting children and young people in the creation of a space in which they can play, and sound is an often overlooked element of this space.

Listening back to sound recordings offers the opportunity to reflect on aspects that may otherwise be overlooked. Aspects of our practice, like our tone of voice, playful or not-so-playful responses, how we interacted with colleagues and how we dealt with particular moments or situations, can be scrutinised. Having the opportunity to listen back through play sessions enables playworkers to draw on their memories and feelings whilst listening. Being one step removed from the situation allows them to look more closely at the way the play may have affected them, although at times that may feel uncomfortable. From replaying some recordings I made, and reflecting on moments that made me feel uncomfortable, I have made an effort to change some of the ways I work. However, as with storytelling, if we limit ourselves only to reflections about "what I could have done better" there will be so much more we do not hear.

In listening back to what was said by the children I also heard themes being picked up and dropped throughout play sessions. For example, at the time of one recording some of the children had been reporting sightings of a ghost on the playground and some had organised themselves into a team of ghost hunters. The sound recordings captured different children re-establishing this play frame (Sturrock and Else, 1998) in different ways and at different times. Thinking about Sturrock and Else's (1998) play cycle; the cues, responses, frames, flows and annihilations, has been very useful to me as a practitioner in building an understanding of how particular incidents of play start, are maintained, might evolve or finish. However, as a playworker, especially during busy times on a setting, you do not always get the opportunity to observe particular playful incidents as they unfold. Instead what the playworker experiences might be shifting snap-shots of many different moments of playfulness as they traverse the space. They are likely to maintain some level of an overview of the atmosphere of the space.

Thinking about Battram's (2008) ideas relating to play, order, complexity and chaos, the recordings certainly captured the sounds of something on the edge of chaos. Regularly in my personal reflection and in reflection with colleagues we talk about the atmosphere of the playground, whether it was "on the edge" and whether it "tipped" over the edge into chaos. According to Battram (2008) play exists in a zone of complexity in the space between order and chaos. Through that sense of a lot happening all at once, with all of the overlapping interactions, I realised just how complex practice must inevitably be and how difficult it is to reflect that back into theory. I thought about Lester's (2013) application of Deleuze's thinking about assemblages, which goes some way to appreciating this. In applying Deleuze's philosophy to play we can move away from reading what happens in terms of direct cause and effect relationships. Instead the possibilities that exist between bodies, objects, spaces, moods and more (Lester 2013) are highlighted. Those moments of playfulness are assembled from them and come together to actualise some of the many possibilities that exist between them. From listening back to the sound recordings, it was difficult to understand particular moments in terms of cause and effect, as in practice it was often difficult to tell where a particular play episode began, ended and evolved into something else. However, it was lovely listening back to those playful moments where playworkers, children, objects, moods, space, time and more all acted together to create a series of unfolding possibilities. Lester's application of Deleuze's thinking also offers playworkers something to reflect on in terms of their role in the play space, and it becomes less clear what the impact on play of the playworker might be. There is a shift from a focus on potential adulteration (Sturrock and Else 1998) towards an exploration of possibilities. The playworker's considerations may shift *from* questions about when and how to intervene in the play they are observing, *to* a recognition that they form part of the assemblage already. Consequently the playworker's role becomes much more enmeshed, not because the playworker seeks to be involved in children's play but out of a recognition that as part of the make-up of the environment they are already interconnected and so need to be sensitive and aware of the impact both of their actions, their inactions and the changes they might make to the play environment. Listening back to sound recordings enabled me to relate these abstract ideas to concrete practice.

There were other surprising things that sound recordings offered the opportunity to reflect on. For example, the sounds that are captured that are not words. I gained an appreciation of the playground's sound landmarks; the church bells which tell us the time on the hour, for example. They can be heard from nearly everywhere on the playground. There were sounds I had not noticed before, like just how loud the bird song is; the way I am accompanied by the jangle of keys everywhere I go, and the squeaking the shutters on the building make when we slide them shut ten minutes before closing time. Listening back to the unspoken elements of sound recordings made me appreciate that these often unnoticed or overlooked sounds were as much a part of the play space as the physical structures. I started to think of examples where they may have impacted on what was going on. We introduced a 3.00pm snack time during school holidays and as a consequence, the children now count the "dongs" from the church when they are feeling hungry to see if it is 3.00pm. One boy asked me, "If 3.00pm is snack time, what is 4.00pm?" There is a developing expectation that something happens when the church bells ring. I have also stopped shouting, "It's 10 minutes until closing time" because the squeak of the shutters closing does the exact same job. The sounds of the play space can contain cues in the same way that the physical environment can.

In 2013 our playwork team was involved in a piece of research based at our adventure playground (Lester et al, 2013). We used sound recordings to try to guess where on the playground snippets of sound were captured; some were easier to guess than others. The play space has its own shifting and changing sound-scape as well as its landscape. Recording and playing back the sounds of play settings can help playworkers to gain a greater appreciation of some of the situated knowledge they use every day in their practice. From this greater appreciation playworkers can then become more sensitive to aspects of sound, how it helps them to make judgements about what is going on, and how sound offers cues.

TOOL THREE: MAPPING

Maps are often thought to represent the truth of something that is "out there" but in fact every map carries its own interpretation. As with the other tools one needs to recognise that what is being captured is always partial and always filtered through personal perceptions and experiences. So long as this is recognised it can be useful in reflections.

The research project mentioned above began with a mapping exercise (Lester et al, 2013). Each member of the staff team roughly sketched an individual aerial map of the playground. Once we had finished we compared our maps. Each playworker had unconsciously included and left out different aspects of the physical environment and we came to appreciate that our understanding of the space is highly subjective. It is based on our relationships and feelings of connection to that particular space. We then worked as a team to create one large collective map. In the process we started sharing stories that had happened in particular locations. We eventually created a map that was both an aerial view of the physical space and one full of connections and meaning. This was an exercise that I would recommend staff teams do, and it is a very useful place to start in encouraging a greater appreciation of storytelling.

The possibilities for mapping are limited only by one's imagination. Since that first experience of mapping, several different methods of capturing something of what is happening within the play space have been tried. In the research project (Lester et al, 2013) we mapped the movement of individual children over a period of time, along with brief notes of gestures and conversation that were noticed. We did the same for playworkers, making a note at five minute intervals of where they were and what they were doing individually and collectively. We mapped objects and their playful journeys through the playground. Whatever formula is chosen it is important to recognise that the process is the most important element, not the finished item. What is produced may not be an accurate representation but is a tool for reflection and discussion.

Most recently I have attempted to create maps of the playground's affective environment; the way the space feels emotionally. These feelings are always in the process of being created by the interactions and relations within the space. Sturrock (2003) talks about the concept of affective topographies, where the aim is to map some of the physical places children choose for particular emotional experiences. An understanding of the affective environment will form part of a playworker's situated knowledge; Where are the places children go if they want to be alone? Are there particular places where conflict is more likely? Playworkers may bring this knowledge to their work already but it is interesting to pause, reflect and discuss in order to understand play and play spaces better and possibly challenge some assumptions.

In order to create an affective topography I used an aerial map of the playground and layered sheets of clear plastic over the top. On the first sheet I thought about a particular child who was a regular visitor to the playground. Using the aerial map as a guide I marked areas that I was aware that child had a particular connection with, on to the sheet. These connections could be the places the child visited each time s/he came in and their habits, as well as the places where specific moments had taken place. I made notes around the edge of the map to explain what the marks related to and repeated this on the other sheets for a total of 10 children of different ages and genders. When placed on top of the map together they created a layered effect which gave a sense of a space filled with meaning that responded differently to different children. It is important to recognise that these marks represented my understandings of the connections different children may have had with specific areas of the playground, and do not necessarily correspond to what was going on for the children themselves. If I try something similar in the future I will ask children to mark spaces that are important to them themselves. I think this would lead to an interesting picture which might highlight ways in which the children use the space that the playworkers may not be aware of.

One of the ongoing discussions within playwork is about the value of staff-led activities or games. Running this kind of activity during a play session might be seen as an intrusion of an adult agenda into the play space. On the playground where I currently work we have found that staff-initiated activities can add to the environment by highlighting some of the possibilities within the space which children and young people can go on to make their own. Since playing big team games like "capture the flag" in the summer holidays, the children now regularly request these games. At times when we have not offered as many staff- initiated games and activities the atmosphere has "tipped" into negativity much more often. As a consequence we offer regular staff-initiated activities or games, particularly in school holidays.

This chapter is looking at different ways playworkers use their situated knowledge. Being able to read and respond to the collective mood of the play setting is one of them.

The process of attempting to produce an affective topography enabled me to appreciate some of my situated knowledge and the way this helps me to see the complexities within the play space. The map makes it clear that the playground is not an empty vessel but is created out of the relationships, connections and meanings it has for those who visit it (Russell 2013).

There have been some major changes planned at the playground which will affect some of the areas that hold meaning for a lot of the children who visit. One of these changes which serves as a good example, is that affecting the London black cab or Taxi.

The Taxi has gained an almost iconic status since it was placed off the ground, within the main wooden playground structure, 4 or 5 years ago. The Taxi provides the location for numerous types of stories for many children. It also provides a focal point for children visiting the playground for the first time as it provides a containment for driving based games including imagined high speed car chases, and journeys to distant and fantastic places. There were occasions when a child would try to fit every single loose item into the back of the cab, and there were many games of dares. Unfortunately the cab has deteriorated over time and we eventually had to take the decision that it needed to be brought down to the ground. Creating an affective topography reinforced how important it was that we treat the Taxi with sensitivity because of the connections so many children and young people had to it and the need for playworkers to be open to the creation of new and different connections that children would make to it as they changed the way they interact with it following its move.

The Taxi has been on the ground for several weeks now and we are watching to see how the children find new ways to interact with it. One thing we had not anticipated was how the children would respond to the gap in the structure where the Taxi used to be. We had temporarily fenced off the area until the children and staff decided what they wanted in its place, but the children instantly climbed straight over the fence and explored the new (just about crossable) space. It made me realise that it was not just the Taxi that held all of the stories, but that the space it had been in had a story of its own which interlinked. In attempting to make an affective topography I was able to give a visual and spatial form to some of the moments and stories that impacted on how I read the play space. The playground and all of its physical elements, both separately and as a whole, has a past, a present and a future (Massey 2005). It is crucial for playworkers to stop and reflect on the living stories within the play space and how the physical features of the site feed into these stories, especially where the playworkers are responsible for the development and maintenance of the space.

In this chapter I have described three playwork tools which capture different elements of what goes on within a play setting. Each of these tools enables the playworker to take a closer look at their own "situated" working knowledge and gain a greater appreciation not only of the complexities of the spaces in which they work but also the diversity of knowledge they draw on in their practice. Many playwork settings do not have behaviour policies with fixed responses to particular types of behaviour. Instead playworkers' responses are specific to that moment in time. This makes it vitally important that playworkers look closely at their working knowledge in order to challenge any dubious assumptions they might hold. As the playworker's role is to support the children and young people's play, they need to maintain a sensitive awareness of what might be going on for the children in the play space.

In the reflections I had following using these tools, I came to realise the importance of telling, retelling and sharing stories, of recognising the complexities of play spaces and the subtle situated knowledge playworkers bring to their work. When playworkers talk about their work it is in the surprising, funny and sometimes challenging stories that we tell about what goes on within play spaces that we pass on why play is so important, what play spaces are and what playworkers do. Straightforward explanations often fall short, but stories from experience can offer subtlety and detail.

I close the chapter with a final story.

> It was Spring and the attendance numbers were growing again after the cold dark Winter. There were a few new faces. One of the regular children aged 8 had been practicing "ninja" skills over the Winter. He would find a long stick to use as a weapon and practice twirling it. Sometimes he would find a piece of foam and ask someone to hold it while he practiced punching it. A new boy, who was 11 joined in and they soon developed a Ninja group. The two of them claimed a base, made weapons from old broom handles and found and protected some treasure (beads). After a week the Ninja group had grown to 6 or 7 members with some of the young children joining in. The new boy was the Captain. He would shout "Ninjas Assemble" from his den and all of the Ninjas would run over. Being a Ninja was not easy. All of the members had to find or make their own weapon. They were allocated tasks by the captain who was a firm leader, regularly expelling people, meaning they had to negotiate their way back in to the group. The Ninja group has been battling enemies, hiding treasure and protecting their base for over a month now. The story continues.

REFERENCES

Anonymous, Everyday Playwork blog at http://www.everydayplaywork.wordpress.com.

Armitage, M. (2005) The influence of school architecture and design on the outdoor play experience within primary schools. *Paedagogica Historica* Vol.41, Nos 4 & 5, August 2005, pp. 535–553.

Battram, A. (2008) The edge of recalcitrance: playwork in the zone of complexity. In: Brown, F. and Taylor, C. (eds) *Foundations of playwork*, Maidenhead: Open University Press.

Gallagher, M. and Prior, J. (2014) Sonic Geographies: Exploring Phonographic Methods. In: *Progress in Human Geography*, Vol 38(2) pp. 267–284. Sage.

Lester, S. (2013) Playing in a deleuzian playground. In Ryall, E., Russell, W. and MacLean, M. (eds) *The philosophy of play*, London: Routledge, pp. 130–140.

Lester, S., Russell, W. and Fitzpatrick, J. (2013) *Co-creating an adventure playground (CAP): reading playwork stories, practices and artefacts.* Gloucester: University of Gloucestershire.

Lorimer, H. (2005) Cultural geography: the busyness of being more-than-representational. *Progress in Human Geography*, Vol. 29(1), pp. 83–94.

Massey, D. (2005) *For space*, London: Sage.

PPSG (2005) *Playwork Principles*, held in trust as honest brokers for the profession by the Playwork Principles Scrutiny Group. [Internet] Available from: http://www.playwales.org.uk/page.asp?id=50 [Accessed 5/8/2013].

Russell, W. (2013) Towards a spatial theory of playwork: what can Lefebvre offer as a response to playwork's inherent contradictions? In: Ryall, E., Russell, W. and MacLean, M. (eds) *The philosophy of play*, London: Routledge, pp. 164–174.

Seath, J., Playworkings blog at https://playworkings.wordpress.com/.

Sturrock, G. and Else, P. (1998), The playground as therapeutic space: playwork as healing. "The Colorado Paper," in Sturrock, G and Else, P. (2005) *Therapeutic playwork reader I*, Sheffield: Ludemos Associates.

Chapter Two

Nonsense, Caring and Everyday Hope

Rethinking the Value of Playwork

Wendy Russell

At the time of writing, the UK is facing the deepest cuts to public services in the history of the welfare state (Slay, 2012). Publicly funded play services are at the forefront of these cuts (CRAE, 2015; Hayes, 2014). Playworkers are seeking different delivery models and ways of articulating value without compromising the playwork ethos. This highlights a fundamental tension for playwork between (in Marxist terms) its exchange value and use value. Put starkly, exchange value links directly to sources of funding for playwork projects and therefore lies in playwork's capacity to address social policy agendas such as play-based learning, development of social skills, crime reduction, physical activity/obesity reduction and community cohesion. Playwork's use value has been articulated in a number of ways, but broadly lies in the co-production of spaces that support children's open-ended and autotelic playing. Any attempt to direct playing towards policy outcomes risks commodifying it and turning it into something other than play. Yet these are not straightforward dualistic oppositions, nor are they the only way of articulating value.

This chapter draws on my research on the dialectics of playwork (Russell, 2013), which focused on open access playwork[1] that tends to be funded in deprived areas, a salient point. It offers a specific dialectical perspective, moving beyond stark either/or dualisms, grand narratives and causal statements, towards an appreciation of the interrelatedness of forms of value and the importance of keeping space open for whatever might emerge. This involves being comfortable with uncertainty and paying attention to ways that spaces are co-produced, in particular to small moments of playfulness, nonsense and perhaps resistance to adult intentions. What is offered here are but tentative steps. I am not pronouncing on a universally applicable strategy for the survival of playwork, but aiming to look beyond existing articulations of playwork's value, not to dismiss them as wrong, but to see what more can be said.

In the UK, playworkers have a set of principles that "establish the professional and ethical framework for playwork" (PPSG, 2005). These are informed by playwork theorizing that emanates mostly from those who were practicing playworkers on adventure playgrounds in the 1960s and 1970s. Given this, it is worth a quick glance at the founding ethos of adventure playgrounds.

In a filmed interview (COI, c1970), landscape architect Lady Marjorie Allen describes her discovery of a *waste material* playground in Copenhagen, Denmark, and how she brought the idea to the UK in the aftermath of World War II. The key arguments from this "propagandist for children's play," as the narrator calls her, are that:

- The environments we expect children to thrive in are barren ("we give them a pretty raw deal"); traditional playgrounds are boring and "not good enough."
- Adventure playgrounds are rough and ready affairs built "entirely by the children themselves" under the permissive supervision of a "playleader," where children are free to build, light fires, meet friends and to a large extent do as they want.
- One aspect Allen highlights is risk, saying "they can take really dangerous risks and overcome them."

Much has happened since those early days of adventure playgrounds. They have evolved, affected by regulations, funding initiatives and gradual shifts in understandings about childhood and play. Despite the ethos of adventure playgrounds being about children's ability to express their own play desires, this permissiveness was seen as a way of meeting social ends. Out of anarchy and freedom would come an understanding of democracy and citizenship. In this sense, adventure playgrounds were sites for education and hope for the moral reconstruction of post war Britain (Kozlovsky, 2008).

Key changes in UK legislation that fundamentally affected adventure playgrounds include the Health and Safety at Work Act 1974, which restricted defining features such as self-built play structures and fires, and the Children Act 1989, which brought playgrounds into the registration and inspection regime and therefore the ethos of early years services. In addition, the rise of neoliberalism and New Public Management ideology that ushered in technical, universal systems for measuring quality, accountability and effectiveness have had a significant impact on the way playworkers articulate value. This is particularly so in funding, tendering and monitoring documents, which privilege measurable and rational outcomes over play's frivolity and nonsense.

THE DIALECTICS OF PLAYWORK (OR "HOW TO MAKE VINAIGRETTE")

In their work playworkers navigate a number of contradictions that stem from adult rationalizations of the nature and value of childhood and of play. Open access playwork can only realistically survive through public funding, which is attached to social policy agendas. Put crudely, policymakers want open access play projects to normalize children deemed to be at risk of poor outcomes. It is understandable that the UK playwork sector seeks to show evidence of its value in policy terms. To this end, the Children's Play Policy Forum commissioned Tim Gill (2014) to write *The Play Return*, which shows evidence of how investing in play provision can reap rewards in terms of children's development, community cohesion, reducing antisocial behavior, reducing obesity, reducing inequalities and helping to create healthier places.

In stark contrast, the playwork sector espouses notions of play's freedoms and autotelicity (that it should be for its own sake rather than attached to specific end goals and outcomes), with developmental and evolutionary benefits accruing from engagement in the widest possible range of play forms untainted by *adulteration* (the imposition of adult desires, intentions and anxieties onto children's play) (Hughes, 2012).

In practice, romantic ideals of fun, "natural" childhoods, innocence and hope for the future, evident in both policy and playwork discourse, rub up against the harsh reality of urban poverty and violence in playwork spaces that can be seen both as safe refuges from chaotic homes and dangerous streets and as volatile places of unpredictability. This is an aspect of playwork in inner city areas that has been poorly addressed in the contemporary literature but emerged as a major theme in my research.

These two expressions of value seem diametrically opposed. The metaphor that comes to mind for this contradiction is of vinaigrette: the oil of one way of articulating value does not readily mix with the vinegar of the other unless vigorously shaken—and then only temporarily. This is where the idea of dialectics comes in. Dialectics is a method, an approach to analysis. In my research I ended up drawing a lot on the work of French philosopher Henri Lefebvre. Lefebvre never talks about dualisms (unless to critique them). For him, there is always a third, and this extends to his version of dialectics. Lefebvre drew on three philosophical influences for this: the work of Hegel, whose philosophy was about ideas; Marx, who looked at social practice; and Nietzsche, who made a plea for not only looking for rational ways to understand the world, but also considered the role of poesy, the irrational and, of course, play (Schmid, 2009).

Currently, the immiscible vinaigrette might look something like this:

Policy paradigms

- Childhood is preparation for adulthood (Wyness, 2006; Moss, 2007).
- Children are economic investments (see, for example, DfE, 2010; Allen, 2011).
- Policies require technical, universal and measurable interventions that lead to desired outcomes (Moss, 2007; Lester and Russell, 2013).
- Play becomes a tool for realizing policy aims (Lester and Russell, 2013).

Playwork paradigms

- Play is a biological, psychological and social necessity (PPSG, 2005).
- It is freely chosen, personally directed and intrinsically motivated (PPSG, 2005).
- There is chronic pollution of children's ludic habitat (Sturrock et al., 2004; Patte and Brown, 2011).
- This leads to play bias and play deprivation (Hughes, 2012; Brown, 2013).
- Playwork acts as compensation for play deprivation and bias (Hughes, 2001; Patte and Brown, 2011).
- For playworkers, the play process takes precedence and playworkers act as advocates for play when engaging with adult led agendas (PPSG, 2005).

I think there is something missing here. Not only do these two perspectives not talk very well to each other, neither of them captures play's irrationality, vitality and frivolity—in other words, its nonsense; nor do they capture how play offers the feeling that life is worth living, at least for the moment of playing (Sutton-Smith, 1997). Both perspectives offer rational, instrumental and future-focused arguments for the value of play and therefore playwork. Dialectics as method may be a form of shaking the vinaigrette, disturbing the way we understand things at the moment, both in terms of policy and playwork paradigms. Shaking up our ideas from time to time must be a good thing, but maybe not sufficient if the oil and vinegar just return to their separate states soon afterwards.

Perhaps another way to keep the oil and vinegar of use and exchange value from separating is to add a third ingredient. An emulsifier, maybe, like mustard. What might playwork's mustard be? Perhaps we can look to Lefebvre's dialectical third, a Nietzschean and playful way of thinking about play. Maybe we have been taking play too seriously, making well-intentioned but perhaps rather overzealous claims for playwork's value as a result. What if an under-considered form of value might be found in play's very nonsense? This was one of the conclusions I came to in my research.[2]

A SPATIAL PERSPECTIVE ON PLAY AND PLAYWORK

I ended up looking somewhere other than the psychological theories our great playwork writers have used. I went to theories of space, and specifically to Henri Lefebvre.[3] Lefebvre had little to say about children, but his analysis of the politics of space has much to offer. For Lefebvre, space is not a neutral container for stuff, but is constantly in the process of being *produced* by the interrelationships between physical and social elements and the actions of individuals and institutions. These interrelationships are political because they are representations of power. Cities are designed to support the processes of capital: production, distribution, exchange and consumption. Land and property are given an exchange value that places the institutions of power at the center with a collection of hierarchically organized and separate spaces for different purposes and different groups of people (Shields, 1999), with poorer people trapped in areas of the city where land value is lowest. Lefebvre describes this as the violence of the state against the individual, and suggests that cities have become

> A collection of ghettoes where individuals are at once "socialised," integrated, submitted to artificial pressures and constraints . . . and separated, isolated, disintegrated. A contradiction which is translated into anguish, frustration and revolt. (Lefebvre, 1972, cited in Shields, 1999, p. 178)

Lefebvre wrote this in the 1970s, since which time cities have continued to grow, and land has continued to be at a premium (particularly in the tiny over-populated island of Britain); we can see this in the processes of regeneration and the current crisis over both housing and city centers. As the Marxist geographer David Harvey (2012) shows, it is always the poor who lose out in this process.

These state actions can be understood as a form of structural violence. Less obvious are the spatial practices that accompany them. There are expected ways for people to behave in specific places; in this sense spaces are disciplined and the relational elements of space are relations of power "coded by dominant embodied conceptions of 'race,' sex, gender, and so on" (Tyner, 2012, p.20). To this we can add Bourdieu and Wacquant's (1992) idea of symbolic violence that occurs through the everyday acts of domination enacted in order to maintain status. Many of these may seem innocuous, and so much a part of everyday life as to seem *normal*.

Many theories of interpersonal violence focus on whether causes can be found in individual traits or environmental factors—the classic nature/culture binary. The sociologist Larry Ray (2011, p.5) offers this perspective that highlights the interrelationship of space, inequalities and violence: "Violence is induced by shame, humiliation and cultures of masculine honour; the conditions for this are closely linked to socioeconomic inequalities . . . ; violence is spatially distributed in ways that coincide with the spatial structuring of global capital."

This brings us back to the salience of open access playwork operating in areas of deprivation. As part of my research, I interviewed several playworkers, including those who were playworkers prior to 1990 and those who worked where I did my fieldwork. When asked about the home lives of children that use the playground, playworkers' responses were often emotional, for example, this response from playworker Tanith[4]: "It tends to be those with a lot of emotional shit [who] access play centres . . . it's amazing how many youngsters have got emotional shit going on in their lives."

Lefebvre's threefold dialectic of the production of space, introduced briefly here, offers a useful perspective on spatial politics, the pervasiveness of violence and the importance of play; applying this to playwork spaces also offers an understanding of the dialectics between the intrinsic and instrumental value of play (and, via a problematic extension, between use and exchange value of playwork).

Spatial practice, also termed "perceived space," refers to the everyday routines of life as experienced through the senses. Much of this is about the humdrum of daily struggles, and can be a site of alienation, a sense of disconnect between daily life and the meaning of life. This is where policy's instrumental understanding of play is most keenly felt and where play becomes a thing, a commodity with market value and understood as something to be "provided."

Representations of space, also called "conceived space," refers to the way that space is conceptualised through planning and maps. For playwork, this might be seen in the naming and zoning of the space (for example, the kick-around pitch, the natural play area or the kitchen) and of materials within the space (paintbrushes, unihoc sticks). This naming assumes that spaces and materials will be used in particular ways, producing desired outcomes—even though playworkers know that children will disturb these assumptions in their play. This is also where playwork theories reside, giving rise to a particular playwork discourse.

Spaces of representation: also termed "lived space," refers to moments of being fully present. It is the space of art, imagination and of course, play. This is when the daily grind is resisted, set aside for things that have meaning and make life worth living. A key aspect of lived space is that it defies the kinds of representations found in conceived and perceived space: it cannot be explained in the modernist, rational science of certainty, determinism and absolute truths, nor in the limits of language. Nor can it be planned, provided, measured or reduced to exchange value.

It should be stressed that these are not separate kinds of space, rather it is their ongoing entanglement that produces space.

This may all sound a bit abstract, so I'll illustrate it with a fairly lengthy, edited extract from my field notes. The Play Centre where I did my fieldwork has a tradition of celebrating Hallowe'en and the children are particularly ghoulish in their play. The October half term also coincided with both Eid and Diwali, and the Play Centre neighborhood has a large Muslim and a smaller Sikh community.

Tuesday 24 October

Playworkers present: Verda, Carla, Tanith, Jem, Gareth

I spent almost all of the morning inside. One table has all the materials to make a mummy, another has henna and associated resources. The mummy idea gave rise to so many different play episodes throughout the whole morning.

A mother comes in with two daughters and explains one has a chest infection so will need her inhaler (she can administer this herself) and to take her off the list for swimming tomorrow. Both Jem and Verda hear her say this. Later, Verda tells Carla . . .

Verda has moved to the mummy table and is starting to work on this with a group of 8–10 children. There are several bags of shredded paper. The idea is to stuff the clothes with the shredded paper. The children start this, and inevitably, one child decides to throw the shredded paper up in the air . . . Gareth comes in from outside and comments "It's going to be a messy day." Before long a paper fight has started, with Gareth and Carla joining in. I missed how it started, but it is short-lived, with quite a few children following Gareth outside when he leaves and some carrying on with Carla for a little while. Throughout this brief moment of mayhem, Verda and Tanith continue with the mummy quietly in the background. Pauline and Jess (11–13 years old) have stuffed shredded paper up their jumpers and are walking around showing their bumps. They come up to me and I say, "My. Have you suddenly got fat or are you having a baby?" They reply, "No, it's paper," and show me. Pauline and Caitlin are now stuffing shredded paper into Tyrone's clothes and he looks like a dummy. They dance off outside singing "Dingle, Dangle Scarecrow." They come back inside and suddenly there is a whole crowd singing the song with Carla. They must range in age from 6/7 up to 13 years old and they are spontaneously singing "Dingle, Dangle Scarecrow." Tyrone now stuffs paper down his back to give him a hunchback, as does Caitlin and they ask for sticks. Carla gives Tyrone a yellow plastic hockey stick, Caitlin gets a blue stump out of a cricket set. They go off hobbling. The mummy making continues . . .

Tanith has taken the mummy and is sewing the stuffed socks to the trousers to the jumper. She surveys the scene—all surfaces are covered with shredded paper—and she wonders if it is worth sweeping up at this stage. I say I will. It takes half an hour because a number of games ensue including pretending to sweep up staff and children, and a small paper fight starting again. Then Moby (5 and very small) decides to sweep up. The wide institutional broom is much bigger than he is, but he is determined. After a while he wants to sweep up outside so I give him the outdoor brush. I go outside to make sure this is OK, and I notice that the hosepipe is running from the toilet window into the (covered) sandpit. Pauline, Jess, Caitlin, Tyrone and a few others are in their bare feet, squirting each other with the hose. Later, children bring sodden clothes in and Carla wrings them out as much as she can. Caitlin finds something else to wear from the clothing left behind on the clothes pegs.

Tanith is still sitting quietly with a group of girls on the floor sewing up the mummy. I admire the girls' mendhi—it is Eid and they are all henna'd up. She has been sitting with them for quite a while and there is a gentle conversation going on about families and places they have visited. They need to turn the mummy over and sew up the back, so they lift it on to the table and Tanith continues there. The girls are making the head and Verda has helped others make the hands using gloves. It has taken most of the morning to get to this point, with a core of children sticking with the project itself and the others dipping in and out and using the resources to spark off other ways of playing. Now they start to wrap the mummy in bandages. There are a couple of enormous reels of white fabric (from the local scrapstore) about 15cms wide that look just like bandages. This new material sparks attention from Caitlin, Jess, Pauline and Tyrone. They start to wrap each other in the bandages and act as mummies. There are a lot of mummy jokes flying around at this stage too. I end up getting involved in wrapping the children in the bandages to make them mummies. With Tyrone, I stand still, holding the bandages taught while he spins round and round and makes himself dizzy. They then use red felt tip pens to give themselves bloody head-wounds. Sometime later I look again at the main mummy and see a group of girls painting henna patterns onto the mummy's bandaged hands.

As we are clearing up, Gareth tells everyone that Jenny from the nursery next door had told him she had seen Leo and Max throwing clay and stones at the little ones. She had gone to ask them to stop and they had run off down the road. She had seen them throwing clay and stones at the tram. One of the difficulties is that Max's mum will not be too bothered by this. Tanith says she knows Max's aunt and she could talk to her and she would then talk to Max's mum and be listened to.

The point about Lefebvre's triad is not that these are separate kinds of space but they combine to produce spaces that have a history, that are reflections of fluid power relations, that are constantly in the process of being produced, and that acknowledge the place of emotions. So, the kinds of planning that take place in conceived space are necessary *and* there needs to be awareness that space can still be left open for moments of nonsense in lived space. The series of playful moments of paper fights, scarecrows, singing, banter, hunchbacks and mummies would not have taken place in the manner described here without the main *activity* being loosely planned and without the culture of the center being as it was, open to whatever might emerge. It is an excellent example of the dialectical and entangled co-existence of moments in conceived, perceived and lived space. It shows how the space is open enough to allow for these different moments and play forms to erupt and die away. Alongside these moments are hundreds of others that combine to co-produce the conditions in which playfulness thrives. Some of this may have been predictable, but largely, the approach is one of creating a situation and then feeling comfortable in just seeing what arises from it.

There is much else besides the playfulness and openness of the space. Much of playwork theorizing has, quite rightly, focused on play, as it is this that makes playwork unique. No other sector within the children's workforce has such potential for working with children on their terms. Yet much of what happens in playwork settings is not play, and these moments are also important in the co-production of a space that supports playfulness. This is illustrated in the extract through the interweaving of mundane bureaucratic matters, quiet chats about this and that, community relations, dealing with anti-social behavior, etc. These elements are all part of the day-to-day work and they can happen in the way they do because of the history of relationships and expectations. The playworkers can have the more didactic conversations with children at times about "kicking off" because they have shared these moments of playfulness. Playwork spaces can also provide a non-stigmatized space for families one step removed from official services such as Social Services or Youth Offending Teams, and I saw plenty of examples of sensitive navigating of those relationships. For example, some playworkers feed children because they know they need it. Another dialectic here is that these services, essential as they are for families, can happen in the way they do precisely because the space is open enough to be responsive in this way. Formalizing them risks closing down that openness.

HOPE AS AN EXPRESSION OF VALUE

This rather over-simplified introduction to Lefebvre's triple dialectics of space provides a grounding for understanding the contradictory emotions that emerged as a theme in my research. Playwork spaces are highly emotionally charged, and it is this aspect to which I now turn, focusing on one emotion that is at the core of adult-child relations, that of hope.

Hope is a defining feature of being human; it helps us stay optimistic if we can imagine what a better life might look like (Lester and Russell, 2013). Children are a repository for our hope for a better life (Kraftl, 2008) and this can be seen in those who work with children, including playworkers. In this sense, hope is closely linked to value. Drawing on work by children's geographer Peter Kraftl (2008), I identified three forms of hope-as-value, another dialectical triad.

Policy Paradigms and Utopian Projects

Social policies relating to children and young people express hope both for and in children. These are manifest in a highly interventionist and technical approach to children and families policies, investing childhood with "a version of hopefulness based on maintaining competitiveness in global markets, couching this both in the moral language of equality and the pragmatic language of economy" (Lester and Russell, 2013, p.41). This future focus, firmly ensconced in Lefebvre's conceived space, territorializes children, rendering childhood a site for adult colonization (Lester and Russell, 2013).

Marxist geographer Cindi Katz (2008, 2011) suggests an understanding of childhood that became pertinent to my political analysis, that of childhood as spectacle. The concept of spectacle is borrowed from French Situationist Guy Debord, who argued that direct experience in the modern world had been reduced to mere representation. Childhood has become a commodified image of real experience, a spectacle. Katz describes the growing sense of insecurity about the future that manifests across three domains: political, geopolitical and environmental. Children become a repository for these anxieties, which play out across three configurations.

Her first configuration is the "child as accumulation strategy," where children become a site of economic, psychic and emotional investment. The quest for perfect childhoods can be seen in practices such as hothousing, competition for entry to the best schools and universities, extra tuition, hypervigilance and myriad parenting guides. Adults invest time, emotion and money into making their children's childhoods the best they can be, equipping them for the future, keeping them as safe as possible through a range of controls and constraints.

The "child as ornament," Katz's second configuration, is the child as bauble and fashion accessory, the doll to be clothed in apparel from a burgeoning children's fashion industry (with its own politics of production). In addition, the ornament is a form of essentializing of childhood innocence so that anxieties over the loss of childhood innocence can be invoked to fuel the desire for vigilance and control.

The third configuration of the "child as waste" has particular relevance here. The fear of a wasted youth feeds the niche marketing that underpins the first two configurations. Those children and families who do not conform to or cannot achieve the normative ideal fulfil this function. Many of the children at the Play Centre fitted into this configuration, and were subject to myriad "waste management" policy interventions through the welfare, education, health and justice systems, and even, perhaps, through playwork itself. Early adventure playgrounds were welcomed by the authorities as a way of keeping delinquent boys off the streets. In my research, the Play Centre received funding from the Children's Fund, aimed directly at working with children deemed at risk of poor outcomes.

Revolutionary Hope

Alongside this future-focused, colonized space of hope runs another, historically based ethos underpinning the playwork sector. In the late 1960s and 1970s, when my "past" interviewees were practicing playworkers, some playworkers were attracted to the work because of its anarchic and democratic nature. Civil liberties underpinned the *zeitgeist*, and many playworkers' favorite books included the anarchist Colin Ward, and children's liberationists such as John Holt, A.S. Neill and Leila Berg. The interviews I did, and the literature of the time, expressed broad optimism in children's futures being *politically* rather than *individually* better through supporting the development of a form of class consciousness.

> Adventure playgrounds were gonna save the world! . . . By offering children a different life experience, yeah. By . . . giving them a real place, and a recognised place, and power . . . [it] was very much about the importance of those sort of children with that sort of position in society having a better deal . . . That was the idea, we can do it for ourselves, we don't need top-down bloody government, you know, we can control our own lives. (Carol interview)

Although this macro level political revolutionary hope is less evident today, vestiges of this anti-establishment recalcitrance remain, mainly in terms of the openness to what social theorist Nikolas Rose calls "minor politics"—small everyday negotiations of power (both in terms of caring and resistance) that might be seen as a form of activism (Horton and Kraftl, 2009). Playwork settings are well placed to support this. In terms of the Play Centre, what was noticeable was how the playworkers *cared* about what some might see as "petty" details of the children's relationships, power struggles and fallings out. They may well be amongst the few adults in children's lives to have this caring response to the exuberances and tragedies of playing.

Moments of Nonsense as "Near Hope"

The third form of hope reflects what Kraftl (2008) terms "childhood-hope." Here we shift our gaze from the dominant conceived and perceived space to an acknowledgement of the importance of moments in lived space. This is to do with alternative understandings of play and an appreciation of children's desire to appropriate time and space for just being and just playing. Rather than play's benefits being deferred until adulthood, they might be understood through play's capacity to enliven everyday life as it is in the here and now (and of course this will affect the future too).

In my research, it was evident that the playworkers got this, and in informal conversations, they gleefully related stories of moments of pure nonsense.

> If I can chase a kid and he's happy and he's coming up to me and giving me a brilliant play cue, you know, and he's laughing at me calling me big nose or whatever and running off and giggling, say a little six-year-old, you've done something for that child, you've made them happy, even for a split second. (Jem interview)

SO WHAT DOES IT ALL MEAN?

The Playwork Principles imply precedence of use value over exchange value. On a purely pragmatic level, unless use value predominates in children's everyday experiences in open access playwork settings, they will stop coming. So, although the funding that paid for staff at the Play Centre at the time of the research was grounded in policies aimed at crime reduction, it also afforded moments of playful nonsense in lived space. The dialectic is that our official articulations about playwork, including the Playwork Principles, reside in Lefebvre's conceived and perceived space, and necessarily so, because lived space defies representation and cannot be planned in any precise way. The dialectic has to remain.

What the extract from my field notes highlights is the importance of small moments in lived space, of caring and openness, of being comfortable with uncertainty, alongside (and often in a dialectical relationship with) the bigger instrumental and universal assertions of the value of play and playwork. Playwork's instrumental value can be articulated in terms of its ability to offer the children the conditions for playful experiences they would not have elsewhere, and all the benefits this has for children both in the here and now and in the future. It can also be articulated in terms of addressing social policy agendas such as anti-social behaviour, skills development, physical activity and so on. Yet, these instrumental outcomes can only be ethically claimed if understood as a part of the overall assemblage that is a playwork setting: the combination of, for example, relationships, material and symbolic objects, space, histories, playfulness and caring that constitutes what is unique about the work. This has implications for how playwork's uniqueness is articulated, both within and outside the playwork community. At the moment, we seek to show just how serious play is, when perhaps we should also be extolling its non-seriousness—in a dialectical relationship of course.

NOTES

1. The term "open access" is used in the UK to differentiate out of school childcare and settings where children are in principle free to come and go and there is no contractual agreement with caregivers. My research looked mostly at adventure playgrounds and play centres.
2. For a more detailed exploration of this understanding of play see the chapter in this volume by Stuart Lester.
3. For a more detailed analysis of my application of Lefebvre's ideas about space to play and playwork, see Wendy Russell. "'I get such a feeling out of . . . those moments': Playwork, passion, politics and space." *International Journal of Play*,Vol.1.1 (2012): 51–63.
4. All names of playworkers and children have been changed.

REFERENCES

Allen, G. (2011) *Early intervention: smart investment, massive savings*. London: Cabinet Office.

Bourdieu, P. and Wacquant, L. (1992) *An invitation to reflexive sociology*. Cambridge: Polity Press.

Brown, F. (2013) *Play deprivation: impact, consequences and the potential of playwork*. Cardiff: Play Wales.

Department for Education (DfE). (2010) *The importance of teaching: the school's white paper*. Norwich: The Stationery Office.

Central Office of Information (COI) (c1970) Lady Allen. *The Pacemakers Issue No. 20*. Available at https://www.youtube.com/watch?v=1pqMXplAI9Y (Accessed 16 Jul 2015).

Children Act (1989). London: HMSO.

CRAE (Children's Rights Alliance England) (2015) *UK implementation of the UN Convention on the Rights of the Child: civil society alternative report 2015 to the UN Committee—England*. London: CRAE.

Gill, T. (2014) *The play return: a review of the wider impact of play initiatives*. Children's Play Policy Forum.

Harvey, D. (2012) *Rebel cities: from the right to the city to the urban revolution*. London: Verso.

Hayes, D. (2014) CYP Now investigation: play services decimated as funding slashed, *Children and Young People Now*, 8 January 2014.

The Health and Safety at Work etc. Act (1974). London: HMSO.

Horton J. and Kraftl, P. (2009) Small acts, kind words and "not too much fuss": Implicit activisms, *Emotion, Space and Society*, Vol.2: 14–23.

Hughes, B. (2001) *Evolutionary playwork and reflective analytic practice*. London: Routledge.

Hughes, B. (2012) *Evolutionary playwork*, 2nd edition. London: Routledge.

Katz, C. (2008) Childhood as spectacle: relays of anxiety and the reconfiguration of the child. *Cultural Geographies*, Vol.15, no. 1, pp.5–17.

Katz, C. (2011) Accumulation, excess, childhood: toward a countertopography of risk and waste, Documents *d'Anàlisis Geogràfica*, Vol.57, no. 1, pp.47–60.

Kozlovsky, R. (2008) Adventure playgrounds and postwar reconstruction. In: *designing modern childhoods: history, space and the material culture of children*, edited by M. Gutman, N. de Coninck-Smith, and N. Piscataway, pp.171–190. New Jersey: Rutgers University Press.

Kraftl, P. (2008) Young people, hope, and childhood-hope, *Space and Culture*, Vol.11 no. 2, pp.81–92.

Lefebvre, H. (1991 [1974]) *The production of space*, translated by Donald Nicholson-Smith, London: Blackwell.

Lester, S. and Russell, W. (2008) *Play for a change: play, policy and practice—a review of contemporary perspectives*. London: National Children's Bureau.

Lester, S. and Russell, W. (2013) Utopian visions of childhood and play in English social policy. In: *Youth sport, physical activity and play: policy, intervention and participation*, edited by Andrew Parker and Don Vinson, pp.40–52. London: Routledge.

Peter, M. (2007) Meetings across the paradigmatic divide. *Educational Philosophy and Theory*, Vol.39 no.3, pp.229–245.

Patte, M. and Brown, F. (2011) "Playwork: a profession challenging societal factors devaluing children's play," *Journal of Student Wellbeing*, Vol.5 no.1, pp.58–70.

PPSG (2005) *Playwork Principles*, held in trust as honest brokers for the profession by the Playwork Principles Scrutiny Group. [Internet] Available from: http://www.playwales.org.uk/page.asp?id=50 [Accessed 25/6/2017].

Ray, L. (2011) *Violence and society*, London: Sage.

Rose, N. (1999) *Powers of freedom: reframing political thought*, Cambridge: Cambridge University Press.

Russell, W. (2013) *The dialectics of playwork: a conceptual and ethnographic study of playwork using cultural historical activity theory*, PhD thesis, Gloucester: University of Gloucestershire.

Schmid, C. (2008) Henri Lefebvre's theory of the production of space: towards a three dimensional dialectic. In: *Space, difference and everyday life: reading Henri Lefebvre*, edited by K. Goonewardena, S. Kipfer, R. Milgrom and C. Schmid, pp.27–45. Abingdon: Routledge.

Shields, R. (1999) *Lefebvre, love and struggle: spatial dialectics.* Abingdon: Routledge.

Slay, J. (2012) 2020: What welfare state? *The NEF Blog*, 22 October, 2012. Available at http://www.neweconomics.org/blog/entry/2020-what-welfare-state (accessed 13 July 2015).

Sturrock, G., Russell, W. and Else, P. (2004) *Towards ludogogy Parts l, ll and lll: the art of being and becoming through play (The Birmingham Paper)*, Sheffield: Ludemos Associates.

Sutton-Smith, B. (1997) *The ambiguity of play*. Cambridge, MA: Harvard University Press.

Tyner, J. (2012) *Space, place and violence: violence and the embodied geographies of race, sex and gender*, Abingdon: Routledge.

Wyness, M. (2006) *Childhood and society: an introduction to the sociology of childhood*, Basingstoke: Palgrave Macmillan.

Chapter Three

The Neoliberalisation of Childhood and the Future of Playwork

Mike Wragg

The Neoliberal Revolution of the last thirty-five years has shaped both the popular paradigmatic conceptualisation of childhood, and the delivery and evaluation of children's services in the UK. This chapter argues that in the face of a seemingly irrepressible force of politico-economic doctrine, playwork, an historically diminutive profession within the wider children's workforce, represents a shrinking bastion of resistance to the principles of neoliberalism that have come to govern contemporary childhoods. Yet within this besieged field of resistance, emerge opportunities for playwork that may define its future in an era of increasing global competitiveness.

Neoliberalism commonly refers to a theory of political and economic practices which propose that the common good is best served by increasing individual entrepreneurial freedom, promoting private ownership, reducing public spending and by maximising the reach and frequency of competitive market transactions. The rise of contemporary neoliberalism as the dominant force in British politics can be attributed to the policies initiated during the Premiership of Margaret Thatcher (1979–1990), and strengthened throughout the 1980s by her unofficial transatlantic partnership with President Ronald Reagan. Whilst initially concerned primarily with matters of commerce and industry, such as market deregulation and the weakening of trade union powers, the policies of the neoliberal revolution, as it has been described, sought also to drive principles of competition into the heart of public policy (Harvey 2005). Throughout the 1980s and beyond, an emphasis on spending reduction, privatization, competition and deregulation led to "the promotion of new forms of public management and a form of governance in which neoliberal principles were advanced" (Jones 2003:107).

So pervasive is the influence of neoliberalism that it has become regarded by many as the dominant ideology shaping our world today (Jones 2003).

Although the pursuit of this ideology has undoubtedly benefitted many, the numbers of those adversely affected, whether they be tribal peoples of Central America displaced by multi-national conglomerates' programmes of deforestation, or the people of Greece rendered destitute by the corporate greed of the international banking system, amount to many more. However, one particular social group universally disadvantaged across socioeconomic strata and income distribution scales is the world's child population (Corsaro 2011). At one end of the spectrum this is evident in the denial of basic human rights to children forced into labour in the developing world. A less extreme, but still worrying example can be found in the concerns of the United Nations Committee on the Rights of the Child for the health impact on children of excessive exposure to advertising (CRC 2013). As this chapter is written the Supreme Court has ruled that the UK government's neoliberal reforms to welfare expenditure breach the United Nations Convention on the Rights of the Child (Butler 2015), and forecasts predict that child poverty in the UK will increase by a third in the decade to 2020, to its highest level in a generation (Doward & Helm 2015). Despite the evident environmental and human costs, neoliberalism has become so ubiquitous that its policies and practices inform the common-sense way we interpret, live in and understand the world, and in so doing have come to redefine and reconstruct children's lived experiences of their childhoods.

A prime example of one of the many practices to begin shaping this contemporary neoliberalisation of childhood in the UK can be seen in the education policy advanced by Thatcher's government and particularly in the Education Reform Act of 1988 (Chitty 2004). Indeed, neoliberal discourses of childhood are perhaps best exemplified in the ongoing political debate surrounding education.

Thatcher's policies of the 1980s were heavily influenced by the Institute of Economic Affairs (IEA), a right-wing think-tank which, during the previous decade, had "worked tirelessly to persuade the Conservative Party to abandon the post-war welfare consensus and embrace social and educational policies based on nineteenth-century free-market anti-statism" (Chitty 2004:47). Most notably the 1988 Act introduced market principles such as consumer choice for parents in where to send their children to school, standardized syllabus content and competitive performance league tables. As tends to be the case with ideologically driven reform, the National Curriculum was devised not by those one might consider best qualified to do so, but by a government quango informed by the IEA. Consequently, and in accordance with neoliberal principles, the role of schools and teachers within the newly defined marketplace was reoriented from that of curriculum innovators to curriculum providers (Chitty 2004).

With the new curriculum came a series of complicated assessment arrangements which were based on the 1988 report of the National Curriculum Task Group on Assessment and Testing (TGAT). This proposed a system of testing at ages seven, 11, 14 and 16 years in which each pupil was to be assessed on ten "Levels" across hundreds of "Attainment Targets" in the ten National Curriculum subjects. This unwieldy assessment regime was arguably concerned less with ensuring academic rigor, and more with the intention of providing marketable evidence of comparable measures of value. This evidence was, and continues to be, advertised in the form of league tables of schools' performance giving parents, theoretically at least, data to inform their free choice of provider. This marketisation of education has continued unabated; reinforced by the policies of the New Labour administration of the late 1990s and 2000s in the form of the Academies Programme, and more recently intensified by the previous UK Coalition government's adoption of the Free School model of education delivery (Chitty 2004).

Whilst the public advertisement of schools' positions in the national league tables drives competition domestically, in an increasingly competitive global economy international equivalents drive competition between nation states. For example, studies such as the Programme for International Student Assessment (PISA), and Trends in International Mathematics and Science Study (TIMSS), provide comparators of school pupils' scholastic performance worldwide (Jerrim & Choi 2013). Neoliberal theory dictates that competition will drive up standards of education and increase future economic prosperity. The desirability of these outcomes is difficult to deny. It is, however, the means by which they are pursued that Playwork resists, particularly the ramifications of that pursuit for the way in which childhood has come to be socially (re)constructed.

Social constructionism refers to the processes by which, in the words of Prout and James (1990:7) "the immaturity of children is conceived and articulated in particular societies into culturally specific sets of ideas and philosophies, attitudes and practices." In a global market in which the value of children is measured by their test results, children themselves have been reconstructed as units of future socio-economic capital. Within this market-defined reconceptualisation the child is perceived as a "proto adult" (James and James, 2004) lacking the basic skills and competencies of the adult they will become. The future orientated temporal focus of this construct trivialises and dismisses the present everyday realities of childhood which is reconstructed as a time of "becoming" rather than "being," and establishes a relationship in which the child is regarded as deficient and subordinate to their adult superior. This construct not only implies that competency and value is something that is acquired the closer one is to becoming "adult," but also that these characteristics are necessarily (and only) belonging to adults, i.e. ones that children cannot possess (James & James, 2004).

Playwork finds itself in a fairly isolated position in resisting this societally dominant paradigm, which it does by equalising the power distribution in the working relationship with the child, and by placing value on the child's immediacy, rather than their future adult-potential. Within this relationship the child is reconstructed as a competent social actor possessing specific skills and abilities *because* not *in spite* of their immaturity (Wragg 2011). Indeed, according to the internationally renowned children's rights advocate, Roger Hart, Playwork is the only profession to work collaboratively or horizontally with children, rather than from a position of power and dominance (Hart 2008). Although within this context children are afforded equal value to adults, it is important not to conflate this with the notion of equal status. Playwork recognises that whilst children are capable autonomous agents, their biological immaturity renders them more vulnerable than adults and therefore in need of greater rights of protection from themselves and others (Wragg 2011).

Nevertheless, based upon this assumption of relational equitability the prime essence and focus of playwork practices is to facilitate the play process, and it is this that takes precedence when engaging with adult agendas (PPSG 2005). This fundamental principle is in itself resistant to the neoliberalisation of childhood which restricts and suppresses the play process. It has been well documented that in the period since the dawn of the neoliberal revolution we have witnessed a sharp decline in children's free play across the Western world (Chudakoff 2007). Many of the factors contributing to this decline, such as the rise of excessive individualism and decline of socially cohesive communities can be attributed to the outcomes of neoliberal policies (Layard & Dunn 2009). Amongst the most detrimental has been the raft of education reforms leading to an ever increasing emphasis on academic attainment and testing in schools (Elkind, 2007). This increased academic burden has led to play time in schools being cut significantly in recent years (Blatchford et al. 2002; Jarrett 2002), and examples exist of UK schools which have removed the time and space traditionally allocated to children's play altogether (Gill 2007). This downward pressure on play looks set to continue as reforms are introduced which further increase the amount of time spent in the classroom (Madsen et al. 2011).

Within a neoliberalised construct of childhood the removal of play from the lives of school children is easily justified by trivializing it as antithetic to the established values of education and academic attainment. For Playwork this is a concerning consequence, but one to which the response is often proactive in increasing the reach and scope of its influence elsewhere in the community, for example the rise of street play and play ranger provision in the UK. A much more pernicious effect, and one which Playwork has arguably been less effective in resisting, has been the promotion of a conceptualisation of play which, since the advent of contemporary neoliberalism, has come to dominate socio-political discourse and public policy development. This conceptualisation, referred to in the literature as Instrumental or Utilitarian (Powell & Wellard 2008), allows for children's play so long as that play can be seen to address a pre-determined aspect of the social agenda, or used to affect a quantifiable positive change in the child. In this context play is regarded as an instrument, at the disposal of adults, for the correction of childhood deficiencies. Play that measurably reduces childhood obesity, or quantifiably improves numeracy, for example, becomes acceptable in the eyes of practitioners and policy-makers. But only if, as Education Minister, Liz Truss explained at a recent conference of early childhood educators, it is "adult-led, planned and purposeful" (Truss 2013).

From a Playwork perspective it would be very difficult to identify three words less apposite to define play than adult-led, planned and purposeful. One of the fundamental assumptions of Playwork is that play is fun, free, and flexible (Brown 2008), which are almost direct antonyms. To paraphrase Stuart Brown, when the purpose or outcome of playing becomes more important than the act of doing it, then it's probably no longer play (Brown 2009). This notion that the process of playing is more important than its outcome is central to the guiding Playwork Principles which state: "Play is a process that is freely chosen, personally directed and intrinsically motivated, the content and intent of which children determine and control by following their own instincts, ideas and interests in their own way and for their own reasons" (PPSG 2005). The concept is summed up rather neatly by Jerome Bruner who describes play as an approach to action rather than a form of activity (Bruner 1989). A discourse of fun and apparent purposelessness, however, should not be mistaken for one of frivolity, nor does that discourse ignore the crucial developmental function of playing.

The Playwork Principles state that practitioners should maintain a sound and up-to-date knowledge of the play process (PPSG 2005), and as the academic study of play grows so too does the accumulative body of evidence which points to play, not as a frivolous activity, but as a deep-rooted bio-psychological drive. That is to say that play is an evolutionarily refined mechanism for survival and adaptation Sutton-Smith 2008), which if supressed or distorted can result in physical and psychological damage. Consequently play is understood as central to all realms of human development. Playing strengthens individual emotional resilience; enhances creative, divergent and innovative thinking, and serves a vital role in maintaining children's physical and mental health (Frederickson, 2006; Isen & Reeve 2006; Pressman & Cohen, 2005; Gmitrova & Gmitrov, 2004). Crucially, however, these benefits are acquired if play is allowed to follow its own course unhindered by unnecessary intervention. To reiterate the words of Stuart Brown, if the outcome is more important than the process, then it probably isn't play. However, despite the relationship between playing and development being long established in the Playwork literature, for example Hughes (1996, 2001, 2002, 2012) and Sturrock & Else (1998), in its bid to resist instrumental and future-oriented constructs of play and childhood, Playwork has traditionally been hesitant about advocating on the basis of play's developmental potential.. Instead it has tended to promote the primacy of play as being for its own sake, and regard the developmental benefits as secondary, deferred, or "windfall." It is perhaps this hesitancy in a society entrenched in neoliberal ideology that has allowed the instrumental construct to gain ascendancy, whilst Playwork's bid for serious political traction has floundered.

Yet whilst play slips down the political agenda in the UK, elsewhere an opposite trend is apparently emerging. In a study for the Department of Quantitative Social Science, Jerrim and Choi (2013) explain that domestic education reforms in Britain have been initiated largely as a response to the disparity in academic attainment between UK and East Asian school children as identified in the aforementioned PISA assessments and TIMSS studies of school pupils' academic achievements. Children's education in East Asian countries has typically involved longer school days with shorter holidays, a greater focus on testing, and a greater expectation to engage with formal learning outside of the school day. However, the study's authors also point out that education reforms influenced by traditional East Asian models might not be the most effective way for the UK to close the attainment gap (Jerrim and Choi, 2013).

Indeed whilst the UK takes direction on education reform from countries such as China and South Korea, those same countries are reforming their own systems in recognition that traditional methods are not best suited to the demands of a changing world economy. Evidence appears to suggest that those graduating from education systems with the highest PISA rankings aren't sufficiently skilled for the jobs of the new global economy. In South Korea, a nation that has also been internationally recognised for the high academic attainment of its school pupils as indicated by test scores, it has been documented that the country's best graduates aren't suited to the jobs on offer (Guilford, 2013). Whilst in China, the phrase *goafen dineng*, meaning "good at tests, but bad at everything else" has become used commonly to describe its school pupils (Gray, P. 2014). In 2011 Xiong Bingqi, a Chinese education expert, told the Los Angeles Times that:

> We have seen the advantages and the disadvantages of our education system, and our students' abilities are still weak . . . they do very well in those subjects the teacher assigns them. They have huge vocabularies and they do math well. However, the level of their creativity and imagination is low. (Klein 2013: 1)

Similarly, reports from employers in the UK and United States are emerging of university and college graduates who are unable to demonstrate the types of "soft" skills deemed increasingly crucial by employers. A study by McKinsey, cited in Mourshed et al. (2012), found that 45 percent of U.S. employers said the main reason for entry-level job vacancies was a lack of these skills in graduates. The same study found that only 42 percent of employers worldwide believe new graduates are adequately prepared for work, and a 2014 study by CareerBuilder found that 40 percent of employers believe students lack problem solving skills, 39 percent aren't sufficiently creative in their thinking and 37 percent have inadequate oral communication (CareerBuilder, 2014).

Whilst causation is difficult to prove, it may be more than coincidence that this generation of ill-equipped graduates is the first to have suffered a significant deficit of play as the neoliberalisation of childhood intensifies. Play is well documented in the literature as a process central to the development of these apparently absent yet highly valued "soft" cognitive and social employability skills, as defined by Universities UK/CBI (2009), such as team-working; communication; critical thinking; creativity; innovation; enterprise and problem solving. For example, play promotes flexible thinking and facilitates the acquisition of personal resources that can be drawn on in times of need (Frederickson, 2006); the enjoyment of playing has benefits for flexible thinking and problem solving and enhances performance (Isen & Reeve 2006; Pressman & Cohen, 2005); there is a positive relationship between cognitive skills and high quality play (Gmitrova & Gmitrov, 2004), and play is linked to creativity in the sense that it involves divergent thinking, symbol substitution, positive affect, problem solving skills and emotion regulation (Russ, 2004).

Those international league table-leading countries' education systems are responding to the aforementioned changes in the types of skills and attributes demanded by growing global industry, and perceived deficiencies in its emerging workforce by *reducing* the academic burden and factoring in more time for free play and self-initiated activity in the school day (Klein 2013). China's Ministry for Education has released draft guidelines for education reform which include 10 regulations to lessen the burden of workload on its school children. One of the regulations states that primary schools may no longer set any form of written homework for students in grades one to six (Klein 2013). Despite taking the number one position on PISA in all three subjects twice in a row (Farrell & Grant, 2005), Shanghai is considering withdrawing from the PISA assessment process 2015 in a bid to reduce the excessive academic workload on children. In place of PISA, Shanghai will develop its own evaluation system which deemphasises the significance of test scores (Zhao 2015).

What is more, companies at the forefront of the expanding knowledge economy and global creative industries are openly citing play and opportunities for freely chosen activity in the workplace as key drivers of productivity, innovation, creative thinking and entrepreneurship. Not only are these companies actively enabling employees to play as a means of improving productivity and performance, they are also doing so in part to compensate for skills deficiencies as identified in graduate employees and which are attributed to a deficit of play in childhood (Brown, 2009).

World-renowned innovators such as Google and 3M implement strategies that allow freedom to play and freedom to fail in the workplace. Erin Fluegge claims that the concept of "having fun at work" emerged with the "dot.com boom" of the 1990s when business first became more associated with play (cited in Vijay & Vazirani, 2011). The ethos of companies such as 3M is to provide employees the freedom to pursue their own interests in the hope of promoting and encouraging creativity and innovation. This ethos encourages employees to engage in "playtime" activities that are traditionally considered a "waste of time" or "unproductive" within business management, such as taking a walk, lying in the sun or playing pinball (Leher, 2012). Organisations which feature regularly on Forbe's 100 Best Companies list are those which have a shift in mind-set from "workplace" to "playspace" in which the creative processes of innovation are highly valued and invite passion and enthusiasm into the business (Meyer 2010). A study by Karl et al. (2005) found that play and fun in the workplace increases productivity; job satisfaction; innovation; morale and efficiency, whilst reducing absenteeism; stress; frustration and illness (Karl et al. 2005).

Whilst the concept of playfulness and fun in the workplace is a broad construct, and several similar, yet slightly distinct conceptualisations have been advanced, Fluegge (2008: 8) provides a working conceptualisation by defining workplace fun as "any social, interpersonal, or task activities at work of a playful or humorous nature which provide an individual with amusement, enjoyment or pleasure." Ford et al. (2003: 22) define fun at work as a "work environment that intentionally encourages, initiates, and supports a variety of enjoyable and pleasurable activities." In respect of play's compensatory value in the workplace, Stuart Brown in his 2009 publication "Play: How it Shapes the Brain, Opens the Imagination and Invigorates the Soul" discusses two consultants, Frank Wilson, a neurologist and author of the book *The Hand:*

How its Use Shapes the Brain, Language and Human Culture, and Nate Johnson, a mechanics teacher in a high school in Long Beach, who found that his students were no longer able to solve problems. In his endeavours to discover why this was the case, Johnson came to the conclusion that it was because they hadn't played enough with their hands in childhood. Johnson and Wilson collaborated to work for JPL, NASA and Boeing as consultants designing play programmes to improve the problem-solving capabilities of newly recruited research and development problem solvers (Brown, 2009).

Throughout history the public perception of play has been driven and bound up in the prevailing childhood construct of the time. For example, during the romantic era, originating in Europe towards the end of the eighteenth century, play was considered a process that made individuals whole and was regarded as comparable in status to adult's work. A century later, coinciding with a reconstruction of the child as "sinful," the prevailing view of play was that it wasted time that could be used for "personal improvement." (Hendrick 1997) Given that the non-outcome driven, child-initiated conceptualisation of play that Playwork has sought to advance during the last 40 years has been largely tangential to the prevailing future oriented construct of childhood it is to playwork's immense credit that it has achieved any political influence at all. Yet in the face of the present government's neoliberal onslaught that modicum of influence dwindles. Within weeks of coming to power the Tory-led coalition government abandoned England's National Strategy for Play developed during the New Labour administration, and Play England, the government's delivery partner on play has been pared back to a state of almost non-existence.

With no credible opposition to this hegemonic political ideology history suggests that the dominant conceptualisations of childhood and play appear unlikely to change any time soon. Consequently Playwork finds itself in a quandary: a political case for play built on Playwork's guiding principles seems increasingly likely to fall on deaf ears, whilst appealing to a neoliberal agenda by promoting play's developmental value risks undermining its own argument. As Playwork's political influence and credibility looks likely to further recede, salvation may be sought in two unlikely arenas. Firstly, the traditionally didactic and instructive teaching and assessment methods of the East Asian countries that the UK is apparently seeking to emulate have been found to correlate negatively with nations' entrepreneurial confidence and activities (Zhao, 2012). In response these countries' education reforms cede control to children because it is precisely the freedom of choice and control in playing which enhances the "soft skills" and entrepreneurial capabilities so highly sought after by global business and commerce. Secondly, business and commerce is itself embracing the "fun, freedom and flexibility" of play in the work place because it drives up profit margins by increasing productivity, efficiency, motivation and morale, whilst reducing stress, illness and absenteeism (Karl et al. 2005). It is the "freely chosen, personally directed and intrinsically motivated" (Hughes 1984) characteristics of play that develops children's creativity, flexibility, problem solving and innovation, which according to Zhao (2012), citing Auerswald (2012), will bring "coming prosperity to the world," and it's difficult to conceive of a neoliberalist worth his salt who wouldn't want to be part of that.

REFERENCES

Alexander, R. J. (2009). *Towards a new primary curriculum: a report from the Cambridge Primary Review. Part 2: The Future.* Cambridge, England: University of Cambridge Faculty of Education.

Auerswald, P. (2012). *The coming prosperity: how entrepreneurs are transforming the global economy.* New York: Oxford University Press.

Blatchford, P., Pellegrini, T., Baines, E. and Kentaro, K. (2002) *Playground games: their social context in elementary/junior school. Final report to the Spencer Foundation 2002.* [Online] Available from: www.breaktime.org.uk/SpencerFinalReport02.pdf [Accessed 14 June 2015].

Brown, F. (2008) "Playwork Theory and Playwork Practice in the UK" In Brown, F. & Taylor, C. (eds.) *Foundations of playwork* Maidenhead: Open University Press.

Brown, S. (2009) *Play. how it shapes the brain, opens the imagination and invigorates the soul.* London: Penguin Books Ltd.

Butland B., Jebb S., Kopelman P., et al. (2007) *Tackling obesities: future choices—project report (2nd Ed).* London: Foresight Programme of the Government Office for Science.

Butler, P. (2015) UK benefits cap is lawful but breaches UN children's rights obligations. *The Guardian* 18 March. p. 22.

CareerBuilder (2014) *The shocking truth about the skills gap.* [Online] Available from: www.careerbuildercommunications.com/pdf/skills-gap-2014.pdf [Accessed 14 June 2015].

Chitty, C. (2004) *Education policy in Britain* Basingstoke: Palgrave Macmillan.

Corsaro, W. (2011) *The sociology of childhood 3rd edition.* London: Sage Publications.

CRC (2013) *General Comment No. 16 (2013) on State obligations regarding the impact of the business sector on children's rights.* United Nations.

Doward, J. & Helm, T. (2015) Child poverty rise across britain halts "progress made since 1990s" *The Guardian* 20th June p. 17.

Dr Foster Research. (2008) *Weighing up the burden of obesity: a review by Dr Foster Research.* London: Dr Foster Research, 2008.

Elkind, D. (2007) *The power of play: how spontaneous, imaginative activities lead to happier, healthier children.* Cambridge, MA: Da Capo Press.

Farrell, D., & Grant, A. (2005). *Addressing China's looming talent shortage.* Shanghai: Mckinsey Global Institute.

Fluegge, E. (2008) *Who put the fun in functional? fun at work and its effects on job performance.* [Online] Available from: http://etd.fcla.edu/UF/UFE0021955/fluegge_e.pdf [Accessed 14 June 2015].

Fredrickson, B. (2006) Unpacking positive emotions: investigating the seeds of human flourishing. *The Journal of Positive Psychology*, 1 (2):57–59.

Gill, T. (2007) *No fear: growing up in a risk averse society.* London: Calouste-Gulbenkian Foundation.

Gmitrova, V. and Gmitrov, J. (2004) The primacy of child-directed pretend play on cognitive competence in a mixed-age environment: possible interpretations. *Early Child Development and Care,* 174(3): 267–279.

Goldin, C., & Katz, L. F. (2008). *The race between education and technology.* Cambridge, MA: Harvard University Press.

Gray, P. (2014) *Give childhood back to children: if we want our offspring to have happy, productive and moral lives, we must allow more time for play, not less.* http://www.independent.co.uk/voices/comment/give-childhood-back-to-children-if-we-want-our-offspring-to-have-happy-productive-and-moral-lives-we-must-allow-more-time-for-play-not-less-are-you-listening-gove-9054433.html [Accessed June 2015].

Guilford, G. (2013). *An elderly crisis and a youth crisis: South Korea's got it all.* [Online] Available from: http://qz.com/76423/an-elderly-crisis-and-a-youth-crisis-south-koreas-got-it-all/ [Accessed 14 June 2015].

Hart, R. (2008) Participation and playwork. *Play for Wales* Issue 24.

Harvey, D. (2005) *A brief history of neoliberalism.* Oxford: Oxford University Press.

Hendrick, H. (1997) *Children, childhood & english society 1880—1990.* Cambridge University Press.

Hughes, B. (1984) *Play: a definition by synthesis.* Ely: Playeducation.

———. (1996) *Play environments: a question of quality.* London: PLAYLINK.

———. (2001) *Evolutionary playwork and reflective analytic practice.* London: Routledge.

———. (2002) *A playworker's taxonomy of play types.* 2nd Edition London, PLAYLINK.

———. (2012) *Evolutionary playwork.* London: Routledge.

Isen, A. and Reeve, J. (2006) The Influence of Positive Affect on Intrinsic and Extrinsic Motivation: facilitating enjoyment of play, responsible work behaviour and self-control. *Motivation and Emotion,* 29(4): 297–325.

James, A. & James, A. (2004) *Constructing childhood. theory, policy & social practice* Basingstoke: Palgrave McMillan.

Jarrett, O. (2002) *Recess in elementary school: what does the research say*? ERIC Digest. ERIC Clearinghouse on Elementary and Early Childhood Education (ERIC Document Reproduction Service No. Ed466331).

Jones, K. (2003) *Education in Britain: 1944 to the present* Cambridge: Polity Press.

Jerrim, J. and Choi, A. (2013) *The mathematics skills of school children: how does England compare to the high performing East Asian jurisdictions?* DoQSS Working Paper No. 13–03. London: Institute of Education. University of London.

Karl, K. et al., (2005) Attitudes toward workplace fun: a three sector comparison *Journal of Leadership & Organizational Studies* 12, no. 2 (2005): 1–17.

Klein, R. (2013) China's education proposal could mean less homework for students. [Online] Available from: www.huffingtonpost.com/2013/09/03/china-education-regulations_n_3862080.html [Accessed 14 June 2015].

Kotz, D. (2002) Globalisaton and neoliberalism *Rethinking Marxism*, Vol.12, Number 2, Summer 2002, pp. 64–79.

Layard, R. and Dunn, J. (2009) *A good childhood: searching for values in a competitive age.* London: Penguin Books Ltd.

Leher, J. (2012) *Imagine—how creativity works.* New York: Houghton Mifflin Harcourt.

Madsen, K., Hicks, K. and Thompson, H. (2011) Physical activity and positive youth development: Impact of a school-based program, *Journal of School Health*, 81, 8, 462–470.

Meyer, P. (2010) *From workplace to playspace: innovating, learning and changing through dynamic engagement.* San Francisco: Jossey Bass.

Mourshed, M., Farrell, D., & Barton, D. (2012). *Education to employment: designing a system that works*. New York: McKinsey & Company.

Pellegrini, AD and Holmes, RM (2006) "The role of recess in primary school," In: Singer, D., Golinkoff, R. and Hirsh-Pasek, K. (eds) (2006) *Play = learning: how play motivates and enhances children's cognitive and social-emotional growth,* Oxford: Oxford University Press.

Powell, S. & Wellard, I. (2008) *Policies and play: the impact of national policies on children's opportunities to play*. London: Play England / National Children's Bureau.

PPSG (2005) *Playwork Principles* held in trust as honest brokers for the profession by the Playwork Principles Scrutiny Group [Online] Available from: www.playwales.org.uk/page.asp?id=50 [Accessed 14 June 2015].

Pressman, S. and Cohen, S. (2005) Does positive affect influence health? *Psychological Bulletin,* 131(6):925–971.

Russ, S. (2004) *Play in child development and psychotherapy.* New Jersey: Lawrence Erlbaum Associates.

Sturrock, G. and Else, P. (1998) The playground as therapeutic space: playwork as healing. In: *Proceedings of the IPA/USA Triennial National Conference, Play in a Changing Society: Research, Design, Application*. June 1998, Colorado. USA.

Sutton-Smith, B (1997) *The Ambiguity of Play,* Cambridge, MA: Harvard University Press.

Sutton-Smith, B. (2008) Beyond Ambiguity. In: Brown, F. & Taylor, C. (eds.) *Foundations of playwork.* Maidenhead: Open University Press.

Truss, L. (2013) *Speech to the Nursery World Conference* https://www.gov.uk/government/speeches/elizabeth-truss-speaks-about-2-year-olds-policy-and-practice [Accessed 14 June 2015].

Universities UK & CBI (2009) *Future Fit preparing graduates for the world of work.* London. CBI.

Vijay, M. and Vazirani N. (2011) Emerging Paradigm—Fun in the Workplace to Alleviate Stress. *SIES Journal of Management.* 7 (2) March 24–30.

Wragg, M. (2011) The Child's Right to Play: Rhetoric or Reality. In: Jones, P. & Walker, G. (eds.) *Children's rights in practice* London: Sage.

Zhao, Y. (2015) *Not interested in being #1 shanghai may ditch PISA*. [Online] Available from: http://zhaolearning.com/2014/05/25/not-interested-in-being-1-shanghai-may-ditch-pisa/ [Accessed 14 June 2015].

Zhao, Y. (2012). *World class learners: educating creative and entrepreneurial students*. Thousand Oaks, CA: Corwin.

Chapter Four

Where Do Playworkers Get the Knowledge that Informs the Responses they Make to Children?

Kelda Lyons

This Chapter asks the question, "Where do playworkers get the knowledge that informs the responses they make to children?" It looks at the kinds of knowledge that playworkers have, where they get it from, and how they use it to inform good responses to playing children, especially when children are playing or dealing with emotionally sensitive content. The importance of non-action in playworker responses or interventions (Hughes 2002) is also discussed.

WHAT IS A PLAYWORK INTERVENTION?

In order to hold the play environment for the children (Wilson 2014), or create a "play frame" (Else and Sturrock 2000, p.84) that may be emotionally risky, difficult, or sensitive for children, playworkers aim to respond to children in ways that support children's play, and the children themselves. In playwork, these responses are called "interventions" (Hughes 2002), meaning an adult intervention into children's play.

An example of a playwork intervention would be: a playworker seeing a child making a model and the child getting frustrated because of the lack of materials, fetching more materials that might be useful to the child, and putting them near the child, thus ensuring that the child has more options for making the model, without being directed in what to do.

METHOD: WHAT IS IN THIS CHAPTER?

1. An observation I wrote as part of a play session on an adventure playground. It looks in detail at how the other playworker and I held the play

frame, how we communicated with each other, and how we responded to the children and intervened. It also discusses what we did not do.
2. An explanation of the process I used to create this chapter
3. A presentation of the information that came out of the interview, analysis and writing process.

ADVENTURE PLAYGROUND OBSERVATION

Please note: Initials have been used in place of children's and playworkers' names, for reasons of confidentiality. Each time you see the word children, please read "children and teenagers," as the ages of children and young people in the observation went up to about 15 years old.

Observation

It was the afternoon session on an adventure playground and G, an eight year old boy, was following his brother M, an eleven year old, around. To me it seemed like G was stalking M. They moved around smoothly and confidently. It contrasted with many of the other children and teenagers who came to the playground, who often looked uncomfortable in their bodies. At some point the brothers stopped moving about, and stood around talking with some other children. M, who was bare-chested, said "When I grow up I'm gonna have a mansion and all the women."

Meanwhile, another playworker and I, and a group of children aged between eight and fifteen years old were sitting at a picnic bench, which was on a concrete area between a shipping container and two sandpits. Objects such as skates, balls, and fancy dress clothes were scattered on the concrete floor, and in big plastic buckets. One sandpit had a boat in it, and was surrounded by a wall with a mural with mismatched landscape objects painted on it (pyramids, pine trees, rivers, etc).

A core group of children attended the playground all year round, even in winter when it was less comfortable because we operated out of a portacabin with no proper heating or hot water. More children attended when it was warmer, in spring and summer. The group of children sitting on the picnic bench were part of the group who attended the playground all year round.

Z, the other playworker, had worked at the playground for five years. I had worked there for about two years. The playground offered five play sessions each week, with summer sessions running from 3–8pm on weekdays, and all day on Saturdays.

On this occasion Z and the children were making necklaces with beads and elastic. I was sitting at the bench. The children made jewellery a lot; it was easy to do, sociable and relaxing. Mothers enjoyed doing it, and everyone made jewellery which they shared with each other as gifts.

The children started talking about C's weight. C, a boy, about thirteen years of age, was popular and well respected by other children. He was normally calm, cheerful, and seemed quite happy in himself. He had changed from being slightly overweight, to being obese over the course of a year. Some of the physical things he used to do, like running, had become much harder for him because of his size. On a playground trip a few months earlier, he had struggled to walk the mile long journey back to the playground. He got very breathless, and his knees and ankles hurt because of his weight. He kept having to stop and sit down, whilst the rest of the group waited for him.

The children who were talking about C's weight weren't being unkind. They were just talking around the subject, and stating in a factual way how his weight now affected his ability to do physical things. This conversation looked difficult for C. Playworker Z and I made a lot of eye contact, and kept quiet. We did not stop the conversation, although a part of me wanted to, as it would have temporarily stopped this difficult situation for C. It was not bullying, which is why I think we chose to keep quiet. I was aware that this was a supported environment for the children (the playworkers were there to support the children), so perhaps it was the best place for the children to have this discussion. I was also aware that this was a reality for the children that one of their peers was too overweight to do basic movements, and that was something they needed or wanted to talk about.

This is an example of playworkers choosing an intervention style, i.e. being non-intrusive, staying near to the children, and using body language and facial expression to try and indicate support to all of the children. It is also an example of good teamwork. Z and I were communicating silently, indicating to each other that we were both aware of and monitoring what was going on. We were not smiling, and we both looked at C from time to time, trying to demonstrate to the children that we took them seriously, and at the same time communicating to C that we knew this was a difficult moment for him.

This is an example of the kind of tension that playworkers encounter on a regular basis; it is difficult to see children you work with experiencing situations they find emotionally challenging, when you know that the other children who are part of that situation are only expressing themselves and discussing their concerns. It is a challenge to sit and listen without stepping in and stopping conversations from happening, when that conversation makes you feel uncomfortable. Playworkers frequently have to try to find a balance between acting on an urge to be protective of children, and actually supporting what those same children choose to do. I believe that when children do these things very near to playworkers and keep them close by—we were all squeezed together on the picnic bench—children are choosing to have that discussion around and near the playworkers, and want them there for backup and support, as they trust that the playworkers will help them out at the right moment if needed. The children could have had this conversation further away from the playworkers.

Suddenly these children started singing loud songs about paedophiles and rape, and started swearing. Nearby there was a mother and her toddler who were new to the playground. Z and I maintained eye contact with each other. We did not want to tell the children to stop, as it was their space. It was made clear in the published playground information that children under eight years old were welcome to come in with parents, but that the playground was there primarily for children aged eight to fifteen, and that the play of this older age group took priority.

The conversation about C resumed, but started to stray into teasing. I got up and moved around, but consciously stayed nearby. I didn't want to stop the conversation, as I knew this was a strong peer group which I felt I should not interfere with. I also knew that if I got up, it would physically change something, in this case, how the children and Z were arranged around the bench. I also thought that if I looked in the plastic buckets near the bench, I might find an object that would serve as a distraction and move the focus from C. This is another example of a playwork intervention. Z had stood up too and although C was trying to sit the situation out and appear to be alright, he looked like he felt vulnerable, and not very happy.

Z asked why people bury themselves in the sand in the desert. I wasn't sure if she was talking about burial, or how people bury themselves in the sand for fun at the seaside. M, a boy of about twelve years old, talked about doing that on the beach. In a deliberate attempt to divert attention away from C, I shouted "who wants to dig a hole and put M in it?" The other children all said "yes," and came and dug a big hole in the sandpit with the boat in. M helped to dig, then got inside the hole. He said "not my head though." The other children buried him in sand right up to the neck, laid a skeleton costume on top of him, and put a pink hat on top of his head.

A Note on the Observation

Readers may have questions relating to what is play, and what is not play in this observation. For the purposes of this chapter, I am asking readers to think of the descriptions of what children are doing in this observation as children (maybe) moving in and out of playful, and non-playful states.

INTERVIEW AND WRITING PROCESS

I began with the question "how do playworkers know what they know?" I decided that I wanted to hear other playworkers views on this and arranged to interview some playworkers. I worked out my interview process, and wrote a set of questions.

I intended to interview three playworkers, one woman and two men. However, I ended up only interviewing the two men. Like me, both of them had done playwork for a long time before studying play and playwork at university. Both playworkers were reflective practitioners, and used what came out of their reflections to improve their playwork practice. Both the playworkers worked on the same playground. I went to their playground on a weekday morning and was given a tour of the indoor and outdoor areas. Then I conducted separate interviews in the staff office.

Each interview went as follows: I gave the playworker a one page printed abstract to read, which outlined what this chapter was intended to be about. I said that we were going to underpin the interviews using three assumptions, which we would each keep in mind for the duration of the interview.

The first assumption was as follows: "For the purposes of this interview: A good playwork decision or response (to the playing child or children)—however you responded at the time—is one that you felt supported the play of all the children as much as possible, and as well as you knew how." The example I gave from my observation, was when Z and I stayed quietly on the bench when the children were talking about C.

The second assumption was: "That when you respond to a playing child, on some level, you make a decision about this response, i.e. you don't just do something."

The third assumption was: "That what playworkers don't do or don't say is often as important as what they actually say and do, and can imply permissions and freedoms to children, thus increasing their opportunities for play."

I asked the playworkers if they understood these three assumptions and asked if they were happy to proceed with the interview on this basis. They said they were. Then I gave them a printed copy of the observation I presented above, and asked them to read it. Then I asked them to think of a similar experience of their own. For example, a time when they were working in a play setting with a child or children who were playing with, or going through something that the playworker knew was difficult or challenging for that child or children. Each playworker related their observation to me. Then I asked each playworker the following questions:

- How did you respond to the children and situation?
- What did you say / not say?

- What did you do / not do?
- How did you move?
- How did you speak, if you did?
- How did you feel?
- What did you think informed your responses to the children and situation?
- Where do you think you got the knowledge that informed your responses to children, or your interventions?

I also asked other questions that aimed to gather more detailed information, or to get clarification about things I thought were important. I took audio recordings of the observations and the questioning process. Each interview was planned to take twenty-five minutes, but actually took around fifty minutes.

Two weeks after the interviews with the playworkers, and after I had transcribed and summarised their interviews, I conducted a fifteen minute interview with a movement specialist about non-verbal communication, and the significance of "not doing" (my phrase), because I wanted an expert perspective on this, and possibly a better description than "not doing."

THE TRANSCRIPTION, ANALYSIS AND WRITING PROCESS

I transcribed the first interview in a mind-map style, in A3 notebooks; then created a summary of this interview, in the same way. I studied the summary; then recorded the broad areas that I thought had emerged from it. They were:

- awareness / attunement
- trust
- relationships
- experience
- learning
- staff team
- values / beliefs
- knowledge
- interventions / decisions

This process was repeated with the second interview.

Next, on a large sheet of paper, I wrote down all of the questions I had asked the playworkers. I also recorded my own answers to these questions, trying to draw from the knowledge that I had at the time of writing my own observation.

I studied both sets of summary notes, and my own notes, and compared them to the broad areas listed above. After doing this repeatedly over the course of three days, I regrouped the broad areas into the following headings, which now form the basis of the remainder of this chapter:

- responses / interventions
- knowledge and/or understanding
- awareness
- attunement
- beliefs and values
- action and non-action
- trust
- learning

I created the above headings because I thought that they would:

1. cover all of the important points from the interviews
2. provide clear sections which all the information I had gathered would accurately and comfortably fit into

I wrote the headings down, evenly spaced, across a 2ft × 5ft piece of paper. Then, on the same paper I wrote down every piece of information from the initial transcription of the first interview. Each piece of information (note) was connected to a heading with a line. I put the initial of the first playworker next to each note, and then added all the notes from the second interview to the large paper in the same way, connecting them to a relevant heading with a line. If I thought that a note from the second interview was similar enough to a note from the first interview, then the note from the second interview did not get written down. Instead, the initial of the second playworker was added to the similar note of the first playworker. Then I went through the same process with my own written answers to the interview questions. If one of my notes corresponded to an existing note from one of the two playworker interviews, I added my initial to it. If my answers generated a new note, I wrote that down on the large paper and put my initial next to it. Most notes had two or three initials by them at the end of the process. A few notes only had one initial, primarily where there was a specific quote next to them that I wanted to use in writing, or because the playworker used a word that did not feature in the other two observations, such as "rage." By the end of the process, all of the information from the interviews related to, and fitted comfortably around one or other of the headings.

I also transcribed the interview I did with the movement specialist in a mindmap format. I wrote summary notes from this interview on the large paper, around a separate heading (the name of this interviewee), so that I could keep reading and re-reading the notes from all three interviews at the same time. Comments from the interview with the movement specialist were integrated into this Chapter after I had written up the information gathered from the playworkers, and from my own answers.

Other Points from Interviewing

One of the playworkers moved from talking about "I" to "We" during the interview, and maintained this for the remainder of the interview. He was referring to the knowledge and actions of his staff team. To me, this implied that he was only able to look at his individual responses to children in the context of him working as part of his current staff team, the "We."

Notes for Reading the Rest of this Chapter

1. The term "playworker/s," rather than "interviewee/s," is used throughout.
2. At various points in the remainder of this chapter I refer to the views of "the playworkers" or "both playworkers," which means the two playworkers who I interviewed. At other points I refer to "one playworker," which means one of the playworkers I interviewed. Sometimes I refer to "we," "our," or "us," which means both of the playworkers I interviewed, and myself. I have tried to be as accurate as possible when specifying who and how many of us talked about any given point.
3. When I use quotation marks without referring to particular texts, names or interviews, it means that this quote comes from one of the two playworker interviews I did. I have not specified which quote is from which interview.

RESULTS: SUMMARIES OF THE TWO PLAYWORKERS' OBSERVATIONS

The First Interview

The first playworker told me about part of a play session that took place on the playground that he was working on. The playground had a good sized building, with a kitchen, office, storerooms and toilets off a large main room. There was a large fenced outside space, with a lot of low level adventure wooden play structures in it, a garden area, and some empty open space.

He described one child starting to jokily tease another child with comments thrown back and forth that developed into conversations about the religions of the respective children. The playworker was stationed in the kitchen, which had a large hatch that looked onto the main room. He was cooking lunch with a group of children, and was listening to the conversation about religion in the main room. He described turning his body around slightly so he could hear what was happening, being careful not to make any sharp movements, deciding to stay in the kitchen and be quiet, and move closer to the sound, with calm movements, tilting his head when he wanted better to hear what was going on. He said that the conversation between the children escalated, and that he was aware of aggression within the conversation. He said that one child played at being a judge. He commented on the fact that some of the children climbed onto and sat on top of a wardrobe near the kitchen hatch, whilst the other child who they were talking about religion with, stayed standing on the floor.

This playworker told me that the children's conversation included talking about:

- the tradition of respecting and not speaking ill of the dead
- Jesus as god, and what the playworker described as "muddled understanding" of religion.
- the discovery and origins of religion
- the concept of a prophet, and Jesus' journey, with one child saying "That's like me, I was born in Margate and moved to London"
- children telling each other "your religion kills and murders"
- children discussing and questioning what people from different religions do and don't do
- a playful court case, with one child in middle of the room pretending to be a judge, asking "Person A, what do you think?"

The Second Interview

The second playworker talked about an experience he had a few years ago when he was a manager in an after school club, where he was trying to "introduce playwork thinking," which there was a "lot of resistance" to. He spoke about rules and the limitations imposed on the use of the building and the children, which he said did not support the children's play. For example, there was a large field outside which staff were not allowed to take children onto for "health and safety" reasons. The playworker described a boy of ten or eleven years old, who often had difficulties with containing his anger. The playworker told me that one afternoon something had triggered a state of rage in the boy, in what was a windowless hall where the club was run, and where there were about twenty-five other children. The playworker said that the boy was shouting, and throwing tables and chairs around.

The playworker described being concerned about the safety both of the boy and the other children in the room. He said that he told the boy "we're going, let's go" and they went through the kitchen (a "banned" room for the children), out of the back door of the building, and into a small outdoors fenced-in space that had a patio, grass with a fire-pit on it that had charcoal in, and a roll of cardboard. The playworker described feeling tense at this moment. He said that the boy started "poking around" in the fire-pit, picking up pieces of charcoal and throwing them around. The playworker told me that he then unrolled the piece of cardboard and told the boy "come on, slap the charcoal down and lets do some art," with the aim of distracting the boy. The playworker told me that the boy crunched the charcoal, laughed, and then together the playworker and the boy decided to smear the whole cardboard black. The playworker told me that the boy eventually calmed down. The playworker then talked to the boy about why he (the boy) was upset.

Why Have I Described Some Moments as Being Emotionally Risky and Sensitive for Children?

Because of the emotional states that children were in during some of the observations; the word "aggressive" was used to describe both the atmosphere and the feeling around some of the conversations about religion. The boy described as being in a state of rage was also described as "not being able to level out again."

Responses/Playworker Interventions

During both interviews, the playworkers used the term "interventions" to talk about what I had initially described as "responses" (to children). Throughout their interviews, both playworkers continued to use this term to describe their actions in the observations they presented.

Each of my interventions and those of both playworkers were based on:

- Previous experience of working with other children
- Trying not to "impinge on the children"
- Making the best available choice in that moment
- Choosing the best space or place to be in at that moment
- Trying to balance the needs of all children present
- Desired empathy, or a degree of empathy with the child/ren
- Being in "normal," or "non-authoritarian" mode with the child/ren

In the interviews, the following things were mentioned by one playworker:

- Using the IMEE (Hughes 2002) model sometimes.
- Asking the child about what they were experiencing, for example "what's wrong?"
- Being able to pay attention to this moment/child/situation, i.e. not being overstretched and having too many other things to do at once. Being and feeling overstretched at work is common for playworkers, due to understaffing, the nature of working in environments where many different things can suddenly happen at once, the mood of the day, etc.

Comments on Intuition and Instinct

Both playworkers said that to some extent they were "making it up" as they went along and working in an intuitive way. Although one playworker did say that interventions still have to "be framed from somewhere," and the other playworker said that interventions have to "be based on something, have to be based on some sort of experience," even when intuition is involved. When questioned about this further, neither playworker was sure about what this frame or base is or might be, although one of them talked about "continuous reading of the environment," and mentioned the concept of "reflection-in-action" (Schon, 1991, p.49).

Knowledge and/or Understanding

Although I used the term knowledge as a starting point in the interviews, I didn't have a clear definition for it and I told the playworkers I interviewed as much. I also said that I hoped that the interviews and my analysis would still reveal, a) "how playworkers know what they know?" and b) "where playworkers get the knowledge that informed the responses they made to children in playwork settings?" Both playworkers said they understood these statements, and we proceeded with the interviews in the understanding that we were not using a clear definition for the word "knowledge." Midway through one of the interviews, one of the playworkers asked if we could move from thinking in terms of playworker knowledge, to thinking more in terms of understanding. We agreed to continue the interview on this basis.

Knowledge and/or understanding that both playworkers and I had:

- We all thought that having awareness of many different aspects of the play environment was important for our understanding of what was happening in the present moment.

- Knowledge of the children was important, and it was thought that this affected the interventions that playworkers made. One playworker and I felt that previous time spent with children, and knowledge of individual children and existing friendships or peer groups meant that we were able to intervene less, as we were able to trust children more, and that this gave them more freedom to experiment.
- Of children's habits, especially of how they use particular areas at particular times.
- Of deep mutual adult child understanding. One playworker spoke about very "quick click" relationships between him and individual children, meaning good relationships that are formed instantly, often without speaking. This is something I have also experienced.
- That children often have emotional resilience, and the capability to negotiate situations that they find emotionally challenging, without the experience causing them harm. We were all aware that conversations and interactions which are difficult for children and teenagers are a normal part of peer group interactions.
- Of previous occasions in play sessions where we had got things "wrong," aggravating tense situations with our actions or behaviour, and making interventions which had not been helpful to children playing. One playworker spoke about learning from mistakes made in the past.

One playworker spoke about having knowledge of:

- How to relate to individual children well, and get on with them.
- How to approach children who are in difficult situations, in a positive way.

The other playworker spoke about having knowledge of:

Children's language, for example being able to quickly understand that a child meant "electrics" or wiring, when they said "Lectric" in response to "I spy something beginning with L" in an I-spy game. This could also be defined as attunement, or the playworker being tuned into children's language and their way of speaking.

None of us had a satisfactory term to describe the type, or types of knowledge or understanding that we have.

Awareness

Both playworkers and I referred to awareness a lot; being aware of the children, being aware of one's self, of what is happening in the moment, and what had happened in previous play sessions. When the playworkers talked to me, and when I made my own notes on this, I noticed that all three of us were easily able to recollect and describe how we felt.

The playworkers and I were aware of:

- (and had recognition of) Children's existing peer groups and relationships.
- Children's energy patterns, rhythms, and routines.
- Of the possibilities of what could happen next (e.g. physical violence stemming from conversations about religion was mentioned as a possibility, as this had happened before).
- Children's cultural backgrounds.
- Children's awareness of the playworkers.
- Our own effect on the children; for example, being conscious of not adding to aggression with our own behaviour or actions.
- What was happening in the moment, or the play that was happening at each moment in time, described by one playworker as "the moments of play that emerged." One example is the moment where one of the playworkers became aware that the boy he was with had started scrunching charcoal with his feet; the playworker was aware that the boy had moved from a state of rage, into doing something.
- Sensory experiences, or what was going on sensory wise for us, in particular, listening and looking.
- The spontaneity of each moment.
- The physical environment, in particular the spatial aspects, including:
    1. What it offers to children (potential play opportunities, privacy, height, the outdoors offering an "away" quality).
    2. Whether there were windows or not in a room, and the potential effects of this on the children.
    3. The size of rooms and areas.
    4. Objects such as a wardrobe, charcoal, dressing up clothes, sand; loose parts (Nicholson 1971) that don't have designated uses in play settings.
    5. The acoustics.
    6. Height, and places for children to be on or in (kitchen with large hatch, boat, sandpit).

Attunement

I am using the term attunement to mean: the playworker being tuned into the detail of what was happening for the children and people in the environment directly around them, and having the ability to read and understand how children were feeling from their actions, facial expressions, language, movements, individual or collective volume, and the tone and inflection in their voices. Attunement also refers to playworkers being able to make meaning of where children position themselves in a room or outdoors area, and understanding the dynamics that this can create amongst groups or larger numbers of children. I am also defining attunement as being able to empathise to some degree with what children were feeling and experiencing.

These different interpretations of the term attunement came from the interviews, when I asked the playworkers: a) what they saw and noticed happening, and b) to describe in detail how they felt, moved, and spoke during the observations they made. Both talked in great detail about what happened around them, and spoke about being attuned to the environment. Each of us experienced heightened awareness of our own feelings; one playworker "felt contained" when he was with, and supporting a child in a state of rage. We all spoke about moments in our observations when we felt "protective."

Both playworkers and I were attuned to:

- Where children were placed within the indoors or outdoors areas, and the potential effect of this on the dynamics of the play. One example was: Three children sitting on top of a wardrobe during a tense conversation, whilst one boy was standing on the floor.
- Physical movements and facial expressions, and the mood and feelings that these indicated in the children.
- Noise levels, tone, inflection of voices, and language the children were using.
- One playworker spoke about "atmospheric attunement." I did not question this further.
- Our own "gut instinct." Both playworkers talked about this. I understood this as being in tune with ones own feelings about how to proceed in a situation.

Beliefs and Values

Beliefs and values played a strong part in informing or defining our interventions in the observations that both playworkers and I presented. After doing these interviews, I think that it is only possible to look at playworker knowledge whilst acknowledging that it is intertwined with beliefs.

One belief was about the purpose of play settings; that they exist to provide time, space and opportunity for children to play. The staff team on the playground where I did the interviews had created this mission statement: "Working to increase possibilities for the time and space for children's play across communities." I was told that it summarised the staff beliefs about what the playground was for, and had "got all the staff values in." What playworkers value in terms of play and play opportunities affects how they set up and manage a play setting, as well as how they intervene in moments of play. One playworker spoke about the "value of providing space for children to be able to have their own emotional repertoires and responses."

For example, we all expressed our belief in children's abilities and capabilities, especially when they were negotiating their own difficulties and differences. The first playworker I interviewed spoke about a child acting in the role of a judge during a conversation about different religions. This could be interpreted as that child helping to support a conversation, which had become "aggressive."

One playworker expressed the belief that children have the ability to read empathic gestures and situations, i.e. that children can understand and appreciate when an adult is trying to empathise with them. Both of the playworkers and I spoke about trying to do this during our observations.

Action and Non-action

I interviewed a movement specialist about the significance of not acting, or not doing. I had taken part in one of his workshops where the group did an exercise that allowed them to explore the significance of silently moving away from, towards, or being still around other people. It was because of this experience that I chose to interview him about not acting, or not doing.

His comment on what I loosely described as non-action was: "It's not non-action," because "the action sometimes is not to react." He said that being highly aware of other people around you is "a very present and active state, to listen with your whole body to what's going on." This echoed what the playworkers talked about, when they listened very closely to the children, and told me about very small movements or actions that they made; a playworker tilting his head slightly in order to hear children in an adjoining indoor space better, for example.

When I asked the movement specialist what non-action generally communicated, he said it can:

- "indicate support"
- suggest an "invitation to continue"
- give out a message that "it is O.K to keep doing this"
- empower the other person

Trust

In my initial notes I wrote the question "what role does trust have in all of this?" Although I did not ask specifically about it in interviews, both playworkers and the movement specialist mentioned it.

Trust seems to span or be connected with several of the headings I am using. It is not knowledge or understanding, or an action, although it can be expressed through an action or communication. A playworker moving far away from a fire to indicate to children that s/he trusts the children to be around it safely, is a good example.

Supportive interventions involve trust. I trusted that the children in my observation were not bullying their friend.

There was a strong sense of playworkers trusting children in all of the observations. One playworker spoke about trusting their gut instinct about the children, and being able to trust themselves to intervene in the right way, because they trusted the children first.

Learning

This section focuses on how learning happened for us. The playworkers and I could not always identify exactly where, how, or when we had learnt particular things. When we could, I have specified it in Table 4.1. I have specified whether learning applied to one, two, or all three of us.

Table 4.1. How did the learning happen for us?

What Learning?	*Where / How?*
Learning about children's "childrenness"—one playworker.	From eye-conversations with children.
Learnt about children from time spent with them—all.	Experience over time, one playworker knows he didn't have this when younger.
Helped to look at own practice in deeper ways—all.	Studying independently and in formal and further education—all.
Expanded ability to question, questioning a lot more now, asking our own questions rather than simply accepting the play theory that we read or hear—all. One playworker is 'now operating in a different bandwidth' after studying.	Studying independently and in formal and further education—all.
Gathering information on what is happening in the moment—all. One playworker talked about 'monitoring emotional impact on children' whilst play is happening.	Learnt to do at work, by observation and experience—all.
Reading helped one playworker's learning, but not directly—he said that it's like a "melting pot that fizzes around in your brain."	Reading
One playworker said that knowledge gained from mapping can inform interventions and improve practice.	Extensive playground mapping: • zones of movement • playworker movement

What Learning?	*Where / How?*
The other playworker was not sure if mapping informed their responses to children.	• loose parts movement • significant and zoned places
How to allow play to happen more.	Past playwork experience—all.
Learning how to trust self and child and not shut play down if it is difficult for the playworker.	
Learning how to trust own instinct.	
We are all still learning (I did not ask about the specifics of this). One playworker said that "more studying is vital for the understanding of space."	Response to me asking if the playworkers think they have finished their playwork learning.
Helped and hindered. One playworker said that some courses are non-questioning, too standardised, and miss the "relational contexts" and "uniqueness" of play spaces.	Training courses and conferences.
One playworker said that theory is often misinterpreted and misrepresented, and that it should stem more from "current practice/observations of children's play . . . contextual to a specific time, place, space." This playworker also said that "when play or playwork theory is discussed in conferences it is often spoken about as a single entity rather than it being linked to the specifics," and that this is unhelpful for playworker learning.	Conferences.
Refer back to the "knowledge/understanding section" to see an overview of our knowledge in the context of these interviews.	One playworker spoke about sharing interpretations of situations, stories and observations, with different colleagues in different ways; during play sessions, at staff meetings, in the pub, at conferences and in online discussions and with friends. We all viewed this as reflective practice. One playworker said that they learnt from hearing experiences of other playworkers, and hearing and understanding their thought processes.
One playworker learnt about de-escalation and distraction techniques, which they used in the observation they shared with me.	On training for working with mentally ill adults.
Finding out what children want and need.	Observing and asking children—all.

Table 4.2. Where did the knowledge come from?

Kelda—What learning?	*Where / How?*
Understanding the meaning and importance of moments of play for children I work with.	Writing observations and reflections. Discussing my work experiences with colleagues, friends and mentors. From time spent with children in play settings.
Appreciating the meaning, value and extent to which children feel and are supported by playworkers.	From working in play settings.
Knowledge of children's abilities and capabilities—informed me knowing when and why I should be silent, not smile, and allow play to happen. Belief that children are trustworthy and ability to trust them.	I knew these things before doing playwork, it was one of the reasons I decided to do playwork. Foundation in playwork course allowed me to articulate these things.
About tensions around space in play settings.	From staff team discussions. Studying and reading about the history of the area I worked in. Talking to local grandparents about their lives on this playground and in the area. Witnessing fights and aggression, and hearing complaints about inadequate play settings.
Learning about if, how and when to intervene. Knowledge of individual children and peer groups. Empathy informing interventions.	From time spent with children. Gathering information in the moment, being aware of what is going on. Foundation in playwork course helped me to understand this should be a conscious choice. Getting it wrong on many previous occasions.

In Table 4.2, I have tried to pinpoint where I think I got the knowledge that I had at the time of writing my observation.

REFLECTIONS AND CONCLUSION

Using observation examples worked well for these interviews. However, if I use this method again, I would ask playworkers to choose more recent observations, so we could look at knowledge gained up to the current moment in time, rather than looking at a combination of retrospective observations and current knowledge, which is what has happened here.

Interviewing playworkers who had a somewhat similar working and educational background to me turned out to be an advantage, in that our backgrounds, in terms of learning about play, seemed to contribute to our having similar kinds of knowledge, although further research with other playworkers would have to be done to confirm this.

The material contained in this Chapter could be a good starting point for further studies about playworker knowledge. It might also be useful for playworkers and other professionals who are thinking about ways to clearly describe and define an existing playwork method; this chapter presents a way of looking at what good playworkers already do, and offers one example of how to analyse and describe it.

Trust, the use of intuition, and playworkers' values and beliefs around children's play might also need to be factored in when looking further at playworker knowledge.

Thanks to: Will Pike, Life and Health Mentor; Joel Seath, playworker; Mike Dessington, playworker; and Dean from Home Build Supplies in Hackney.

REFERENCES

Else, P., and Sturrock, G. (2000) *Therapeutic playwork reader one*. Hampshire: Common Thread Publications Ltd.

Hughes, B. (2002) *The first claim—desirable processes*. Cardiff : PlayWales.

———. (2012) *Evolutionary playwork*. London: Routledge.

Nicholson, S. (1971) How not to cheat children: the theory of loose parts. In: *Landscape Architecture Quarterly*. Vol.62, No.1, October 1971, pp.30–34.

Schön D. (1991) *The reflective practitioner: how professionals think in action*. London: Temple Smith.

Wilson, P. 2014. *Good enough: D.W.Winnicott and playwork*. [Online] Available from: http://theinternationale.com/papers/goodenough.pdf [Accessed 24 April 2017].

Chapter Five

Playwork in America

Past, Current, and Future Trends

Michael Patte with contributions from:
Alex Cote, Rusty Keeler, Suzanna Law
and Morgan Leichter-Saxby

INTRODUCTION

This chapter documents how I became acquainted with the field of playwork, provides a brief examination of the historical roots of playwork in America, offers a glimpse into innovative programs adopting a playwork philosophy that are flourishing in America today, and makes recommendations for growing the field of playwork throughout America in the future.

The road leading to my interest in the field of playwork was curvy and included a few interesting destinations along the way including a rich childhood play life, professional training in child development and early childhood education, working both as a preschool and fifth grade teacher, and playing an active role in The Association for the Study of Play (TASP). As a child, my siblings and I enjoyed a rich play life where my parents provided an abundance of time and space to explore, risk, challenge, negotiate, construct, deconstruct, succeed, fail, laugh, cry, and be bored. They endorsed this parenting style intuitively without any formal education or training; perhaps they were both playworkers in a past life. These experiences nurtured my resiliency and an ethos that I was able to direct/chart the course of my own life. To date, this is the most precious gift that I ever received.

My professional training in child development and early childhood education featured world-renowned programs (Waldorf/Steiner, Reggio Emilia, Bank Street, Montessori, etc.) and scholars (Bruner, Dewey, Froebel, Piaget, Vygotsky, Sutton-Smith) all of which championed the role of play as an integral element throughout the lifespan. Experiencing these programs firsthand through fieldwork, and digesting the seminal works of the scholars mentioned above, had a profound influence on my desire to advocate for play on the local, state, and national levels in America.

Working as a preschool teacher for five years and as a fifth grade teacher for ten presented two distinctly different worlds that both reaffirmed and challenged my ardent views about the role of adults in directing children's lives. My teaching experience in a Reggio-inspired preschool that endorsed an emergent curricular approach growing out of the children's interests was exceptional. In this environment we explored topics for extended periods of time with no external pressure to rush on to the next topic at hand. Socio-dramatic and other forms of play were abundant throughout the day and children spent at least 60-minutes outdoors exploring in a nature area (a semi-wild play space of trees, rocks, sand, water, and wildlife). These five years affirmed my views about the beauty of childhood and the influence of positive teachers so beautifully articulated by American educationalist Jonathan Kozol (2007) in his book *Letters to a Young Teacher*,

> I think that teaching is a beautiful profession and that teachers of young children do one of the best things that there is to do in life: bring joy and beauty, mystery and mischievous delight into the hearts of little people in their years of greatest curiosity. (p. 1–2)

The ten years of teaching fifth graders (9–11 years olds) stood in stark contrast to my preschool teaching experiences with the biggest differences revolving around the concepts of control and intentionality. Whereas the preschool schedule and curriculum were child-driven and open-ended, those in fifth grade were adult-driven and prescribed. Initially, there were several extra-curricular activities dispersed throughout the school year to keep things interesting, but they eventually fell by the wayside in an ever-expanding culture of accountability. Elementary school teaching for me was always more of an artistic endeavor than a scientific one, but under these oppressive circumstances, teaching for me had lost its soul.

It was at this time that I stumbled upon The Association for the Study of Play, recognized as the premiere professional organization in academia dedicated to interdisciplinary research and theory construction concerning play. I attended the annual TASP gathering first in 2004 and shared the results of an empirical study documenting my experiences as a fifth grade teacher struggling to thrive in an oppressive accountability culture (Patte, 2009). The presentation was well received and the sessions I attended on all aspects of play offered by scholars across multiple disciplines were fascinating. At long last I had found an organization to serve as my professional home. At the 2006 TASP meeting in St. Catharines, Ontario, I attended a session offered by Fraser Brown titled *The Impact of a Playwork Project on a Group of Children in a Romanian Pediatric Hospital* that changed my life forever. This served as my introduction to the field of playwork.

Fraser's presentation inspired me to study the field of playwork and the more I studied, the more I came to realize that the foundational principles of the field seemed well suited to address societal factors devaluing play in America (Brown and Patte, 2013; Patte and Brown, 2011). In 2010 I was awarded a Distinguished Fulbright Scholarship Grant to study the field of playwork in the United Kingdom under Fraser's direction. One of the goals of the Fulbright was to build upon the work begun in America around the field of playwork by various individuals and organizations. As my colleagues will document later in the chapter, the field of playwork and adventourous play spaces in America is today gaining some traction.

HISTORICAL ROOTS OF PLAYWORK IN AMERICA

In the early part of the twentieth century, the Playground and Recreation Association of America produced *The Normal Course in Play—Practical Materials for Use in the Training of Playground Recreation Workers* (NCIP). The content of the manual was implemented throughout normal schools (teacher training programs) and universities that offered training courses in play for specialist workers across the country. In 1916, over 100 schools throughout America offered such training courses. According to Frost (2010), in 1924 over 700 American cities were providing community recreation leadership training, overseeing some 5,000 playgrounds, and employing nearly 16,000 workers whose focus was substantially on the play of children.

A foundational principle of the NCIP was that children must learn to govern themselves since government must be acquired as an experience rather than taught as a theory. From this frame, the playground and team games stressing democratic values were seen as important components for thriving in a democratic republic. The two stated purposes of the NCIP were:

1. To lay before the instructor, in as vivid a way as possible, the main facts about the play movement and program, its significance in the life of the individual and community, and the sources of information regarding it (PRAA, 1925, p. v).
2. To make community recreation vital; to give the spirit of play value as a philosophy of life; to give a conception of the scope of play and its influence on life which will challenge the student, as well as to give practical information, is the purpose of the NCIP (PRAA, 1925, p. v).

The NCIP defined play as "what we do, when we are free to do what we will" (PRAA, 1925, p. v) and drew upon multiple disciplines including psychology, sociology, child study, anthropology, civics, pedagogy, physical education, dramatics, and storytelling. Finally, the NCIP was comprehensive in scope including program planning, the nature and function of play, play leadership, play facilities, organization and administration, and the history of the community recreation movement.

THE BIRTH OF JUNK PLAYGROUNDS

During the years of World War II a controversial concept in playground design emerged in Denmark. Junk playgrounds or adventure playgrounds as they are known today were advanced by the Danish landscape architect Sorensen (1936) who drew upon the natural instincts of children to play with anything and anywhere often beyond the watchful eyes of adults. Although these playgrounds were to be staffed by trained playleaders, both the content and context of what happened in the space was to reflect the interests and imaginations of the children, and not the adults. The concept of junk/adventure playgrounds made its way to America around 1950 with playgrounds popping up in Minnesota, Massachusettes, California, Texas, Pennsylvania, and Georgia (Hogan 1974; Frost and Kline, 1979; Frost and Sunderlin, 1985). However, due to a variety of societal factors including a high priority on aesthetic value for play spaces, national safety guidelines, the litigious nature of society, lack of funds, inadequate training for playleaders, and no long term play advocacy strategy, most of the adventure playgrounds disappeared soon after they were initiated.

The state with the best track record for sustaining its adventure playgrounds into the present day is California, and as of 2017 three adventure playgrounds in Berkley, Huntington Beach, and Irvine were thriving. All of these venues offer children opportunities to experience what Hughes (2012) calls the four essential elements of all adventure playgrounds: wind, earth, fire, and water.

Although America has exhibited marginal success in sustaining adventure playgrounds in the past, the tide is beginning to turn. Due in part to organizations like *The Association for the Study of Play, The International Play Association, The Alliance for Childhood, The North American Adventure Play Association, The U.S. Play Coalition, and Pop Up Adventure Play* adventurous play spaces are beginning to sprout up throughout America. Following are descriptions of innovative programs that endorse a playwork philosophy flourishing across America today.

POP-UP ADVENTURE PLAY: NORTH AMERICAN TOUR 2014, *SUZANNA LAW*

When a child is at play, playworkers do not intervene. If needed, playworkers employ the lowest level of intervention so that the play can continue without disruption. What happens when a child asks you to participate in their play? What happens when a child sends a direct play cue? That is when the playworker instinct activates (following the child's lead, meeting their needs in play, and respecting the play frame). Playworkers draw upon extensive training and research from the field to make informed decisions about how to support the play process.

Applied on an organizational level, the playworkers at *Pop-Up Adventure Play* endorse the lowest level of intervention possible in meeting the needs of our clients. Sometimes, those needs are simple, like reaching out to see if others believe that play is important. Other times the needs are more complex, like rallying to support a fellow play advocate in a crisis. As a business, we keep an eye on these inquiries, examining our clients' interests and how best to meet them. As a playwork-based charity founded in 2008, we observed what the wider world was saying about play (priority to achievement culture, marginalization of recess, limited opportunities for community-based play) and devised a strategy to combat these barriers head on. We want to support adults in creating communities that encourage child-directed play by finding innovative ways to meet their needs.

In the Summer of 2013, we reached out to our American friends to help their neighborhoods foster a culture of play. Community-based play advocates sent us invitations to play, and after much discussion and reflection—another handy tool in the playworker arsenal (Jeffrey, 2008)—the team devised a strategy to meet the needs of those friends by connecting them all. Thus, the first ever Pop-Up Adventure Play Tour was hatched, and what an adventure it was.

We started our journey on February 19, 2014, where a heavy snowstorm threatened the tour's first event. After wading across snowdrifts with wet and soggy cardboard boxes and loose parts, we arrived at the Berkshire Museum where the Pop-Up Adventure Play tour began. Staff at the museum had meticulously lined a huge, architecturally significant hall with cardboard to allow themselves and visiting children the permission to play without damaging the space. Just seeing that thoughtful response of saying "yes" to play was quite emotional. This was going to be a tour that provided the opportunity to literally think outside the box in support of play.

The tour's mission was simple; to meet the play needs of each community visited. Our initial traveling playwork team included Morgan Leichter-Saxby and Suzanna Law and was supplemented by Grant Lambie and Andy Hinchcliffe to ensure we were able to meet the specific needs of each community on the tour. Grant offered many years of playground slow build experience and Andy shared his passion for community embedded playwork. They both took turns driving the thousands of miles and helped to maintain the comically small yellow car; playworkers also need a good support network to keep going.

The dramatic landscapes on the trek from east to west gave rise to something we had not expected: the warmth and joy of the playful recipient hosts. People we had never met in person greeted us with open arms, brought us into their homes, and discussed their play needs over home-cooked meals. We listened to their stories and fears, and shared a common loneliness as play advocates. We had not expected that our presence alone and the message we brought would bring joyous tears to folks who were once strangers but were now friends. These passionate play advocates needed to be heard and to let the world know that they were shouting about play. We provided the confidence to pursue play advocacy with renewed vigor by encouraging them in their work. After talking to an audience of fifty at Portland Children's Museum about the benefits of play, we were described as "the Johnny Appleseeds of play," spreading the joys of self-direction in children's play.

While watching the children play at our pop-ups on tour, it was difficult to understand why play could be so under-valued. Children were fully immersed in play, building forts, making homes, engaging in magical battles, and painting themselves blue. They did not need to be taught how to play, rather they just needed the space, time and permission to do so. For a few hours at our play events, they followed their instincts and did just that, much to the astonishment of on-looking parents. The children also saw that child-directed play was not always accepted, and feigned a tamer type of play on occasion in case they would be stopped. "This is not a gun," said an 8 year old in earnest, "this is a sixteenth century artifact replica."

The tour was an 8 week trek across America from sea (Massachusetts) to shining sea (California) and back again. Although the team aimed for eight events throughout the eight-week tour, by the time we set off in our little yellow car, 16 events were scheduled across 12 states (Berkshire, MA; Ithaca, NY; Louisville, KY; Houston, TX; Newhall, CA; Manhattan Beach, CA; San Diego, CA; Seattle, WA; Portland; OR; Chicago; IL; Port Clinton, OH; Raleigh, NC; Buffalo; NY; Philadelphia, PA; Lakeview; MA; and Brookline, MA). We traversed through 27 different states to deliver 30 separate events to over 2,000 adults and children; the tour was bigger than anyone had thought possible.

On the journey home we reflected on the impact of the tour now documented in a book titled *The New Adventure Playground Movement: How communities across the USA are returning risk and freedom to childhood* (Leichter-Saxby and Law, 2015). We had driven 10,000 miles to talk about playwork, a little recognised concept in the USA, but something our charity is deeply passionate about. We had an inkling that folks would find playwork interesting, and would apply some of the ideas that we spoke about. We did not expect them to embrace the concept with open arms, just as they physically embraced us on arriving in their community. People are warming to the idea that play can take priority, and that a whole profession, complete with a professional framework (PPSG, 2005) can exist. The passion that we saw and continue to see from different communities of people across America suggests the start of something important, and that something is grassroots, adventurous, and filled with play.

THE PARISH SCHOOL ADVENTURE PLAYGROUND, HOUSTON, TEXAS, *MORGAN LEICHTER-SAXBY*

Branching Practice

The adventure playground at The Parish School is an after-school program at a small private school for children with communication delays and learning differences located in Houston, Texas. The most common diagnoses are expressive and/or receptive language disorder, autism spectrum disorder, apraxia, ADHD, and social (pragmatic) learning disorder. Jill Wood opened the program in 2008 and has run it since. She is also the school librarian—a position which she finds "totally analogous" to playwork, saying "play is like exploring library shelves; it's much better when there are a lot of choices and no one is telling you exactly what to use."

Jill's late boss was part of the Houston Adventure Playground Association, which managed 3 sites in the 1990s. Jill had missed her enormously since her passing in 2013, and told me how she'd run into her office to say "I found a way to get playwork training without going to Europe! Now I can meet other people who do what I do!" We met her in person for the first time during our 2014 national tour, where she hugged us and showed us the binder her boss and mentor had provided. It was full of multiple-generation photocopies, articles about other adventure playgrounds and pieces of theory, and ideas of things to make from wood and tires.

When staying with Jill, I got to do playwork with her at four settings: the adventure playground after-school, elementary school recess, Shriner's hospital, and at public pop-up adventure playgrounds. The adventure playground sessions will also serve as fieldwork for my PhD in playwork.

Adventure Playground

A group of children are sitting on the front porch of what we call the fire truck, sharing out nail polish. A young, newly enrolled boy is having his fingernails painted in alternating colors and blows delicately to help them dry. Around him there is a gentle argument on whether boys can have their nails painted, or if it's "a girl thing." Then another boy, who has been attending the adventure playground for several years, asks to have his done as well. "In black," he says, "to match my cape." This settles the discussion.

To one side, a couple of children are directing water from the hose across a carefully constructed landscape in the sand pit and laughing at its devastation. Another child has taken apart a scrap vacuum cleaner and put it together again. Having found an external plug on the school building, he plugs it in and starts cleaning the grass. One playworker runs past in the middle of a chase game, while another circulates peaceably. At the far end, a group of children have taken up a long pole each and set off across the field of tall, waving grass towards the ridge line beyond.

Children attend the adventure playground for up to two and a half hours, four days a week, and often for several years. No adult knows its secret corners and wildlife like they do.

The Hidden Prerequisites of Play

I've worked in inclusive settings before, but never one like this. The children's issues are extremely varied, but what most have in common is trouble with communication. These difficulties can overlap in very particular ways. Some do not understand that a person who is far away cannot hear them calling, and get angry that they're being "ignored." Many play alone, but we're not sure how much of that isolation is a choice when playing with others must seem so baffling and fraught. Jill has been explaining some of the essentials of an approach called Social Thinking, which makes explicit the unspoken rules of social engagement. At first, this seems interventionist to me and potentially in conflict with a playwork approach. Do we really need to be explaining or narrating? But I trust Jill's instincts, and her knowledge of these children and watch how she will present information about a social situation to a child who is struggling and then let them decide what to do with that information.

Playwork has a whole language of cues and frames (Sturrock and Else 1998), but we rarely discuss what is required to establish and hold a play frame, to perceive them or communicate their shape to others. We do not think to explain that proximity helps, if you want to play with someone else. We do not think to make explicit the meaning of facial expressions with words because neurotypical people assume that they would match automatically. Over time, I can see how expecting every child to "pick up on" social skills organically may ignore their very real differences, and even be cruel. We make all sorts of tools available to children so that they can build the material world they want; is there a parallel framework for supporting social interactions?

Loose Parts Recess

We've gathered a large plastic box and filled it with fabric, ropes, buckets, clamps and small plastic animals. We put up hammocks and swings on the unused elements of fixed equipment, and children weave ropes around the climbing frame to "make it much harder." They create pulley systems and lift wood chips onto the higher levels to trickle down the slide. They gather handfuls of plastic dinosaurs and wash them in a coffee can, then imprison them beneath a milk crate. One brings me a fitted bed sheet and asks me to tie him "at each corner," then explains he's a flying squirrel. Another pulls a piece of string from his pocket and sets about making a leash for the lizard he found sunning itself contentedly on a wall.

Jill and I have been training the paraeducators, who are out there every recess, in basic playwork practice but both of us underestimated the difficult position this would put them in. If their teachers don't understand what we're doing, they work against it—either by setting new rules for their students specifically, or by teaching them how to use these loose parts before sending them out to recess. We hear that there are classes on the "appropriate" use of a cardboard box, and how "pool noodles" must never be used to hit a person. Then the children come out to play and get caught in the differences between their teachers' rules and ours, and those of other classes. It's clear that children are getting a lot from loose parts recess, but this isn't what we had in mind.

Visiting Shriners Hospital

Twice a month, Jill and another volunteer take two large suitcases of materials to a local hospital. These sessions are open to children across the wards, including short-term patients and repeat visitors. On tables, we set out a rainbow of homemade play dough, small plastic animals, colored rice, and magnets. I'm brushing an upturned fan with bubble solution, watching a child's face go from solemn to fascinated as he directs the air and changes each bubble's course. Jill sprinkles white rice for a child over a scene she's created from dough. Both laugh and say "lluvia" to each other (Spanish for rain).

Bayou City Play

Jill and her husband started delivering pop-up adventure playgrounds around Houston in 2014, and have attracted a small team of volunteers. They've covered a trailer in chalkboard paint and have enormous tubs of rope, fabric, bamboo poles that they unpack in parks and nature centers. I go along to help, one very windy day on a peninsula, where we help children and families to build, tear, decorate, run, smash and—for a few brief moments—fly.

Studying Risk

Jill and I have gathered data on injury rates from five years at Parish School, comparing the rate of injury-per-hour on the adventure playground and at recess (before we brought out loose parts). It's made us question a lot of our own assumptions about what constitutes risk, and what allows adults to trust an adventure playground from the outside. Fixed equipment over wood chips is set against hammers, nails, child-built battleships, and fights with giant sticks. Although both are "safe" by any reasonable measure, we find that a child is 4.3 times more likely to be injured during recess than at the adventure playground. Even though we'd suspected that the adventure playground was safer, the margin seems astonishing. We check the numbers again and again, but they stand. Taking a rough look at the data across the school day, we suspect that the most dangerous time is actually the transition between classes. None of this matches the way that both critics and advocates talk about adventure playgrounds, as wild "risky" places. The data instead suggest something we've long suspected, that it is in fact a place where children are deliberate and very careful.

Into the Future

It's the last week of school, and my last week in town. Jill has been clear that she's looking for the next generation of adventure playground leadership to emerge, and has had trouble keeping good staff. A new candidate comes to interview and hang out on the adventure playground for an afternoon. He shakes everyone's hand politely and looks around. Smiles. We all take turns hanging out with him while the children do their infinite things, rotating through conversations. We watch him watch the children.

He leans back against the white tube, looking relaxed. The sun is on his face and he smiles left and right over the mud flats and the paint explosions, the broken pipes and skinny trees, and says how beautiful all this is.

THE HANDS-ON-NATURE ANARCHY ZONE AT ITHACA CHILDREN'S GARDEN, ITHACA, NEW YORK, *RUSTY KEELER AND ALEX COTE*

Introduction and History

The Hands-on-Nature Anarchy Zone is the wild and messy space at Ithaca Children's Garden in Ithaca, New York, where children are free to climb trees, dig in the mud, build forts and dens, make their own swings, cook over fires, and more. The environment itself is made up of undulating earth mounds and weedy berms, hot sunny areas, and shaded spots. On top of all that are strewn loose play and construction materials—boards, tires, stumps, rope, buckets, shovels, rakes, straw bales, sheets, sails, and the list goes on. And the things that go on here are what you'd imagine seeing in vacant lots in cities, in fields in the country side, and on the great adventure playgrounds in Europe—basically: child-directed adventurous play.

It started with a group of excited community members striving to start a play-based space that connected children to nature with the spirit of adventure playgrounds. I had seen images from those wild spaces for years as a playground designer and was thrilled to tour various examples in Germany, England, and Denmark. The places were all so amazing and had what every child needs: access to time, space, and materials to do as they like. Fires, saws, hammers, mud, animals, and freedom—these places were filled with the good stuff of childhood. We knew we wanted this for our children in Ithaca, but we also wanted to help spark a movement to bring adventure playgrounds back to America.

With big dreams we started small. We began with a blank slate and playwork training. We knew that training would be key to the success of the Anarchy Zone and we let the Playwork Principles (PPSG 2005) guide our philosophy and practice as we began our Anarchy Zone adventure. After getting the green light from health officials, insurance agents, and city offices, we kicked off the first season by celebrating International Mud Day (June 29). Loads of topsoil were delivered, the fire department hosed it down into a soupy mess, and in jumped the community. We continued that first season with playworked special events as well as drop-in times for families every day. Since the beginning we've teamed up with the U.S. Fish and Wildlife Service who have supplied startup seed money, in-kind donations of heavy equipment time (moving earth mounds, building snow mountains), as well as sharing their Americorp staff to help us plan activities and events. It's inspiring that the federal government has worked to help the North American adventure playground movement!

Evolution and Future

The Anarchy Zone continues to evolve. We've been open four years now, and the space looks very different from when we started. We started small—new loose parts on a grassy area with a few trees, surrounded by berms to contain the anarchy a bit. In the first year, playworkers pulled out loose parts from a shed and put them away after every play session. It was laborious to haul out shovels, pots and pans, pieces of wood, and buckets for every session, but both the Children's Garden and the community at large were new to this idea and we couldn't conceive of leaving out a mess in a public space. As the years rolled on people began understanding that a space filled with layers of materials offered a more complex play environment for the children. Now we leave out more and more things. It looks quite junky now, just how the children like it. There are more than enough materials for children to play with even when playworkers are not present.

I'd like to expand on that last point: playworkers are not always present at the Anarchy Zone. When I give tours, I explain to people that I only call it an adventure playground when our trained playworkers are present. Much of the time, the space is an adventurous nature play zone with loose parts. Because the Anarchy Zone is located within a public park whose mandate is to be public and open every day of the year from dawn till dusk, we can't possibly provide staffing during all open hours. So, like all good adventure playgrounds, the Anarchy Zone has responded to its context. I am confident that many children have fantastic play experiences in the Anarchy Zone with their caregivers when playworkers are not present. I see evidence of their play in the bowls of acorns hidden in forts and boards carefully stacked to build a platform in the branches of the sycamore. That being said, the play that can occur during our summer camps, when we have 40 children age 5 to 12 with only trained playwork staff, is the reason the site was created. The play supported by playwork is complex, risky, sometimes challenging, and always child-led.

Our understanding of playwork has been essential to our evolution. We have been guided by Pop-Up Adventure Play, especially Morgan Leichter-Saxby, who trained us originally for a few days and then for a full summer camp season in our second year. The Playwork Principles and reflective practice have led to us expanding our loose parts offerings and adding elements to the site: big logs to climb, places to hide, and small world elements. The children push us to examine our practice closely every year and we have Morgan and other playworkers on call frequently to help us support challenging play.

With our increasing playwork knowledge we brought playwork beyond the bounds of the Garden. We've shared loose parts and our playwork staff with a variety of other sites. We've also hosted three Play Symposiums—small conferences where playwork-curious folks from around the country gathered to learn from each other. The last symposium led two local public schools to begin exploring the expansion of play opportunities and support at recess.

It is essential to emphasize the importance of playwork training in the expansion of adventure play in America. Since there are so few sites of best practice here, currently most people see adventure playgrounds in photos, online articles, or film and the subtle art of playwork is not always easily apparent in these media formats. In these early stages of re-interest in adventure play and playwork, America is fertile ground for new models of provision—afterschool clubs, summer camps, children's museums, and parks. It's an incredible opportunity to innovate, as long as informed playwork practice is kept front and center. Therefore, it will also be imperative to identify fiscal models that can support qualified playwork staff while still providing equitable opportunity for play whenever possible.

Growing Playwork in America

From the beginning of the twentieth century concerned citizens in America began a movement leading to the creation of national organizations advancing an understanding of the significance of play in the lives of individuals, communities, and our democratic society. These pioneering play advocates lead the *Playground and Recreation Association of America* (1925) in creating *The Normal Course in Play—Practical Materials for Use in the Training of Playground Recreation Workers* which served as the roadmap for training playworkers at normal schools and universities throughout the country. Due to their diligence, thousands of trained playworkers made community recreation and the enduring spirit of play a vital aspect of the American landscape for years to follow.

Fast forward to today, and on many fronts, play in America's schools and communities is under siege (Patte, 2015) due to a variety of societal factors that include: fear (Gill, 2007; Marano, 2008); hyper-parenting (Skenazy, 2009); overly structured lives (Elkind, 2007); heightened academic demands at school (Miller and Almon, 2009); and a scarcity of quality venues for children to play (Colabianchi, Kinsella, Coulton, and Moore, 2009). The play advocates of yesteryear have been lying dormant, frozen and numb to the consequences of marginalizing play: risk aversion (Gill, 2007); inflexibility (Bekoff and Pierce, 2009); stunted creativity and imagination (Kim, 2011); heightened levels of anxiety and depression (Gray, 2013); emotional fragility (Marano, 2008); and impaired social competence (Gray, 2013) for children in America waiting for the spring to come.

I believe the field of playwork, guided by the strong belief that, "All children and young people need to play. The impulse to play is innate. Play is a biological, psychological, and social necessity, and is fundamental to the healthy development and well being of individuals and communities (PPSG, 2005)," is well suited to re-engage the present-day community play advocates necessary to destroy the societal factors marginalizing play in America (Patte and Brown, 2011). The following recommendations are offered to grow the field of playwork in America to achieve these goals.

- Build capacity through establishing partnerships with public and private national, state, and local organizations that support the significance of play in the lives of individuals and communities.
- Focus on advancing the field of playwork in all public and private schools using the playpod model (http://www.playpods.co.uk) from the UK that melds playwork training and loose parts play for children on a daily basis.
- Use the resources provided by play advocacy, policy, and research organizations to promote the field of playwork throughout America (Alliance for Childhood, Academy of Pediatrics, American Association for the Child's Right to Play, American Specialty Toy Retailing Association, Association for the Study of Play, Association of Children's Museums, Children and Nature Network, Children, Youth, and Families Education and Research Network, Children's Play Information Service, Connect for Kids, Good to Grow, Hands On, Europe Institute of Play, International Play Association, International Toy Library Association, The Joan Ganz Cooney Center at Sesame Workshop, The Judy Center Partnership, KaBoom, Kiwanis International, The Media Group of Connecticut, Inc., National Association for the Education of Young Children, National Institute for Early Education Research, The National Institute of Play, National Toy Hall of Fame, The Parent-Child Home Program, Parenting Counts, Parents Action for Children, Parents' Choice Foundation, PBS Ready to Learn, Play England, Play Wales, Project Play, Pop-Up Adventure Play, Toy Industry Association, Inc., Teachers Resisting Unhealthy Children's Entertainment, The International Council for Children's Play, United Way Born Learning Campaign, United Way of America, Voice of Play, Youth Service America, Zero To Three, The US Play Coalition).

- Establish and promote annual national, state, and local events (play days, mud days, cardboard challenges, pop-up adventure playgrounds, festivals of street games, etc.) facilitated by playworkers that promote the significance of play in the lives of individuals and communities.
- Conduct and disseminate empirical research on various aspects of the playwork profession as a means of introducing this field to the broader public.
- Connect with members of the North American Adventure Playground Association to advance the field of playwork on the local, state, and national level.
- Develop high quality playwork training programs throughout America in collaboration with universities and agencies endorsed by the UK's Skills Active organisation
- Identify a variety of venues (before and after school care, summer and holiday play schemes, school recess, community centers, children's museums, local, state and national parks, children's hospitals, prisons, mobile playranging units) for playworkers to facilitate play throughout America.
- Develop a national, long-term play policy advancing the significance of play in the lives of individuals and communities.

REFERENCES

Bekoff, M. and Pierce, J. (2009). *Wild justice: the moral lives of animals*. Chicago, IL: University of Chicago Press.

Brown, F. and Patte, M.M. (2013). *Rethinking children's play*. London: Bloomsbury.

Colabianchi, N., Kinsells, A.E., Coulton, C.J.,and Moore, S.M. (2009). Utilization and physical activity levels at renovated and unrenovated school playgrounds. *Preventive Medicine, 48*(2), pp. 140–143.

Elkind, D. (2007). *The power of play: how spontaneous, imaginative activities lead to happier, healthier children*. Cambridge, MA: Da Capa Press.

Frost, J. (2010). *A history of children's play and play environments: Toward a contemporary child-saving movement*. New York: Routledge.

Frost, J. and Kline, B. (1979). *Children's play and play environments*. Boston: Allyn and Bacon.

Frost, J. and Sunderlin, S. (Eds.). (1985). *When children play*. Association for Childhood Education International.

Gill, T. (2007). *No fear: growing up in a risk averse society*. London: Gulbenkian Foundation.

Gray, P. (2013). *The play deficit*. Aeon Magazine, 1–8. Retrieved from: eon.co/magazine/being-human/children-today-are-suffering-a-severe-deficit-of-play/.

Hogan, P. (1974). *Playgrounds for free*. Massachusetts: MIT Press.

Hughes, B. (2012) *Evolutionary Playwork*. London: Routledge.

Jeffrey, J. (2008). Storytelling and the reflective playworker. In F. Brown and C. Taylor (Eds.), *Foundations of Playwork*. Berkshire: Open University Press.

Kim, K. (2011). The creativity crisis: The decrease in creative thinking scores on the Torrance Tests of Creative Thinking. *Creativity Research Journal,* 23 (4), pp. 285–295.

Kozol, J. (2007). *Letters to a young teacher*. New York, NY: Three Rivers Press.

Leichter-Saxby, M., and Law, S. (2015). *The new adventure playground movement: how communities across the USA are returning risk and freedom to childhood.* Notebook Publishing.

Marano, H. (2008). *A nation of wimps: the high cost of invasive parenting*. New York, NY: Broadway.

Miller, E., and Almon, J. (2009). *Crisis in the kindergarten: why children need to play in school*. Alliance for Childhood, College Park: MD.

National Recreation Association. (1925). *The normal course in play: practical material for use in the training of playground and recreation workers.* New York, NY: A. S. Barnes and Company.

Patte, M. (2015). *From pick up games to play dates—the decline of child-initiated, unstructured play and the rise of hothouse parenting*. White paper for Playworld. Lewisburg, PA: Playworld.

Patte, M. (2009). All in a day's work: Children's views on play and work at the fifth grade level. In: D. Kuschner (Ed.), *Play and Culture Studies, From Children to Red Hatters: Diverse Images and Issues of Play*, 8, pp. 113–130.

Patte, M. and Brown, F. (2011). Playwork: a profession challenging societal factors devaluing children's play. *Journal of Student Wellbeing,* 5 (1), pp.58–70.

PPSG (2005) *Playwork Principles*, held in trust as honest brokers for the profession by the Playwork Principles Scrutiny Group. [Internet] Available from: http://www.playwales.org.uk/page.asp?id=50 [Accessed 5/4/2017].

Skenazy, L. (2009). *Free range kids: how to raise safe, self-reliant children without going nuts with worry*. San Francisco, CA: Jossey-Bass.

Sorensen, C.Th. (1951). Junk playgrounds. *Danish Outlook,* 4 (1), p.314.

Sturrock, G. and Else, P. (1998) The playground as therapeutic space: playwork as healing. In: P*roceedings of the IPA/USA Triennial National Conference, Play in a Changing Society: Research, Design, Application*. June 1998, Colorado. USA.

Chapter Six

Playwork and the Co-creation of Play Spaces

The Rhythms and Refrains of a Play Environment

Stuart Lester

INTRODUCTION

Playwork's primary role is to support children in creating an environment where they can play, yet little attention has been given to this co-creation process and the relationship between playing and the production of space. This chapter will extend this foundational playwork principle (PPSG, 2005) to propose spaces are always produced through on-going intra-actions between bodies, materials, symbols, memories, ideas and so on (Barad, 2007). It will offer, albeit briefly, a perspective on the process of life itself as continuous movement and change. Given this, a "playspace" may be distinguishable as a co-constituted formation of moving bodies and things with a certain affirmative style, flow and intensity. Such movements produce a degree of temporary stability, a refrain that is generative of new possibilities and wandering beyond the familiar (McCormack, 2013). Playwork is thus concerned with discerning patterns of relationships as they constitute space and the possibilities they contain for the emergence of playing. It is above all a pragmatic ethical stance that takes account of the moment by moment flows of movements and encounters and acts responsively to maintain a prevailing playful atmosphere.

At the outset it should be noted that the ideas presented here follow a different line of enquiry than is generally pursued in play and playwork studies. While play studies range across disparate disciplinary fields, what most have in common is a desire to distinguish playing from other forms of behaviour, to classify and categorise boundaries and defining features, and identify developmental value. Through this process play is reduced to a specific activity that exists in a binary relationship with other forms of behaviour. It is indicative of ways in which things become fixed by resemblance, opposition, analogy and identity to produce a stable account of the world (Deleuze, 1995).

Everything can be put in its proper place, located by relative terms (work/play, bigger/smaller, human/non-human, inside/outside etc.). Further elaborations and sophisticated classifications are then overlaid on these productions of difference which in play studies may include, for example, the identification of ages and stages of play, different play behaviours, incremental benefits, and so on. It adopts a pseudoscientific approach that resonates with Sutton-Smith's (1997) assertion that all too often play is treated as a separate text in which the presumed form and products of playing take precedence over formation, process and flow. The modern progress rhetoric of play and its utilitarian association with learning, reinforced by particular readings of play as identity-forming/fixing and self-actualisation, dominate minority world perspectives. Play is presented and valued as an individual affair, often depicted as an innate drive of self-possessed organisms that interact with other bodies and things.

Notwithstanding the valuable contribution of biological and psychological studies to understanding play and its associated functions and benefits, they come with various degrees of caution and statements of limitations that are often ignored or conveniently left aside in common-sense attributions of play's purpose and value (Fagen, 2011). Fagen (2011, p92) continues by provocatively suggesting a "place remains for novel perspectives on play, imaginative and bold as play itself" and before play can be fully understood a new, or partially new, story about the universe is needed. Following Fagen's lead the discussion pursues a different trajectory by eschewing the idea of a single "life" and the individual humanist subject. Individualism is not an intrinsic part of human nature but rather a particular and powerful way of thinking, representing and making the world—what could be called mutually shaping material-discursive effects (Barad, 2007)—that has gained increasing prominence in minority world contexts to the exclusion of other ways of thinking about life. The intention of this chapter is to add difference to the world rather than more of the same; it is a generative "what if" position that will present life as more-than-human and consider the possibilities this presents for a different outlook on the formation of a "*playspacetime*" before finally exploring the implications for playwork practice.

AN INDIVIDUAL AND ISOLATED LIFE

Teasing play apart into classifications and component subject-object relationships is indicative of the wider presumption that the process of life is an individual self-contained affair and organisms come with their own pre-figured potential waiting to be filled as one grows-up. From this point of view playing is an expression of individual freedom, personal choice and self-fulfilment. It marks an increasing individualisation of life in which humans are required to be autonomous, self-regulating and independent. Playing is "cut" in a particular way, a representation of wider dominant economic and political forces of neoliberalism and globalisation (see Lester, 2016) that would appropriate play for its own nefarious purposes to develop productive and consuming citizens; forces of individualisation are inextricably tied to principles of profit. Thus playing is valued for the contribution it makes to developing skills such as creativity, problem-solving and flexibility, desirable qualities of the capitalist project. But playing must also be kept in check for fear that it might escape this purpose; thus certain forms of play (irrational, disgusting, destructive, risky, nonsense and so on) warrant adult intervention and sanction. While a fuller discussion around this awaits another occasion; the main point to reinforce is the way in which material-discursive forces of individualisation become entangled across multiple scales of organisation, insidiously permeating all aspects of life to perform acts of inversion by which beings "are closed in upon themselves, sealed by an outer boundary or shell that protects their inner constitution from the traffic of interaction with their surroundings" (Ingold, 2011, p68).

This section of the chapter reverses this movement; the idea that bodies have an outline and the mind is the command centre enclosed within an individual body according to modernist accounts of the liberal human subject is increasingly disputed by advances in, for example, contemporary physical and life sciences, complexity, information and technology studies and neuroscience. Equally certain strands of what might be referred to as materialist philosophy and its application in the humanities (politics, anthropology, geography etc.) have countered the idea that there is a fixed body boundary that ends at the skin by emphasising the body's specific situatedness in, and openness to, the world. While obviously there are many differences between such a disparate collection, what they have in common is a view of life going on through continuous and discontinuous self-organising connections and relations that collude in various formations to produce a degree of indeterminate and temporary stability, what Ingold (2011, p.63) refers to as a "meshwork of entangled lines of life, growth and movement." The shape of these arrangements is not determined in advance by intrinsic properties of already formed things (Colebrook 2005; Barad, 2007; Braidotti, 2013). The world and humans are not separate entities but are co-created through on-going complex processes of differing that occur in entangled relationships with multiple other things, mutually shaping in all sorts of iterative and prospective patterns (Barad, 2007). The body is a system of processes that are continuously in-formation with the environment or milieu of which it is a part, always "a node of relational processes, not a form *per se*" (Manning, 2013, p19). A stable body is extremely short-lived—it cannot be seen as something that holds together across space and time and can never pre-exist its movements (Manning, 2014).

It is this process of dynamic and continuous differentiation and emergence, or intra-action (Barad, 2007), that is at the heart of this analysis. Rather than difference being a comparative state between pre-existing entities (which is implicit in the term inter-action) every aspect of life is evidence of difference rather than sameness. To emphasise the point before moving on, intra-action is productive of indeterminate, non-linear, emergent meshworks that actively partake in the very process of the world's ongoing generation and regeneration (Ingold, 2011). From this perspective, attention shifts from reducing life to its presumed separate parts to paying attention to the continuous formative currents of things making a difference in unique, singular and particular ways. Life is always in process, relational and open-ended; representation is superseded by giving attention to pre-conscious, embodied movements, affective intensities, rhythms and patterns that collude to form a particular arrangement or "reality" that always contains within it the prospect for being differently arranged, always in-formation (Lorimer, 2005).

Now this all sounds very abstract, but stay with it and hopefully the exciting possibilities that this presents for thinking/acting differently will be revealed in what follows.

LIFE ON THE MOVE

When looking at children's play the focus traditionally falls, not so much on the process of playing, but invariably the determination of subject/object relationships traced back into individual bodies, or more frequently minds, to attribute some intention and meaning and the benefits that might accrue for the individual player. Playing is an activity or product that can then be classified with similar or different productions, reducing things to various degrees of sameness, establishing cause-effect relationships and formalising concepts that explain the world; whatever happens can be explained by these universal rules. By this means, the processes of emergence and intra-action are disassembled to fit into existing schemes.

The idea briefly presented in the previous section offers another way of thinking about life and the process of playing: the idea of continuous variation implies constant movement and novel formations, indeed, wherever there is life, there is movement (Ingold, 2011). What follows is a brief observation of two children and an adult. Before presenting this, it is important to highlight that this meshwork, composed from intra-actions between all sorts of things in motion, is a unique occurrence that only relates to itself. There is nothing in this instance that can be extracted and applied to something else; no concepts borrowed from outside the example can adequately explain it (Massumi, 2002). Indeed "to unravel this meshwork and to reassemble the resulting fragments on the basis of their intrinsic similarities and differences is to destroy its very meaning and coherence" (Ingold, 2011, p155). Everything is singular and should be treated as such, but nevertheless it has vital importance because of its particularity (Lester, 2015).

An example—playing in a café

> The following observation occurred in a café, a chance encounter with two young children sitting with an adult at an adjacent table. The adult was looking at/playing with his mobile phone, sitting opposite the 2 children, both of whom had glasses of soft drinks with straws on the table. One child nudged the other's elbow as he was about to take a drink; the child who was nudged managed not to spill the drink and laughed, put his drink down and jostled the other child. The attendant adult looked up from his phone and the children became still, the adult returned attention to the phone and after a very short period the first child lightly flicked the ear of the other which brought a muffled cry of pain and laughter, and a move away from the other child by sliding to the edge of the seat and half turning away while at the same time sucking some of the drink into a straw, turning around quickly and spraying the other child. At this point the adult told them both to "stop messing about." The children paused, one child saying "he started it" while the other child denied this and said he had "sprayed him;" both were smiling as they aired their grievances. The adult again told them to stop messing about after which they sat quietly until the adult's attention returned to the phone, before a highly furtive process of nudging and jostling started again, with extremely quick and light touches passing backwards and forwards between the children above and below the table and further muffled cries and laughter. The pace increased and movements became more vigorous until the adult said "come on, drink up, we're going;" the children quickly finished their drinks and left with the adult—as they moved off there were further jostling movements between the children as they became entangled together, almost as if in a dance routine with haphazard steps.

The collective movements and sensations in the cafe establish diffractive, rippling patterns that agitate, disturb, resonate, interfere, and intensify; patterns that are felt before known (Manning, 2013). The slightest movement of a body reverberates within the meshwork and brings about a qualitative difference by initiating sensations that fold into each other in unaccountable and unpredictable ways to unfold again in further movement (Massumi, 2002). From this perspective movement may be presented as a form of emergent wondering/wandering (Manning, 2014) that brings about differences in the world. There is no central locus of control in the café example but the patterns may at times cohere to establish a temporary stability that we might recognise as "messing about" or playing; movements become attuned to produce a recognisable pattern but always retain tendencies to produce different forms. Thus, for example, the response from the adult temporarily alters the formation of playing, children become passive but remain open to the possibility for further mo(ve)ments of disorder. This is not something out of the ordinary; wondering the world occurs all the time even in the most banal of everyday encounters (Manning, 2013). Bodies (adults and children), movements, materials (drinks, straws, chairs and so on) collectively compose this moment and it will not occur in this manner again, although there may be something of this encounter that remains for the future, what Bennett (2004) refers to as anticipatory readiness, or alertness to the possibility for further outbreaks of playfulness as the children wander off with the adult. While crafted from seemingly ordinary contexts, they have great value in enlivening the practice of everyday life by creating moments when life is more vital and worth living (Lester and Russell, 2014), simply generating greater satisfaction in being alive (Sutton-Smith, 2003). And while it is a singular event, as previously noted, this moment of playing has the potential to become extensive, circulating beyond the specific details to connect with other examples; it always has some room for extend-ability beyond itself by activating more and more detail, not a move from the particular to the general but from the particular to more particularities (Gambs, 2013). Being faithful to the movements and their affects has potential to reconfigure sensibilities to such moments and defer the imposition of proofs and universal meanings.

A "PLAY SPACE"

The world is in a state of perpetual flux and life is not fixed to any specific location, indeed any environment can be seen as the production of a meshwork or entanglement brought about by the intra-active movements of different materials. The argument presented here suggests that "space" rather than being a fixed container or pre-existing surface emerges through a dynamic process of intra-action. Playing, as quintessentially the process of life going on in an affirmative manner (Lester, 2015), is always productive of space imbued with certain qualities (pleasurable, spontaneous etc.). The play space in the café does not pre-exist its actualisation and co-creation by all the assembled components and after children and adult move off there is no "playspace" remaining. As such, a play space is generative in "bringing forth new worlds, in engaging in an on-going reconfiguring of the world" (Barad, 2007, p170). Bodies are not simply situated in particular environments but environments and bodies are intra-actively co-constituted. From this perspective spaces are always under construction and open to the future; there are always connections yet to be made (Massey, 2005). It implies exchanging a vocabulary of stasis, representation, fixity and closure with one of intensities, capacities, forces, rhythms, encounters, movements, flows, affects, and entanglements. Thus a "play space," so often used to describe a specific adult determined location for playing is something totally different and far more intriguing from a processual, relational and performative perspective. As Colin Ward (1979) reminds us, children will play everywhere and with anything, and play spaces can intra-actively emerge in a museum (Lester, Strachan and Derry, 2014), art gallery (Lester and Russell, 2014a), bus-stop (Lester, 2016) the street (Lester, 2011) and adventure playground (Lester, Fitzpatrick and Russell, 2014); wherever children are, is where they play (Opie and Opie, 1969).

RHYTHMS AND REFRAINS OF A "PLAY SPACE": A PLAYFUL ATMOSPHERE

The discussion to date suggests the connection between moving bodies, materials, and so much more, generates "*playspacetimes*,"[1] a milieu that is imbued with a particular atmosphere, spaces whose qualities are vague but sensed as a distinctive affective register of pleasure, nonsense, uncertainty, unpredictability, and so on. Affect is used here as an expression of processes and forces by which spaces come into being, the affective attunement (Stern 1985) of bodies and things in motion to produce singular events. Affect is a quality of life; bodies have a desire or enthusiasm (Manning, 2013) to affect and be affected to produce an optimal state of being from the prevailing conditions; it is not an individual quality but flows through the meshwork as a distributed, dispersed and intensive force within and between bodies. It may be presented as the active outcome of an encounter that leads to an increase or decrease in the power of a body to act (Thrift, 2004); bodies are shaped from the milieu as much as they shape it. In this mutually entangled and dynamic process bodies and space are indistinguishable as they enhance and limit each other as the following brief observation of wandering/wondering at a train station illustrates:

> An adult (male) with 2 young girls, one who appeared slightly older than the other, were making their way to the platform, the two girls each holding a bag of sweets. As the adult walked ahead, the two girls paused to look inside each

> other's bags and the older one said to the other "Wow, you have got pink mermaids, they can do magic," while waving her arms in the air as though holding a magic wand and performing a pirouette; the younger girl held her bag open and peered closely into it, smelling the contents as the older girl continued "they are lovely and made from strawberries." The other girl half smiled at this, faced the older child, but looked a little unsure and said, "I don't think I like strawberries." Her friend calmly said "Never mind, I'll have them" and then quickly added "but I am not going to give you any of mine." Both girls closed their bags and skipped together to catch up with the adult.

Affective environments are composed of fragile, fleeting, fragmentary combinations of sensations and movements; various rhythms and ways of thinking, feeling and acting align in novel compositions (who can say when playing begins and ends?). The intensity and flow of playful intra-activity sustains an affirmative mood and disposition that is alert to further possibilities for joyful encounters; more extensive connections can be made that continue to enhance life. It is a refrain or point of order (after Deleuze and Guattari, 1988) with a certain style that constitutes a territory or block of playspacetime:

> These territories are not necessarily demarcated or delineated, however, they can be affective complexes, "hazy, atmospheric," but sensed nevertheless, as intensities of feeling in and through the movement of bodies. (McCormack, 2013, p7)

But there are also many formations that inhibit possibilities for playful and affirmative compositions. Multiple practices, habits and routines consciously and pre-consciously actively organise and operate on moving bodies by producing dominant affective registers that shape and constrain possibilities for becoming different (McCormack, 2013). Though not fixed and static, they tend to attune movements to a particular end, what Lefebvre (2004) refers to as a form of dressage or entrainment through repetitive patterns that inculcate habitual ways of being. Thus, for example, it is possible to discern how habits, practices, routines, material arrangements, and so on produce a patterning or rhythm in a school classroom (material-discursive effects) to establish a purposeful atmosphere which choreographs movements of both adults and children alike. However, this is not totalising: there are multiple arrhythmic movements that temporarily break apart order and stability and potentially generate creative expressions.[2] No matter what dominant productions of space intend there is always something which escapes and gets out of order.

The composition of affective encounters cannot be reduced to universal accounts (Harrison, 2007). Rather than fix and explain this relational messiness by drawing on pre-established concepts that prise entanglements apart, the question becomes one of how to account for the ways in which bodies, materials and space co-produce each other. The specificity of playful moments demands approaches that are "tuned to the particularities of the entanglements at hand" (Barad, 2007, p74) and the differences they bring about. It suggests attention is given to the affective qualities of space combined with a commitment to experimenting with different ways of becoming attuned to these qualities (McCormack, 2013). This will be further developed in the next section which turns specifically to consider the implications for playwork practice. As noted in the introduction, the line pursued at this stage emphasises this is a pragmatic ethical stance to co-create a playful atmosphere where adults and children can get on and go on together. It is also suggested that this is not the preserve of playwork but has wider implications and application for all adults who have a professional role with children.

PLAYWORK AS CARTOGRAPHY

As with other childhood institutions, adult-designed and managed segregated locations designated as sites for play have their own rhythm. Unlike most other settings, however, the intention is not to progress children along a predetermined line towards independent, self-regulating adults but rather offer potential for the emergence of *playspacetimes* of becoming different or otherwise. While the dominant rhythm, habits and practices of most adult-designed locations for children act as processes of dressage and produce normalising effects (notwithstanding moments of arrhythmia), playwork is co-productive of an environment or territory that is marked by a persistent playful refrain. Although there will be periodic repetitions and habits, it is the creation of difference and not the reproduction of sameness which is constitutive of their unique rhythms. Playworkers are not detached and passive observers of what happens in these settings; neither neutral nor non-interventionist. Practice emerges through and as part of their entangled intra-actions with children, materials and everything else that is part of a "play environment" (bearing in mind all that has been discussed to date about these terms). Playwork is intimately caught up in processes of affecting and being affected to constitute conditions in which there is a greater possibility for "*playspacetimes*" to emerge. It cultivates affirmative modes of relations as well as transforming negative forces which seek to constrain the desire to affect and be affected in a playful manner. Practice is concerned with everyday relationships as the following example reveals:

> In conversation with a playworker in a residential setting, a discussion took place about the apparently trivial and mundane stuff that happened in the

> previous session. The playworker struggled to respond, falling back on describing play activities that took place and when gently pushed to go beyond this, a smile played over her face and she recalled a moment when she was sitting alongside a child, both silent, when the playworker turned to the child and said "Can I put you in the bin?" The child turned and smiled at the playworker and moved closer before silence returned.

The playworker acknowledged that she wasn't fully aware of where this question came from, other than it "felt right at the time." Such apparently mundane moments matter; they are singular instances that generate a refrain of difference in the making—the playworker is not a social worker, teacher, parent or other adult, the child is not a "problem." It is a shared moment of becoming together and makes a minor contribution to maintaining a play territory. But they largely escape explicit articulation and become lost in externally derived technical accounting systems.

Given that a constellation of such moments constitute a playful atmosphere, critical attention needs to be paid to these everyday rhythms. It requires a set of practice techniques that hold off forces of individualisation, counter the privilege afforded to representation and defer the imposition of interpretations and meanings for as long as possible. Such techniques may be presented as cartographic approaches that pay attention to mapping the unpredictable, indeterminate and multi-sensory intra-actions, the spaces of in-between, and the refrain of the environment. They do not seek to represent something that already exists but are drawn towards movements and sensations; they are concerned with wayfaring as a process of continual movement rather than destination-focussed tracings (Ingold, 2011). This approach is further elaborated in the mapping/diagramming experiments developed with playworkers at an adventure playground (See Lester, Fitzpatrick and Russell, 2014) that foregrounded movement through the environment to reveal hitherto unnoticed patterns, rhythms and habits. The diagrams generated from increasing attentiveness to everyday arrangements of bodies and things are forms of composition which draw expressive lines of movement that are imbued with sensations and entangled with all sorts of matter; they are processual rather than products. When these diagrams are overlaid they begin to reveal complex patterns and affects that continually and intra-actively constitute a playground territory that has a degree of consistency (i.e., a predominantly playful feel) but not in any continuous manner; there is no beginning or end to these movements but they form a refrain with habits and routines that always contain the potential for moving otherwise. When complemented by other techniques (for example story-telling, moving and still images, observational commentaries, soundscapes) cartography generates lively materials of subtle movements and flows, encounters, resistances, avoidances and so on. The following abridged observation of two children playing on an adventure playground (Lester and Russell, 2014b, p251/252) is another example:

> It was apparent that the game had a rule of not going on the ground, which constrained the two adversaries to the platform and other structures. There was also another implicit rule which meant that these two could engage in reciprocal bouts of tagging. This led to the two children standing facing each other, in very close proximity, but not touching. The person who was "it" would tag, and immediately receive a tag back from the other, often increasing the force of the contact in an attempt to push each other away and create a moment to flee; and then there were brief moments when both stood poised ready to tag without actually doing anything. There was a restless dance between the two, as one looked to retreat, the other followed; it was almost balletic in the choreography of action, bodies and affects, tensions and laughter and so on.

The desire is not to fix and reduce play by classification (a game of tag) but to be more attentive to affective resonance and the ways in which *playspacetimes* emerge and temporarily cohere and fall apart. It is a performative practice concerned with the event as if presenting a radio commentary to describe the distinctive rhythms, movements and style as they unfold (McCormack, 2013). But it is more than mere description as it incorporates a state of enchantment or "the capacity to move and be moved by bodies at a distance" (McCormack, 2013, p140). It adds more to the picture by sensing perturbations, novelty, tensions, and surprises and the promise these hold for keeping the territory open in all sorts of unpredictable ways.

Reading these materials is "diffractive" (Barad, 2007), that is, it focuses on processes that produce different flows and patterns when encountering other forces rather than seeking resolution and stability by measuring and reflecting against some pre-established and ideal image. The superimposition of diverse processual materials bring to attention the dominant forces at play and makes them available for critical scrutiny to form temporary and incomplete judgments about their capacity to maintain an open environment for playing. It forms the basis for experimental interventions as this example from conversations with playworkers at an after-school club reveals:

> One playworker drew attention to a line of masking tape running across the floor in one of the main rooms, leading to a square, again marked out by tape and recalled what had happened following this spatial intervention. One child arrived at the setting, asked the playworker "what was the line for?" and received a casual response "I dunno." The child balanced along the line and jumped into the square, pronouncing that they had been turned into something different (the exact creature was indistinct), this was followed by other children repeating this movement and as they jumped into the square, announced their transformation

> into a creature—and a pattern of creating creatures that began with the first letter of their name emerged. Children discovered other taped symbols throughout the building and this temporarily transformed movement before a child asked if they could take it up and move it around, precipitating further novelty.

This is not simply a random act but arose from becoming more attuned to the patterns of movements and habits leading to a minor experiment with no prediction or expectation of what might happen other than a desire to affect and be affected to see what if and what more bodies and things might do in this setting.

CONCLUSION: THERE IS NO CONCLUSION

Playwork practice is speculative, curious, engaged and enchanted with experimentation designed to develop methods that co-produce and augment the playful openness of the territory. The refrain of *playspacetime* attunes bodies to produce playful meshworks of difference (messing about in a café, enchanted by mermaids, dancing on a platform and following lines to become different). They are grounded in habits and practices that are foundations for movements away from a pre-determined future; children and adults tentatively expose and explore the environment through different ways of moving and relating, creating new juxtapositions of bodies, symbols and materials, simply to enliven the productive possibilities of space.

Playwork practice is also sensitive i.e., it privileges senses over thought, or rather focuses on sensory expressions that give rise to thoughts by attending to the fine detail of entanglements, patterns of movement and the ways in which things appear to fit together without imposing some external "thoughts" or concepts on them or effacing their singularity. Experimenting with cartographic techniques cultivates the capacity to make good judgments in the midst of encounters; to intra-act in open and affirmative ways to enable life to flourish. The intention is to make a difference in the world, to perform choices and make critical interventions that favour certain movements while avoiding others. This does not presume any cause-effect relationship or sense of determinacy (i.e., by doing this playing will happen) but necessitates paying attention to and acting responsibly with the on-going generation of affective atmospheres conducive to the emergence of unknown and yet-to-be created playful configurations of bodies, materials and ideas. As such, playwork is always an ethical stance—not concerned with the imposition of universal moral standards—but paying attention to the details of everyday lived moments. It is an on-gong practice that is alert and open to the possibilities that each encounter offers, to take account of this and develop a response-ability to maintain a playful refrain.

NOTES

1. Given the limitations of space for this chapter, little mention has been made of "time"; the assumption made is that as with play and space, time cannot be broken down into discrete units but should be merged with space to produce an event or "spacetime" that is always open and therefore always in the process of becoming different.

2. See, for example, Hannikainen's (2001) study of ways in which children and kindergarten teacher establish different rhythms throughout the school day by sharing moments of playfulness and nonsense that deregulates, "throws out of order and disrupts . . . it can also produce a lacuna, a hole in time, to be filled by an invention, a creation" (Lefebvre, 2004, p44).

REFERENCES

Barad, K (2007) *Meeting the universe halfway*. Durham: Duke University Press.

Braidotti, R (2013) *Posthuman.* Cambridge: Polity Press.

Colebrook, C (2005) Introduction. In A Parr (ed) *The Deleuze Dictionary*. Edinburgh: Edinburgh University Press.

Deleuze, G (1995) *Negotiations 1972–1990.* New York: Columbia University Press.

Deleuze, G and Guattari, F (1988) *A thousand plateaus*. London: Continuum.

Fagen, R (2011) Play and development. In A Pellegrini (ed) *The oxford handbook of the development of play.* Oxford: Oxford University Press.

Gambs, D (2013) Experimental research methods after critique: on the example, affirmative methods, and making connections. *Cultural Studies ↔ Critical Methodologies*, 13(5): pp.383–389.

Hannikainen, M. (2001) Playful actions as a sign of togetherness in day care centres. *International Journal of Early Years Education*, 9(2): 125–134.

Harrison, P. (2007) "How shall I say it . . . ?" Relating the nonrelational. *Environment and Planning A,* Vol. 39: pp. 590–608.

Ingold, T (2011) *Being alive. Essays on movement, knowledge and description.* Abingdon: Routledge.

Lefebvre, H. (2004) *Rhythmanalysis: space, time and everyday life*. London: Continuum.

Lester, S. (2011) The pedagogy of play, space and learning. In A Pihlgren (ed) *Fritidspedagogik.* Lund: Studentlitteratur.

Lester, S. (2015) Post-human nature: Life beyond the natural playground. In: E. Ryall, W Russell and M. Maclean (eds) *Philosophy of play II*. London: Routledge.

Lester, S. (2016) From the margins to the middle: Children's right to play. In: M. Ruck, M. Peterson-Badali and M. Freeman (eds) *Handbook of children's rights: global and multidisciplinary perspectives.* New York: Taylor and Francis (in press).

Lester, S., Fitzpatrick, J. and Russell, W. (2014) *Co-creating an adventure playground: Reading playwork stories, practices and artefacts.* Gloucester: University of Gloucestershire.

Lester, S. and Russell, W. (2014a) Children's right to play. In E. Brooker, M. Blaise and S. Edwards (eds) *The sage handbook of play and learning in early childhood.* London: Sage.

Lester, S. and Russell, W. (2014b) Turning the world upside down: Playing as the deliberate creation of uncertainty. *Children*, Vol. 1: pp. 241–260.

Lester, S., Strachan, A. and Derry, C. (2014) A more playful museum: Exploring issues of institutional space, children's play and well-being. *International Journal of Play*, 3(1): pp.24–35.

Lorimer, H. (2005) Cultural geography: the busyness of being `more-than-representational. *Progress in Human Geography*, Vol. 29(1): 83–94.

Manning, E. (2013) *Always more than one. Individuations dance.* Durham: Duke University Press.

Manning, E. (2014) Wondering the world directly—or, how movement outruns the subject. *Body and Society*, 20(3/4): pp. 162–186.

Massey, D. (2005) *For space*. London: Sage.

Massumi, B. (2002) *Parables for the virtual*. Durham: Duke University Press.

McCormack, D. (2013) *Refrains for moving bodies*. Durham: Duke University Press.

Opie, P. and Opie, I. (1969) *Children's games in street and playground.* Oxford: Oxford University Press.

PPSG (2005) *Playwork Principles*, held in trust as honest brokers for the profession by the Playwork Principles Scrutiny Group. [Internet] Available from: http://www.playwales.org.uk/page.asp?id=50 [Accessed 5/8/2013].

Stern, D. (1985) *The interpersonal world of the infant: a view from psychoanalysis and developmental psychology.* New York: Basic Books.

Sutton-Smith, B. (1997) *The ambiguity of play*. Cambridge, MA: Harvard University Press.

Sutton-Smith, B. (2003) Play as a Parody of Emotional Vulnerability. In Lytle, D. (ed) *Play and educational theory and practice, play and culture studies 5.* Westport: Praeger.

Thrift, N. (2004) Intensities of feeling: Towards a spatial politics of affect. *Geografiska Annaler,* 86 B(1): pp. 57–78.

Ward, C. (1979) *The child in the city.* Harmondsworth: Penguin.

Chapter Seven

Therapeutic Playwork

Theory and Practice

Fraser Brown

INTRODUCTION

Although the different schools of psychology often appear to be strongly at odds with each other, one of the key arguments of this chapter is that they all have something to offer to the therapeutic role of a playworker.

- Behaviorists such as Watson and Skinner suggest that behaviour is largely a consequence of the child's personal history, especially in relation to their experience of punishment and reward.
- Cognitive psychologists such as Piaget and Chomsky see the mind as a computer, having the ability to find answers to its own problems, so it should be possible to help a troubled child by the careful application of logic.
- Humanistic psychologists say that individuals are inherently good, and constantly trying to self-actualize, and so theorists such as Maslow and Rogers encourage a focus on creativity and self-awareness
- Psychoanalysts such as Freud and Klein believe that outward disturbances are a reflection of the unconscious mind, and in the case of children that is revealed in their play.

Nevertheless, it is true to say that psychologists have largely ignored the significant role of play in children's lives, but that does not mean playworkers should follow suit and ignore what psychology has to offer. To do so would be to limit the potential for playworkers to help those troubled children with whom they work. The psychiatrist Stuart Brown (2009) has shown that when children are deprived of play, the consequences may be catastrophic. This was confirmed during my own work with abandoned children in a Romanian pediatric hospital (Brown 2014). This quote, from the developmental psychologist and play theorist Brian Sutton-Smith, sums up the powerful nature of the play experience very succinctly:

> The opposite of play—if redefined in terms which stress its reinforcing optimism and excitement—is not work, it is depression. Players come out of their ludic paradoxes . . . with renewed belief in the worthwhileness of merely living. (Sutton-Smith 1999, p.254)

In fact play can be such an all-encompassing force for good in a child's life that a whole profession has arisen just to promote and protect it. At its most positive, Playwork is essentially about "creating environments that enable children to take control of their playing" (Brown 2014, p.160). That can only really happen when the environment is substantially adaptable, thus lending itself to the compound flexibility process, which I have discussed in detail elsewhere (2014, p.150–160). The substantial benefits that accrue are then largely a consequence of the children's playful interaction with the environment, and with each other. These benefits are both immediate and longer term, and they range right across all aspects of child development. However, the Sutton-Smith quote also touches on the awful consequences of a lack of play, which begs the question, what does this mean for playwork?

UNDERPINNING PLAYWORK THEORY

The playwork theorist Bob Hughes has explored this in some detail, suggesting that many of the children with whom we work may be exhibiting signs of either play deprivation or play bias. He describes play deprivation as resulting from "a chronic lack of sensory interaction with the world, or a neurotic, erratic interaction" (Hughes 2000, p.21). Play bias refers to, "a loading of play in one area of experience or another, having the effect of excluding the child from some parts of the total play experience" (Hughes 2003, p.68). He suggests that these conditions are the result of a range of factors, including fear of traffic, perceived stranger danger, parental fears of children engaging in risky activity, poor housing or diet, violent neighbourhoods, or play which does not involve contact with other living things.

Clearly, these factors do not impinge on every child's life to the same degree, and so it would be reasonable to suggest that play deprivation and play bias are spectrum conditions. For example, at one end of the spectrum we may find a child who is mildly play deprived as a result perhaps of not being allowed to play outside very much. At the other end of the spectrum might be a child who has suffered chronic neglect or abuse, perhaps of the kind seen in the plight of the Romanian orphans that filled our television screens in the 1990s. Both are play deprived, although there is obviously a world of difference between the two levels of damage. The same variation is true of the play bias spectrum. At one end of that spectrum we may find a child who has been able to engage in a wide range of play types (Hughes 1996), but has never been allowed to take risks. At the other end might be a child whose parents have been trying to live a vicarious existence through their child, by forcing them to do nothing but play a specific sport, or devote their childhood to becoming a ballet dancer. Again, both have experienced play bias in their childhood, but with different levels of damage.

The root causes of the problems faced by modern day children are nicely summarised by Kilvington and Wood (2018, p.229):

> For many children these days . . . adults make decisions on their behalf, watch over them constantly, regularly interrupt to "teach" them all they need to know, and rush to protect them from anything that is deemed harmful. . . . Sadly for many other children the opposite is true and for them there is insufficient or absent adult care and oversight as they struggle to find themselves and survive.

Thus, we have a confusing mixture of over-protection, fear and neglect on the part of adults towards our children. The resulting symptoms are witnessed on a daily basis by playworkers.

Given all this it would not be unreasonable to expect to find some reference to these issues in the Playwork Principles (PPSG 2005), and indeed the idea that playwork might have a therapeutic benefit is not entirely absent, in as much as they refer to children's "wellbeing." Principle 1 states that play is "fundamental to the healthy development and wellbeing of individuals and communities." In addition, Principle 8 states "All playworker interventions must balance risk with the developmental benefit and well being of children." However, this all feels a bit half-hearted, so it is not surprising that a recent study by Smith (2017) found playworkers do not generally recognize the therapeutic role they often perform.

Nevertheless, both Hughes (2012) and Brown (2014) argue that an effective playwork approach can go some considerable way to re-balancing things, and enabling the child to achieve a level of homeostasis. Through their empathy, and their ability to interpret the children's play cues effectively, playworkers are able to create strong trusting relationships, which in turn helps to enhance the children's self-esteem.

Perhaps the most influential piece of writing about the potentially therapeutic nature of playwork may be seen in the work of Sturrock and Else. In their *Colorado Paper* (1998) they argued that we should view play practice from an interpretative and analytic perspective—the study of the mind or psyche at play, which they termed *psycholudics* (p.4). As such they were not so concerned about the more physical aspects of the playwork setting, but instead concentrated on the interpersonal and emotional aspects of playwork. Making strong use of Bateson's (1955) concept of the *play frame*, and Sutton-Smith's (1984) concept of *play cues*, they suggested a model ludic cycle with which we may understand the actions and interventions of playwork. Put very simply, they suggest that children's play takes place within a metaphorical frame. When playing, children issue play cues to all aspects of the play environment (including their playmates and the artifacts they are playing with). In an ideal world they will get an appropriate response to their cue, and the play will take its natural course. Sadly, that does not always happen, and the consequences can be seriously damaging.

Sturrock and Else offer their own view of the significance of play. They reject the commonly held view of play which sees it as having certain indefinable qualities. Instead they say that the primary element of play is a consciousness or an awareness that is the prefiguring element of all creativity. They suggest that this consciousness is the source of all mental health, and therein lies a means of healing trauma, neurosis and psychic ill (through play). Their thesis rests on the proposition that "prior to each act of creativity . . . lies an imaginal realm or zone that is playful *(ludic)* and symbolically constituted. The playworker joins and works with this *emergent material* and content" (p.4). Thus, playwork is not about encouraging play activities, nor is it an attempt to control or manage the child's play. Rather, they suggest that the true value of playwork rests in the richness of response that a play exchange, setting or artefact generates (p.5). The play frame contains the material that enables the playworker to "develop insights and interpretative responses, aiding further, and perhaps deepening, expressions of this *ludic content*" (p.5). For Sturrock and Else *dys-play* occurs where the meaning of play goes unrecognised, the adult's response is inappropriate, the containment breaks, or the cycle becomes hybrid (p.5).

This is potentially damaging, because as Sturrock and Else suggest, "the playworker is active at the precise point where potential neuroses are being formed" (p.5). They argue that an active playworker can be said to be *freely associating in the free associations* of children. Playworkers are engaging with both an obvious level of playing, and also a deeper layer of unconscious, but emerging content. Therefore, if the playworker's response to the child's play cue is inappropriate the child is likely to feel let down. If those responses are consistently inappropriate the child's neuroses are likely to deepen, as they are not getting the support they need. As a result of this train of thought, Sturrock and Else ask two key questions relating to the therapeutic role of playwork:

- might playworkers enable the "playing out" of actual neurotic formation as part of their practice?
- could playwork be seen as being curative?

Some elements of the playwork setting may contribute to the child's emotional equilibrium. At the deeper levels of functioning, children express, in symbolic form, unconscious material crucial to their psychic development. This also requires containment, reflection, return, and thoughtful engagement by the playworker. All this means that playworkers must develop a consistent interpretative or analytic perspective out of which to issue their responses.

THE THERAPEUTIC POTENTIAL OF A PLAYWORK ENVIRONMENT

Most playworkers will encounter troubled children at some time during their practice. This is true of playworkers in any setting, whether it be an adventure playground, after school club, children's centre, etc. So long as the child feels truly free to play without interference, then the type of setting may not be especially relevant.

In the first instance children are likely to use the play environment to "play out" their problems, as suggested by Sturrock and Else (1998). Freud (1900) calls this "reconciliation" (one of his three reasons why children play). He suggests that children use play to reconcile themselves to traumatic events in their lives. For example, I was once told of an adventure playground where two children who had sadly lost their mother, spent several weeks playing funerals. At first the playworkers found this difficult, but when other children joined in they realised that the game was actually helping everyone. In Freud's thinking, these children were achieving the double benefit of:

- deepening their understanding of what had happened, and
- metaphorically taking control of the event

Eventually the focus of their play moved on to other things, because they had been enabled to say goodbye to their mother through their play. If their play had been stifled, or the playworkers had felt the need to protect them, it is likely that their anguish would have been internalised, only to surface in later life in some sort of neurotic form.

Although there is a substantial difference between therapeutic playwork and most types of play therapy, it is nevertheless true that many of the conditions that a play therapist tries to create are actually available to the child in the atmosphere of "fun, freedom and flexibility" (Brown 2003) that characterises playwork settings. In general play therapy is rooted in the idea of enabling the child to return to a developmental stage, where they previously felt safe and secure. In some cases this will involve their very earliest memories. Thus:

> What play therapy provides children with is the opportunity to go back to the earliest developmental point in order to understand their experiences and find some meaningful resolution for early traumatic or distorted experiences where the gaining of a sense of the body self has been denied. (Chown 2014, p.102)

The renowned drama-therapist, Sue Jennings (1999) sees this in terms of her EPR developmental paradigm, i.e., embodiment, projection and role. However, that is just one example of the many ages and stages views of child development that educational psychologists are fond of. The point here is, if we accept Axline's (1969) view that children have it within themselves to solve their own problems providing they have the right environment, then it should not surprise us to find that children will do just that within a playwork setting.

What is it about a playwork setting that enables reconciliation to happen? Clearly playwork offers an environment of safety and security, but that is not unique to playwork. Most schools would claim to be able to offer that; so would most children's care homes (although that has been thrown into doubt recently). Jennings suggests, "It is important to have contact with nature and for damaged children, it can be a very healing experience" (2011, p.163). There can be little doubt that this is important, but again contact with nature is not unique to playwork settings, nor is it even the primary feature of a lot of playwork settings.

So what is it that is so uniquely therapeutic in a playwork setting? The slightly simplistic answer would be to say playwork settings are characterised by all the things that children subconsciously recognise as being play. In other words, the environment provides lots of stimulation; there are lots of exciting things to do; the children are free to make their own choices about what they want to do; and there is no obstacle to them manipulating the environment in whatever way they wish.

The playwork environment lends itself to this feeling on the part of the child because it is consistently applying two interlinked principles. The first is Simon Nicholson's *Theory of Loose Parts*, which says: "In any environment both the degree of inventiveness and creativity, and the possibility of discovery, are directly proportional to the number and kind of variables in it"

(1971, p.30). The second is summed up in the words of the creative artist John Portchmouth (1969, p.7), "It helps if someone, no matter how lightly, puts in our way the means of making use of what we find." In other words, one of the main roles of the playworker is to provide "loose materials" for children to manipulate, and the tools to enable them to do so. That sort of environment is rare in a child's life. In fact it is so rare that Hughes (2014) says it may be necessary to reassure the children and confirm these realities to them, because they are likely to assume the opposite. In the words of the educationalist Mine Gol-Guven (2016), "Children do not feel free of adults' decisions and judgments even in play where they are supposed to be free from everything . . . even the idea of getting into trouble could stop play" (pp.124–127).

Obviously there will be circumstances where a playworker will have to intervene, but this should only be where a child is a danger to themselves or to other children. On my own adventure playground in the 1970s we just had one rule, which was that children could do whatever they wanted so long as it didn't interfere with the enjoyment of another child. This was once described to me as "a load of 60s hippy claptrap." However, a more purist view might be that the rule didn't go far enough, i.e., it's not necessarily about protecting the children's enjoyment, but rather protecting their right to play. The playworker (and so the whole playwork environment) must essentially adopt an attitude of *negative capability*. Fisher (2008) suggests that playworkers are only there to support what the children are doing, and so they need to internalise negative capability as a creative approach. In so doing they will be approaching the children in a completely unprejudiced, non-judgmental and open-minded way.

All these conditions confirm in the child's mind "this is an environment that I can control, an environment that responds to me." Axline (1969) suggests that in an environment of permissiveness, openness and honesty, children are likely to develop the self confidence to explore their own ideas and feelings. Axline's thinking is reinforced by the play therapist, Mark Barnes (2013), who suggests that the therapeutic process consists of six broad elements: a safe space; a mode of expression; freedom; some boundaries; an accepting therapist who offers a trusting relationship to children; and the guarantee of confidentiality. As we have seen the first four of these can be offered in a playwork environment, and they are substantial contributors to enabling children to "play out" their own troubling issues. The final two factors apply more to the special one-to-one child-playworker relationships that are very often developed in playwork settings, and which are explored in more detail in the next section.

THE THERAPEUTIC POTENTIAL OF THE CHILD-PLAYWORKER RELATIONSHIP

If a child is not able to reach closure through "playing out" their issues, then they will probably seek more immediate help from an adult. In that regard, playworkers are very likely to be chosen. In fact, I would argue that they are more likely than any other adult to be confronted with a child's serious issues, and often without any warning. There is a good reason for this. Children are taught during their earliest attachment experiences (Bowlby 1988) that adults are the solution to their problems. However, as they get older they begin to realise that the adults in their lives have their own agendas, so they are not necessarily to be trusted with serious problems. Coupled with this, children's only experience of being fully in control of their own lives is when they are playing. A good playworker does not intervene unnecessarily in the detail of the child's play. Instead they follow the child's agenda. So, a troubled child, in search of help, finds themselves in the company of an adult who is not taking control, not "adulterating" the child's agenda. In such circumstances it is not surprising that the child feels they can trust that person. Thus, at a very fundamental level there is something unique about the child-playworker relationship that makes it highly suited to a therapeutic exchange. However, there are various subtleties about the way in which the playworker relates to the child that make the relationship especially powerful.

Firstly, at its heart playwork adopts an approach of *unconditional positive regard* (which is not quite the same as unconditional love). At the end of a recent conference I was asked to sum up the playwork approach in a few words. I think the questioner probably expected me to fall back on my usual "fun, freedom and flexibility" (Brown 2003), but I had just been talking about the therapeutic aspects of playwork, and so I said "unconditional positive regard." In this response, I was drawing on the work of the humanistic psychologist, Carl Rogers (1961) and the play therapist, Virginia Axline (1969). Humanistic theory would see the playwork environment as characterised by respect, understanding and openness on the part of the playworker—an environment where the child is free to express their feelings completely. In such an environment the role of the playworker is that of a selfless helper, whose task is to satisfy the child's fundamental need to play, while at the same time developing warm human relationships. All this may eventually enable the child to come closer to Maslow's (1943) concept of self-actualisation than might otherwise be possible. "Unconditional positive regard" is the term that applies to the fundamental attitude of the playworker towards the children. The playworker who adopts this approach deeply values the humanity of the children and, most importantly, is not deflected from that attitude by any particular child behaviours. The attitude is constantly reconfirmed by the playworker's "acceptance of and enduring warmth towards the children" (Mearns and Thorne, 1988, p.59—slightly paraphrased).

Secondly, whenever possible playworkers should be giving positive feedback to the children about how truly great they are. This is important for both short term relationship reasons, and also for long term developmental reasons. Playworkers are there to support the children in what they are doing. Although most playworkers are more interested in the "being" child than the "becoming" child (Sturrock 2007), they are nevertheless aware of the fact that the act of playing is likely to enhance the development of the potential inherent in all children. Indeed, Uprichard (2008) draws on Prigogine's (1980) discussion of time as "being and becoming" to suggest that "viewed from this alternative angle, children and childhood are always and necessarily being *and* becoming" (Uprichard 2008, p.303). By consistently giving positive feedback to the children, the playworker shows respect for the children's immediate interests, which will in turn help the development of self-respect in the child. At the same time this type of feedback is likely to have a longer term positive influence on the child's future development. Providing consistently positive feedback is extremely important as we now know that the brain wave patterns of a young child are similar to those of someone who has been hypnotised (Sunderland 2006). Clearly, if a young child is repeatedly told they are worthless or stupid or annoying, they will begin to believe it. It is therefore crucial that all messages from a playworker are positive.

Thirdly, the nature of the child-playworker relationship that has already been touched upon, lends itself very readily to the powerful therapeutic technique of *joining* (Kaufmann 2017), which is very closely aligned to the basic playwork tenet of working to the child's agenda. The Autism Treatment Centre of America developed this approach as part of their Son-Rise Programme, specifically for working with autistic children. The approach is rooted in a fundamental belief that, contrary to the received wisdom of Wing's (2003) *Triad of Impairments*, autistic children are actually very keen to communicate. Sadly, they don't have the tools to do so in a way that non-autistic people can recognize. Also, contrary to the lazy view that autistic children have no imagination, and therefore cannot play, this is a technique that has a complete acceptance that the child wants to play. Unfortunately, their play doesn't always look like something that we take to be "normal." Therefore, instead of trying to drag the child into our "normal" world—a world which they struggle to understand—Kaufmann recommends a first step of "joining" the child in their world.

> The idea is that children with autism are performing their behaviors for reasons that are important to them. . . . When parents show interest in what their children

are doing, they establish a powerful bond. In response, children begin to display a genuine interest. Once a child is willingly engaged, the door is open to help that child to learn and grow. (Kaufman 2014)

This is just as true of non-autistic children. A disturbed child will often display unusual and sometimes repetitive behavior patterns. This may well be a convoluted plea for help. By joining the child in their behavior the play-worker then demonstrates a level of empathy. This is likely to encourage the child to feel she can trust this person. Once that trusting relationship begins, then a stronger bond is likely to follow, often with powerful outcomes. The following examples are taken from Sophie Webb's research diary, which was kept during her time working with a group of abused children in a Romanian pediatric hospital. The first is an example of using "joining" to encourage a 10 year old boy to walk unaided for the first time. He had previously played with shoes and gloves, to the exclusion of anything else.

I made sure I spent some time with Nicolae today. I have played "shoes" with him for the past two weeks and that appears to have led him to trust me. Today, after playing "shoes" yet again, I stood him in the middle of the room, about four steps away from me. Usually he just sits down, but this time he walked towards me with his arms stretched out for a hug. I think these may have been his first independent steps (after 10 years!). (Webb 2000, Day 18)

The second example is of a 6 year old girl who would not play with the other children, and resisted all contact with the playworkers. She seemed at her happiest when standing in a corner by herself, making the same repetitive sound—a bit like a melodic ambulance siren. Sophie was keen to find a way for her to be confident of beginning to make social contact with us and the rest of the children in the group.

Today I started to repeat the noises that Elena makes "waaaaoooo waaaaoooo" and her reaction was amazing! The look on her face was just like someone had spoken her language. It felt like a little break through as you can rarely communicate with her. Touch is so important to her. I started to repeat this noise back to her and she responded by instigating the sequence when she saw me, exploring my face and trying to decide where the noise was coming from. By offering myself as the play environment Elena was comfortable to allow herself the freedom to communicate and investigate. (Webb 2000, Day 29)

These two examples are from the most extreme circumstances in which therapeutic playwork is likely to occur. However, there is no reason why a similar approach should not be applied in everyday situations, when it becomes obvious that a child is exhibiting signs of disturbance. In most cases therapeutic playwork is about relieving a small to medium one-off emotion that could be affecting the child. It is certainly not for a playworker to adopt the role of a qualified play therapist, but we often have no choice but to offer immediate help, because the child is in urgent need, and no-one else is better placed. Hopefully, once a serious need has been identified it will be possible for the child to be referred to an appropriate specialist. This process may actually be hurried along as result of the strong relationship between child and playworker, and the advocacy role of the playworker.

THE THERAPEUTIC POTENTIAL OF THE CHILD-CHILD RELATIONSHIP

Having proposed all this concerning the significance of the playwork environment and the child-playworker relationship, I finally want to highlight the importance of the child-child relationship. The work in Romania has already been mentioned (Brown 2016), but without touching on the most significant factor in the remarkable recovery of those severely damaged children—namely the fact that the children were at last able to play with other children. It is hard to imagine a more play deprived group of children, some of whom had been tied in their cots for 10 years. Yet as soon as they were provided with the opportunity to play with each other, their development took off, and increased exponentially. This should not be surprising since social play, especially the act of playing with other children, is a powerful trigger for most other play types, and as Hughes (2012) suggests, children need to access a full range of play types in order to develop in a well-rounded manner.

The developmental psychologist Lev Vygotsky highlighted the role of play in a child's development. He suggested:

> Play creates a zone of proximal development of the child. In play a child always behaves beyond his average age, above his daily behaviour; in play it is as though he were a head taller than himself. As in the focus of a magnifying glass, play contains all developmental tendencies in a condensed form and is itself a major source of development. (1978, p.102)

So, the very act of playing brings the child into contact with the social and physical environment in a potentially flexible interactive way. Playing inevitably means the child will have new experiences, and the most stimulating of those experiences is interacting with other children. This means they are able constantly to enter, and re-enter, their own *zone of proximal development* in a completely natural way, without the active guidance of anyone else.

Furthermore, it is only by interacting with other human beings in an informal environment that children are able to learn essential life skills, such as sympathy, empathy, mimesis, affective attunement, and our use of rhythm as a basic building block of development (Brown 2014). We are born with the potential to develop these sophisticated skills, but that potential is only actualised while playing with other children. For example, mimesis, which Donald (2002) describes as the act of using the body to represent meaning, cannot be taught in a classroom. We are never taught that running around with both arms outstretched is a representation of an aeroplane. Instead we learn that sort of thing while playing with other children. This example might seem slightly trivial, but it is the accumulation of numerous such lessons that builds the essential life skills, without which it would be difficult to survive.

Thus, a play-full environment enables children to learn and develop for themselves. In the case of a troubled child that process will be naturally therapeutic.

SUMMARY

The following summary of the main characteristics of therapeutic playwork does not claim that each point is unique to playwork. Rather, it is suggested that taken together they represent a unique way of working with troubled children.

In their underpinning thinking, therapeutic playwork:

- Draws on elements from most of the major strands of psychology
- Understands that play is a basic human drive
- Believes in the uniqueness of every child
- Respects the child's ability to solve their own problems through playing
- Accepts that children may use play as a reconciliation mechanism
- Accepts that children's play has elements of both "being" and "becoming"
- Aims for the development of the potential inherent in all children

In their practice, therapeutic playworkers:

- Work with groups of children, while paying close attention to the needs of individual children in the group
- Create an atmosphere of safety and security
- Create a resource-full play environment
- Create an environment characterised by fun, freedom and flexibility
- Establish a permissive environment of openness and honesty
- Adopt an attitude of unconditional positive regard towards the children

- Work as far as possible to the child's agenda, in a non-directive way
- Emphasise the development of the child-playworker relationship
- Internalise negative capability as a creative approach, and thus adopt an open-minded attitude towards the children
- Use the technique of "joining" where appropriate
- Encourage the development of fundamental life skills, e.g. sympathy, empathy, mimesis
- Recognise the fundamental role of rhythm in early child development
- May sometimes act in an advocacy role for a child

REFERENCES

Axline, V. (1969) *Play Therapy.* (rev. ed.) New York, Ballantine Books

Bateson, G. (1955) A theory of play and fantasy. *Psychiatric Research Reports,* 2: 39–51.

Bowlby, J. (1988) *A secure base: clinical applications of attachment theory.* London: Routledge.

Brown, F. (2003) Compound flexibility: the role of playwork in child development, In: Brown, F. (ed.) *Playwork—theory and practice.* Buckingham: Open University Press.

———. (2014) *Play and playwork: 101 stories of children playing.* Maidenhead: Open University Press.

———. (2016) The healing power of play: therapeutic work with chronically neglected and abused children. In: Navidi, U. (ed) (2016) *The role of play in children's health and development.* Basel: MDPI. pp. 474–488.

Brown, S. (2009) *Play: how it shapes the brain, opens the imagination, and invigorates the soul.* London: Penguin Books.

Chown, A. (2014) *Play therapy in the outdoors.* London: Jessica Kingsley Publishers.

Donald, M. (2002) *A mind so rare: the evolution of human consciousness.* New York, NY: W.W.Norton & Co.

Fisher, K. (2008) Playwork in the early years: working in a parallel profession. In: Brown, F. and Taylor, C. (eds.) (2008) *Foundations of playwork.* Maidenhead: Open University Press.

Freud, S. (1900) The interpretation of dreams, In: Freud, S. (1974) *The standard edition of the complete psychological works of Sigmund Freud.* 24 volumes, translated from the German under the general editorship of James Strachey, in collaboration with Anna Freud; assisted by Alix Strachey and Alan Tyson. London, Hogarth Press, Institute of Psycho-Analysis.

Gol-Guven, M. (2016) Who is holding the longer stick? the power of adult presence on children's play. *International Journal of Play* Vol.5:2, pp. 123–127.

Hughes, B. (1996) *A playworker's taxonomy of play types.* London, PLAYLINK.

———. (2000) *A dark and evil cul-de-sac: Has children's play in urban Belfast been adulterated by the troubles?* Unpublished MA dissertation, Cambridge, Anglia Polytechnic University.

———. (2003) Play deprivation, play bias, and playwork practice. In: Brown, F. (2003) *Playwork theory and practice*. Buckingham: Open University Press.

———. (2012) *Evolutionary playwork.* London: Routledge.

Jennings, S. (1999) Introduction to developmental play therapy. London: Jessica Kingsley Publishers.

———. (2011) *Healthy attachments and neuro-dramatic play*. London: Jessica Kingsley Publishers.

Kaufman, R. (2017) *The Son-Rise Program versus ABA.* The Option Institute. [Internet] Available from: www.autismtreatmentcenter.org/contents/other_sections/aba-vs-son-rise-program.php [Accessed 12 June 2017].

Kilvington, J. and Wood, A. (2018) *Reflective playwork: For all who work with children.* London: Bloomsbury.

Maslow, A. (1943) A theory of human motivation. *Psychological Review*, Vol.50:4. pp. 370–396.

Mearns, D. and Thorne, B. (1988) *Person-centred counselling in action*. London: Sage Publications Ltd.

Nicholson, S. (1971) How not to cheat children. the theory of loose parts. In: *Landscape Architecture Quarterly.* Vol.62, No.1, October 1971, pp. 30–34.

PPSG (2005) *Playwork Principles*, held in trust as honest brokers for the profession by the Playwork Principles Scrutiny Group. [Internet] Available from: http://www.playwales.org.uk/page.asp?id=50 [Accessed 25/6/2017].

Portchmouth, J. (1969) *Creative crafts for today.* London, Studio Vista.

Prigogine, I. (1980) *From being to becoming: time and complexity in the physical sciences*. San Francisco, CA: W.H.Freeman.

Rogers, C. (1961) *On becoming a person*. Boston, MA: Houghton Miflin.

Smith, K. (2017) *The therapeutic benefits of adventure playgrounds.* Unpublished undergraduate paper. Leeds Beckett University.

Sturrock, G. (2007) Towards tenets of playwork practice. In: IP-DiP Issue 1, Sept–Dec 2007. Eastbourne: Meynell Games.

Sturrock, G. and Else, P. (1998) The playground as therapeutic space: playwork as healing. In: *Proceedings of the IPA/USA Triennial National Conference, Play in a Changing Society: Research, Design, Application*. June 1998, Colorado. USA.

Sunderland, M. (2006) *What every parent needs to know*. London: Dorling Kindersley.

Sutton-Smith, B and Kelly-Byrne, D (1984) The Idealization of Play. In Smith, P.K. (ed.), *Play in animals and humans.* Oxford: Blackwell.

Sutton-Smith, B. (1999) Evolving a consilience of play definitions: playfully. In S. Reifel (Ed.), *Play and Culture Studies, Play Contexts Revisited*, 2: 239–256. Stamford: Ablex.

Uprichard. E (2008) Children as "being and becomings:" children, childhood and temporality. *Children & Society* 22(4), pp. 303–313.

Vygotsky, L S (1978) *Mind in society*. Cambridge, MA: Harvard University Press.

Webb, S. (2000) Therapeutic playwork project: extracts from a reflective diary. In: Brown, F. (2014) *Play and playwork: 101 stories of children playing.* Maidenhead: Open University Press.

Chapter Eight

The Might of Play as Possibility and Power

Sylwyn Guilbaud

From wonder into wonder existence opens.

—Lao Tzu

It seems, as many have noted, that we cannot know a child's experience of play. While it is accepted across fields of knowledge from hard science to philosophy that we do not know another's experience, to recognise this in respect of a child's play can, perhaps, be understood as more than a segment of that generalised obvious. Though such recognition offers on the one hand a ready disengagement with the nonsensical unsubstantial inventions of the young, on the other it holds the potential to wonder at the details of those perpetually created play experiences. Each instant that we recognise as play meshes myriad sensations, thoughts, sounds, movements, imaginings, unknown to all but the player, and yet calls forth our identification with play's tone. Every detail of a child's play that we notice holds, in our noticing, a juxtaposition of meaning and mystery—a meaning and mystery contextualised at once by individuality of experience and by play's reconfiguration of what is held to be, in fields of knowledge. Here then is perhaps a hint of the nub of the difference between generalized acceptance of the gap between my experience and yours, and an adult's unknowingness in response to a child's play. To embrace with humility a sense of wonder at the detail of a child's play, subverts for a moment the power dynamic between the worldly wise and the fanciful growing, flipping the positions of real and unreal, slipping in a question of what might be, and a willingness to believe that which is beyond our bounds.

Interestingly when noticing of play is retold in this vein, without abstraction into the rhetoric of various disciplines, the nature of the play seems to travel through the wor(l)ds, with an impression tangibly un-dissected by knowing.

Webb's description of a moment of play in the playroom of a Romanian paediatric hospital is illustrative of this. "I watched Elena play with Virgil—it was absolutely beautiful, and the best representation of play I have seen. All they were doing was chasing each other, it was so gentle and silent and it was as if they were flowing in and out of one another. . . . Just like two butterflies" (2001, preface)—the wonder of her experience can be found re-presented in her poem.

> Play as the conduit for change
>
> I watched as they moved
> Beautiful in the sunlight,
> Chasing one-another like balloons
> Caught by the breeze
> So gentle . . .
> And the room seemed silent
> As they flowed in and out
> Of one-another . . .
> Just like two butterflies.
> —Sophie Louise Webb, June 11, 2000

If we wonder at the wellspring of our capacity for wonder, its fit as a means to transmit play begins to unfold and within that integral quality of possibility Lao Tzu's translated words, with which I opened this contribution, suggest a fundamental perpetuation. This chapter seeks to tease apart the filigree of the relationship between play and wonder. Drawing on my doctoral research, accounts from the playwork field and other resonant descriptions of childhood moments, this chapter will explore the possible patterns of such a relationship through three refractive lenses:

- The role of play in what is and what might be,
- The inherence of mistake and unpredictable possibility in that relationship,
- The ripple affect of being sensitized to the world of existence by the detail of childhood play.

WONDER'S RECEPTION OF PLAY

It seems that through a willingness to let the play of a child affect our perception of what might be, our sense of existence and what exists becomes open to undefined possibilities. Several times I have been privileged to hear Bob

Hughes tell the story of his experience of being invited into his grandson's den, constructed of walls and properties that Hughes couldn't see. Hughes tells of his sense that for his grandson the structure existed in detail and of how important it was to enter and navigate appropriately there. I remember the feeling of being asked many years ago by my young daughter to join her in moving paper fairies through a circle of air in a ceremonial gathering which I did not know but which was certainly obvious to her. I remember the feeling of clumsiness while I tried to follow her instructions, moving my fingers through three-dimensional arcs and pathways, which were indecipherable to me, and how gradually my hands started to feel the atmosphere above the table and my contributions became intuitively evident. Air is both empty and full for the playing into, holding patterns that are made visible by birds, seeds, smoke. Babies babble intently at spaces, seemingly creating or responding to something there. In Hughes' most recent telling to me of the story of his grandson's play, he spoke, as before, of the magic of play he experienced by being taken into these worlds that he didn't even know existed. He then shared his wondering about whether what was happening was that his grandson "was projecting changes in his brain to the space outside himself, and the pain if you didn't get it right was that he had to re-juggle his own brain to be able to deal with that" (Guilbaud 2015).

These impressions can be further wondered about in context with Abram's exploration of the "forgetting and remembering of air." Abram (1996) tells of the Navajo understanding that, "Air—particularly in its capacity to provide awareness, thought and speech—has properties that European alphabetic civilization has traditionally ascribed to an interior, individual human 'mind' or 'psyche'" (p.237 original emphasis).

He then traces the etymology of air through different languages, noting that the Latin word anima from which we draw *animate*, signified both soul and air (ibid p.238 original emphasis). Air may be the most undefined of mediums to form through play; its potential dependent and constrained by the player's imagination. There, what is and what isn't rests in the player's perceptual frame. Yet the inspiration which the air offers towards what might be, the presence of waves and the dusty patterns of ancient ancestors,[1] the ripple of a breeze that has blown through tall trees, is hard to discount or qualify. As such that which air carries to and from each player, can surely only be wondered at. When discussing properties of liminality and of play Spariosu writes,

> The liminal, in its most radical form, points to boundless freedom or "stillness"—what Zen Buddhism calls the "luminous void," out of which all structure emerges and into which all structure is dissolved. In turn, play is an active principle—a creative activity that draws upon this luminous void continuously to generate, reconfigure, or dissolve structures. (2013, p.7)

Playing into air can be perceived as expansively generative of, and responsive to, that vast possible—an unfettered bringing about of the as yet unreal; thereby at once in each unique experience, offering a metaphoric reflection of play's nature, a seed within the flower, the macro of many micros. Though Spariosu (2013) sits play within liminality and not all liminality within play, what of our perception of the liminal and what of our poetic relationship to air's properties? Are these capacities not connected to play, and our perception of play? What of the mind's flexibility?

THE POTENTIAL OF WHAT MIGHT BE, TO FORM WHAT EXISTS

The possibility that inhaling the vast unknown into thought and word might make aesthetic sense, suggests an instigation of that sense making, the presence of like to recognise like.[2] Such questioning is offered ground by Sutton-Smith's discussion of *the neurological player* (Sutton-Smith, 1997, p.60). Similarly to Abram's noting of the attribution of air's properties to the internal workings of man, Sutton-Smith refers to Spariosu's (1989) analysis of the polarity between "the openness of science to the metaphor of play" and the more rigid rational view of physical philosophers, "they do not really allow for imagining as a subversive activity or allow themselves to be seriously attracted to an irrational view of the universe" (Sutton-Smith, 1997, p.59–60, for original discussion see Spariosu 1989, *Play and anarchistic epistemology in contemporary philosophy of science* pp. 292–311). Sutton-Smith then expands the view of flexible lability, of flux and unpredictability in epistemology (Spariosu 1989), proposing that play defends against rigidification of potential. To this end he interweaves findings and speculations from perspectives of anthropology, biology, philosophy and neurology, which "prompt us to see a brain at play that is as universal as that kind of play envisaged for the gods and the physical universe" (Sutton-Smith, 1997, p.62). He shows us a mind which is part of, made by and creative of its perceptual environment, suggesting that "play might imitate the fluidity and value-driven character of the mind's own internal processing, but with a transference to the agencies, agents, acts and spatio-temporal scenes of the external world. Play is, as it were, a halfway house between the night and the day, the brain and the world" (ibid, p.61).

I recently came across a small extract of an article and video clip about Helen Keller's visits to Martha Graham's dance studio. Within this happening, drawing on the perspective of understanding offered by Sutton-Smith, it is possible to add a layer of materialization to the questioning awareness of playing formatively with air, initiated above. Here, that which might to many be imperceptible in the air seems to merge through play with the mind as it interacts with the capacity and forming of the physical body. The video shows Keller with her hands in the air above a drum feeling and playing out the rhythm without touching the drum itself, but her hand does not stay above the drum it seems to follow the vibration up into the air. The text extracted from Brown (2013) recounts Keller's question to Graham: "Martha, what is jumping? I don't understand?" So Graham asks Merce Cunningham, one of her dancers to jump with Keller's hands on his waist, and recalls:

> Her expression changed from curiosity to one of joy. You could see the enthusiasm rise in her face as she threw her arms in the air.
>
> Cunningham continues to perform small leaps, with very straight legs. He suddenly feels Keller's fingers, still touching his waist, begin to move slightly, "as though fluttering." For the first time in her life, she is experiencing dance. "Oh, how wonderful! How like thought! How like the mind it is!" she exclaims when he stops. (Brown, 2013, p.16)

These interactions and Keller's expressive responses point delicately at a mind's flexibility to create itself in relationship to the sensible world, and within this there seems to be tangibility to Sutton-Smith's suggestion of imitation between play, the mind's internal processing and the external world. Between the drummer, the drum, the air, Keller's hand, her mind, her expression, those around her, there is a patterning recognisable as that wonder of new discovery resonating, of responding jubilantly without pre-determination; in the same way as a child might engage with a wave on the shore.

The awareness expressed by Cobb (1993) can be found to contribute another refraction to this developing picture. When reflecting on the work of Heisenberg, Bohr and Thorpe—she questions "the creative effect on perception and mind of those rhythmical continuities, visual, auditory, tactile, or metabolic, that support the system of the body and unite its organs of research with systems in nature" (Cobb, 1993, p.98), suggesting that "we are not extrapolating too far in relating the principle of organization in nature's behaviour directly to human imagination, the organizing behaviour of mind that creates novelty of thought" (ibid, p.99). Keller's response to the vibrations in the air, and the movement of dance, are well situated within Cobb's synthesis "that the physics of the body and nature as universe remain the generating forces, but evolution, rather than growth, is the proper metaphor for the process of the developing mind" (ibid, p.99). Together and discretely these views are lit by the lability by which Sutton-Smith (1997) conjoins the playful brain with nature and the gods, with palpable wonder in his tone, as well as content.

Within the metaphor of evolution rather than growth and, in verification, within the very capacity to perceive metaphorically, we are reminded that play does not belong to us. Though our capacity for definition permits us to view play anthropomorphically, differentiating species who play by our own awareness of as-if-ness (Bateson 2000; Burghardt 2005; Bekoff & Pierce 2009; Henricks 2015), the potential for the evolution of play within our being, is beyond our deliberation. Our recognition of human like play in other species dichotomously offers a telling realisation, as Huizinga notes "Since the reality of play extends beyond the sphere of human life it cannot have its foundations in any rational nexus, because this would limit it to mankind" (1955, p.3). However perhaps a greater representation of the synergy in nature's organisation and human imagination (Cobb 1993) is offered in Bateson's (2000, p.401) description of the unfertilized frog's egg "uncommitted potential for change." The egg's becoming awaits and is determined by the entry point of the spermatozoon, but, perhaps playfully, it can also be begun by an "as if" prick from a camel hair brush. Bateson identifies this quality in the unfertilized egg as not-structure but that from which new structure is generated. The synergy of nature's organization and human imagination is complexly demonstrated in the interplay of subject and process. Using this phenomenon as a lens he applies the flexibility within the egg and within the metaphor he makes from it, to view the economics of flexibility both in the relationship between organisms and environment (ibid, pp.346–363) and within societal ecology (ibid, 502–513). In the later section he notes that when something does not change it becomes hard programmed, and that "to maintain the flexibility of a given variable, either that flexibility must be exercised, or the encroaching variables must be directly controlled." He proposes that while in the valuing of freedom within society, "We try to prohibit certain encroachments . . . it might be more effective to encourage people to know their freedoms and flexibilities and use them more often" (p.511). The integrity of the unmappable to existence is similarly pointed to by Thomas's (1979) description of the impossibility of deliberate creation of a molecule. He notes that if we had attempted to replicate it, deliberateness would have fatally omitted the integral possibility for mistake (p.28). Further to this, is Bohr's (1958) proposition that the essence of life is not available to the dissecting knife, but is entwined with our perception of aliveness. It seems that we reflexively recognise the potential of possibility of that which we did not intend, and that resonance is complicit in the mood of wonder, and the might of play. In my own questioning of the relationship between play and what might be via different lenses (Guilbaud 2008; Guilbaud 2011; Guilbaud TBA), the integrity of possibility to play and to perception of aliveness is inescapably resurgent, leading to a synthesis that "the decisively constructed life form would not contain what it needs to regenerate, to become, to exist in that play-full differentiation which we call life" (Guilbaud TBA).

THE PLAYFUL INVITATION OF THE UNINTENDED

Without our propensity for mistake and for following the sense of rightness in the surprise or the flow of indeliberate happenstance how could play be? What parent does not remember and sometimes rue the day they picked up and gave back the toy or spoon that fell initially accidentally from highchair or buggy, opening the way for that delightful game? The unforeseen alteration of form offered by mistake can be seen along the smudge line from which play draws life or disintegrates, the intersection between players' awareness and unawareness of its occurrence seeming integral to the incorporation. Together the following five observations touch on the complexity of such interweaving.

Observation 1

Angel: Mummy come here, you're not allowed to touch the floor at all today, you have to walk on the things.

Mummy: Ok but how can I make my cup of tea?

Angel: Hang on I'm just going to make a pathway. (she gathers tea towels etc and lays them on the floor)

Mummy: But Angel you're walking on the floor.

Angel: Yeah but I'm being the mum, and the mum is one of the painters, isn't she.

Honey: No I'm being the mum.

Angel: No, you're being the teacher aren't you, she's also one of the painters.

Honey: Pretend she's (herself) putting down drying powder to make the floor dry faster.

Angel: No, we don't want the floor to dry faster.

Honey: Actually the drying powder makes the floor really, really wet (Collusive laughter). (Guilbaud 2008)

Observation 2

In the kitchen getting louder and louder, two girls are layering stories about what a playworker has said about washing hands and wiping bums. They are drawing other people in and telling and retelling the story with exuberance and laughter. The playworker has her hair in a ponytail. Her hair and hair-bands have been part of an excited game with other children earlier. With a link to the playworker's perceived seriousness regarding the hand washing, which they are teasing her about, the girls move into the next story. It goes something like this: "Ponies have tails, unicorns are ponies but the horn means they're happy, H (playworker) has a ponytail but she says she's serious, but she's happy because it's a ponytail and unicorns have tails and unicorns are like ponies and if you take the uni and tail, but unicorns have horns and it means they're happy. . . ."

This story evolves with each telling. The girls come out of the kitchen and accost everyone, including playworkers, to tell the story to, jumping up and down in front of the person to tell it, layering their stories into and on top of each other, finding it so funny that they often lose their places and have to start again—louder and louder, the story seems at its loudest point to evaporate out of shear excited effort. (Guilbaud 2011)

Observation 3

Children Talking to a Researcher (K) About How Musical Playground Games Change.

Hong-Soo: But when . . . you learn a new version of something that you already know, like "See See My Playmate" like we've already seen, you sort of let go of what was and then catch hold of what is so you can't remember the one before it.

K (researcher): So you can't remember the previous one. It just goes out of your mind? . . .

Sheila: You can remember the actions but you can't remember the song or you can remember the song but you can't remember the actions.

Alicia: Yeah. What usually happens—how different versions often spread, and this is what happened to me—what happens is, I learn something off Sadie and then I might have one movement which I think is right but isn't quite right. Then I'll teach Hong-Soo that, and she'll probably catch on to what I had. And then she'll probably get one movement wrong and so different versions will just spread all over the school. And if you catch on every version of the person before you then, like, you've taught one that's been gradually changed through so many people teaching [it]. (Marsh 2008)

Observation 4

She is shelling broad beans and talking about bunnies "I want a bunny," she says. One of the broad beans hops out of the pod and across the table, landing in one of the holes in the slotted breadboard. "Oh look it hopped," she says, "Must have been because I was talking about bunnies." She smiles. (Guilbaud 2011)

Observation 5

> *The Slide Might Also Be Known As a Zip Wire or Flying Fox*
> JC, Jarod, Morris and Mickey are all on the slide at once—unsurprisingly, it sags so much that they touch the ground. Jarod tightens the ringbolt at the bottom to raise the cable a bit.
> Barry and Corin run across as Mark comes down the slide: "I nearly killed you," he says.
> Some children take a run before they launch off, thereby increasing the speed of the slide and crashing into the end stop. Wesley announces "I'm trying to whack into that black thing" (he means the tyre that acts as the end stop). He tries a few times, then mistimes his run and falls off the slider seat—turns it into a joke by lying spread-eagled on the ground as if injured. He enjoys this so much that he does it again, on purpose. Later he manages to get his "whacking," but he also goes on doing the comedy act. (The Slide, Mark Gladwin—play researcher p.94, in Brown 2014)

As part of its unexpectedness, mistake offers as yet unspecified meaning, a readiness to become, an invitation to and reliance on being appropriated, lived into by the player. Similarly to the welcome with which the playing children in the instances above incorporate mistake, bricoleurs (Levi-Strauss 1983) and improvising artists rely on the fusion of materials un-fit-for-purpose with their capacity to reconstrue error. Nachmanovitch (1990) describes the sudden humidity induced slackening of a violin string. He points out the options, to retune and pretend it didn't happen, or to go with the unexpected sound. "Out of tune with what?" he asks, "with my perceived benchmark of 'in tune.'" He then shares the appeal of this string's less-than condition, "A low, thick string, when it goes flabby, not only becomes lower in pitch, but because of the flabbiness will give to the bow's weight much more easily and will produce (if lightly touched) more breathy and resonant tones than a normal string" (p.91). He tells of the potential fun to be had with this string and questions whether he might be inspired to detune it further. The same awareness can be seen in the approach of the photographer Miroslav Tichy (2008), who made his cameras out of scraps, old cotton reels, cardboard tubes, plexiglass, saying "Photography is something concrete, a perception, what you see with your eyes, and it happens so fast that you may not see anything at all! To photograph is to paint with light! The flaws are part of it. That's what makes the poetry, and for that you need a bad camera" (Tichy 2008, synopsis). It is also in the recognition of the playworker who values the rocking chairs made with big round tables, which don't really work to play on for long but "contribute to the permissional and out of the ordinary ambience we attempt to construct" (Guilbaud 2015).

BEING AND GROWING SENSITIZED TO PLAY

Such conjunction between potential for perception and perception of potential can be seen deeply rooted in the playwork psyche. The cumulative spiral of "compound flexibility" proposed by Brown (1989; 2003), rests on the interaction between the degree of unfixed possibility within the child's experiential environment and their evolving capacity for play's flexibility. Such conjunction between the playing child, the flexibility of the physical and human environment, and the dawning awarenesses of the responsive playworker, can be found underpinning such fundamental perspectives as the play cycle (Sturrock & Else 1998) and play types (Hughes 1996b; Hughes 2006). Furthermore young players' inclination for reinterpretations and appropriation of spaces in transition—destroyed, degraded, abandoned or in partial construction—can be seen reflected in the foundational dynamic of Adventure Playgrounds, wherefrom playwork draws its ethic (Hughes 1975; Hughes 1996a; Hughes 2001; Chilton 2003; Brown 2007; Gill 2008; Cranwell 2009). Under the title "The secret life of objects: building transformative places for play," Leichter-Saxby (2009) poetically transmits the complex subtle de-establishing re-creative qualitative strands in the liminal landscape of relationship between discarded de-purposed material and the playing child. In a richly tangible furnishing of Nicholson's (1971) recognition of loose parts—a theory which has ironically since fallen prey to the very abstractive commodification[3] of adult organisation that Leichter-Saxby identifies as rendering things less malleable to play—she brings notice to the power held in the specification and reification of objects' use and position in the order of things. She brings awareness to the undeliniated power offered through freedom from the established configurations, both to objects and the player who notices such openness to repositioning within the order of existence. The way she does this has a similar resonance to that which Spariosu (2013) engenders when discussing those dwellers of liminality, ejected, rejected or divergent from societies' assimilative norms. Through the atmospheric detail of her writing Leichter-Saxby demonstrates the sensitization of her perception to play, while her subject matter grounds awareness of the reliance of the playing child on the adult's capacity for such perceptiveness.

> These articles of rubbish are troubling, in part because they remind us that the systems we use to organize and navigate the world are imperfect, arbitrary and insecure. Because rubbish can be seen as anarchic, disobedient and dangerous, and because children can be seen as all those things and vulnerable as well, adults went into those bomb sites where children were playing, built fences and swept away the glass. (Leichter-Saxby 2009, p.ii)

The dichotomy of intervention is integral to every dimension of playwork awareness, from our raison d'être through every theorised discussion. Yet the practice of being in the presence of playing children responsively is perhaps too transient to fix into idea. For that moment-by-moment responsiveness is sometimes an action towards a request, towards the cumulation of flexibility; but is often an internal shift, a pricking of potential realisation towards the incomprehensible, that cannot be preconceived.

For as an abstract concept, even neophilia, may disturb the delicate biosphere of laid down play, affecting the players experience very similarly to imposed concerns for health and safety, litigation or propriety.

> When we, as adults, build structures, we are shaping children's play. When we purchase new pieces of equipment or arts and crafts materials, when we bring new objects into a site or remove things that we have found there we are setting boundaries on what children might do. We are creating a system for ordering the materials onsite, rather than letting the children develop their own on a daily basis. We are keeping the site fixed, rather than letting it evolve. (Leichter-Saxby 2009, p.iii)

Where adults are stewards of a play space, the nature of their perception cannot but affect the play's materialisation. To hold an interpretive reference point creates a lens into which play tends, in its flexibility, to fit. An instance of play has no single meaning, value or category. Our recognition that "this is play" exists in the synthesis of what we sense and what we conceptualise.

In an interview from which I quoted earlier, in which he also talks about the freedom of his childhood play and how the patterns of his thinking are saturated with the play he has noticed and absorbed over many years, the playwork theorist Bob Hughes demonstrates his openness to being altered by the sensing of play. This telling accepts the way that awareness of play slips in as inspiration while evading direct figuring and Hughes cherishes such means in the conjunction of his play orientated practice and musings.

> I came into playwork really to help children, so I came in as an interventionist as well, what was strange is that I went through a metamorphosis in the first couple of years I was there, and couldn't work out what my function was for at least that period of time. Every time I looked at the kids, I thought that isn't what I need to be doing. I need to be doing something else, and what came to pass was this. The site of the playground was on an old farmyard on the outskirts of the town that I'd lived in and I'd played there as a child. That whole area had been a playground for me. It was out on the outskirts of town when I was a kid, but I actually played there, but the resonance of that and the resonance of the children playing on that spot again, began to make me realise, or at least I began to acknowledge, that there was another function and that is really where

> I got the title for that little red book,—*Notes for Adventure Playworkers*. It was only then that I began to realise that our primary function was not intervention but in making sure those kids were able to play. It's taken me ever since to try and work out what I meant. (Guilbaud 2015)

As a researching playworker, I too found myself becoming cumulatively altered by the atmosphere of the playing and the things and spaces that were being played with. My ways of noticing seemed to be becoming attuned to what I was noticing. I found myself sensing more and more as I observed, by letting my mind drift rather than through deliberate attention. I gradually developed the capacity to notice peripherally, as opposed to with the seemingly more intrusive direct attention of every-day inquisitiveness. The internal state of being, which became knowable and re-accessible as this differentiation, is describable as "encountering as an act of believing and accepting, rather than of questioning and interrogating" (Guilbaud 2011, p.344). This capacity in me felt as if it grew from a palpable sense of a playing child's drifting into things around them as they seem to open themselves up to finding exactly what they needed though perhaps could not pre-specify, in what came to hand. The sensitization of my play diffused senses, allowed me to notice such moments as when a boy who had been bashing a metal pole repeatedly on stone steps, and throwing each broken off piece from the end in turn onto the grass beyond, suddenly said quietly to himself, in the midst of this "It's a story." Something in this happening suggested to me that the pieces of metal pole should be left to be on the grass for a time, and that then they should be put together in a corner of the shed. When I mentioned to the boy that this is where I had put them there was the merest moment of recognition, but the feel of it was often there in our future interactions (ibid. p.226 & pp.282–283).

Seath writes and speaks in a way that feels similarly familiar, of the subtle almost indescribable awarenesses that permeate and re-form his perception of play while it is happening, and of the playground after the children have gone home. He shared with me his sense of the traces left by the day of play, and of the fizz in the air that builds whilst children are playing (Seath 2014/15). In the following self-revealing description there is an overlap in his perception of the drifting wood smoke, the hazy sun and the sense of play in the atmosphere of the playground, an echoing of the diffused way of noticing play that allows the playworker to be altered by what is happening, as opposed to being, by our perception, its shaping influence.

> Looking out over the playground, over the new and already evolving fire pit in the foreground, through its upright palette wall and the drift of wood smoke, into the hazy sun, the crisp blue February sky over the recently sodden site, there is a sudden sense of wonder. It isn't new, this feeling, but it returns in moments

> made both of clarity in its general whole and in a certain inability to capture all its constituent elements there and then. It is a well-being of the spirit. It's a moment like a haiku. Later, when I think on it all, I try to do it justice with words that don't seem to quite sum it up so well. (Seath 2014)

In the sensitization to play which play seems to afford we can find the might of play in the power of possibility. This ripple into the perception of the playworker, into the very creation and constant reforming of the playworker, can be understood as a humble materialisation of the endless refraction of play with what might be. It can be felt as unpredictability in the flux of existence, the affect of being sensitized by play perpetuating the potential for new possibility to form. Hughes' experience of resonance from the landscape of his childhood play generating new awareness in his early playwork practice and the continuous assimilation of a life of play-reception into the patterns of his thinking; Seath's communication of play saturated atmosphere beyond the bounds of his description, yet held by the kite strings of his expression; my own experience of how my noticing as a researching playworker grew ever sensitised from exposure to the detail of the children's play; are all responses to the possibility of what might be in our world, and to what *is* in the fundamental unarguable truth in the personal manifestations of play within the experience of each playing child's transient and returning moments. In such ways play lives free and remains wonderfully freeing from the dissector's knife (after Bohr 1956).

Yet though the playworker sways in wonder noticing the smoke of the half way house between night and day, accepting that they know not what they perceive, they are not immune to the urge to capture, to define, to reify play. Interestingly, by its very flexibility play affords us both the capacity of thought and the malleability of its essence, which fits and forms by the dimensions that we invite it into. This dichotomy is perhaps the greatest demonstration of integrity of mistake within this medium of becoming. No separation can be made between the delighted infants kicking into air and the awareness that air, kicking and delight are discoverable by all the means that we accrue, nor is there any need for separation between such initial discovery and the inquiry of thought.[4] Yet those who would orientate their being in response to play, might be aware that even philosophers, in their explorations which once began in wonder (Plato cited in Stewart & Mickunas 1990) seem vulnerable to rigidity (Spariosu 1989). It could be argued that all atrophy provides the liminality of future playscapes, the dust to be re-configured. Yet recognition of such unspecified potential might rely on perception having been formed by and ever encountering its like, in air, in play, in the wonder of possibility, an infinitude expansively expressed in the Emily Dickinson poem, which begins:

I dwell in Possibility
A fairer House that Prose
(from *I dwell in Possibility* by Emily Dickinson 1862)

NOTES

1. "Your next breath will contain more than 400,000 of the argon atoms that Gandhi breathed in his long life. Argon atoms are here from the conversations at the Last Supper, from the arguments of diplomats at Yalta, and from the recitations of the classic poet" (Shaply 1967, p.48).

2. In supposing that the potential of our aesthetic sense corresponds with the possibility which it absorbs I draw on the impression which was created in me when reading Goethe's understanding of the forming of the eye "The eye may be said to owe its existence to light, which calls forth, as it were, a sense that is akin to itself; the eye, in short, is formed with reference to light, to be fit for the action of light; the light it contains corresponding with the light without. We are here reminded of a significant adage in constant use with the ancient Ionian school—'Like is only known by Like'" (Goethe & Eastlake 1840).

3. http://www.playforce.co.uk/product/loose-parts-kit/; http://www.oneperfectdayblog.net/2013/09/16/preschool-math-games-loose-parts/; http://earthwrights.co.uk/products/12.

4. Joseph Campbell (2008) notes that "whenever the poetry of myth is interpreted as biology, history or science it is killed" (p. 212). While such forewarning may be amply evidenced, the dislocation is not inherent to the subject or means of inquiry of biology science or history. More common is, as noted by Spariosu, the use of play orientated metaphor in expressing the experience of discovery.

Marie Curie said, "A scientist in his laboratory is not a mere technician: he is also a child confronting natural phenomena that impress him as though they were fairy tales."

The physicist Richard Feynman describes the playing that led to him winning Nobel prize:

> I was eating lunch some kid threw up a plate in the cafeteria which has a blue medallion on the plate, the Cornell sign and as he threw up the plate and it came down it wobbled and the blue thing went around. And I wondered, it seemed to me the blue thing went around faster than the wobble and I wondered what the relation was between the two so I was just playing—no importance at all. So I played around with the equations of motion of rotating things and I found out that if the wobble is small the blue thing goes around twice as fast as the wobble goes around. And then I tried to figure out if I could see why that was directly from Newton's laws instead of from the complicated equations and I worked that out for the fun of it. (Feynman 2008)

Elsewhere (Gadamer 2004, discussed in Guilbaud 2011, p.175) I consider Gadamer's suggestion that it is only when play exists, continues to exist beyond the player, transformed into structure, within for example a piece of art or a dramatic play, that it becomes real, as opposed to the rhythmic open ended playing-itself-out of play in the elements, or in children's play. Yet he recognises that such play, even in this becoming real, is never completely separated from its origin, for though it exists transformed into something in itself, it has to be experienced/enlivened as play for it to really exist. In this attempt to grasp at play's slippery malleability we must consider the inherent potential for atrophy within the artefacts that await, reliant as they are on being encountered with play sensitive eyes. There is an inseparability therein of the prior perceptions of play in air, of childhood play. For those elemental experiences are vital in the forming of that which will find, and by recognition re-enliven, play's traces, bringing them to relevance in the existence of the moment, futhermore creating the awareness that might thrill to their resonance.

REFERENCES

Abram, D. (1996) *The spell of the sensuous: perception and language in a more-than-human world.* New York, NY: Pantheon Books.

Bateson, G. (2000) *Steps to an ecology of mind.* London: The University of Chicago Press.

Bekoff, M. & Pierce, J. (2009) *Wild justice: the moral lives of animals.* London: University of Chicago Press.

Bohr, N. (1958) Light and life. *Atomic physics and human knowledge.* New York: John Wiley & Sons. pp. 3–8.

Brown, C. (2013) *Hello goodbye hello: A circle of 101 remarkable meetings.* New York, NY: Simon & Schuster.

Brown, F. (1989) *Working with children: a playwork training pack.* Leeds: Children First.

———. (2003) Compound flexibility: the role of playwork in child development. *In:* Brown, F. (ed.) *Playwork theory and practice.* Buckingham: Open University Press. pp. 51–65.

———. (2007) *The Venture: a case study of an adventure playground.* Cardiff: Play Wales.

———. (2014) Play and playwork: 101 stories of children playing. Maidenhead: Open University Press.

Burghardt, G. M. (2005) *The genesis of animal play: testing the limits.* London: MIT.

Campbell, J. (2008) *The hero with a thousand faces.* Novato, CA: New World Library.

Chilton, T. (2003) Adventure playgrounds in the twenty-first century. In: Brown, F. (ed.) *Playwork theory and practice.* Buckingham: Open University Press. pp. 114–127.

Cobb, E. (1993) *The ecology of imagination in childhood.* Dallas, Tex.: Spring Publications.

Cranwell, K. (2009) Adventure playgrounds. In *Encyclopedia of play in today's society*, Vol.1, London: Sage. pp. 11–12.
Dickinson, E. (1862) I dwell in Possibility. *Emily Dickinson Archive* [Online] Available from: http://www.edickinson.org [Accessed 2 August 2018].
Feynman, R. (2008) *The late great physicist Richard Feynman*. Australia, ABC Radio National.
Gadamer, H., Weinsheimer, J. and Marshall, D. (2004) *Truth and method.* London: Continuum.
Gill, T. (2008) If you go into the woods today, why nature and adventure matter to children and young people *In:* Brown, F. & Taylor, C. (eds.) *Foundations Of playwork.* Maidenhead: Open University Press.
Goethe, J. and Eastlake, C. (1840) *Goethe's theory of colours.* J. Murray.
Guilbaud, S. (2008) Play makes the world and the world makes play. *IP-DIP* (2), pp. i–viii.
———. (2011) *A phenomelogical inquiry into the possiblity of played-with-ness in experiences with things.* PhD Thesis, Leeds Metropolitan University.
———. (2015) Sharing playwork identities: research across the UK's field of playwork. *International Journal of Play Special Issue, Play and Playwork: notes and reflections in a time of austerity.* Volume 4, Issue 3, Winter 2015.
———. (TBA) Extrapolating the might of play. *In:* Bateson, N. (ed.) *forthcoming publication, title as yet unknown.* The International Bateson Institute.
Henricks, T. (2015) *Play and the human condition* University of Illinois Press.
Hughes, B. (1975) *Notes for adventure playworkers.* London: Childs Play.
———. (1996a) *Play environments a question of quality.* London: Playlink.
———. (1996b) *A playworker's taxonomy of playtypes.* London: PLAYLINK.
———. (2001) *Evolutionary playwork and reflective analytic practice.* London: Routledge.
———. (2006) *Play types, speculations and possibilities.* London: London Centre for Playwork Education and Training.
Huizinga, J. (1955) *Homo ludens: a study of the play-element in culture.* Boston: Beacon Press.
Leichter-Saxby, M. (2009) The secret lives of objects: building transformative places for play. *IP-DIP* (11), pp. i–ix.
Lévi-Strauss, C. (1983) *The raw and the cooked.* Chicago: University of Chicago Press.
Marsh, K. (2008) *The musical playground, global tradition and change in children's songs and games.* Oxford: Oxford University Press.
Nachmanovitch, S. (1990) *Free Play.* New York: Penguin Putnam Inc.
Nicholson, S. (1971) How not to cheat children: the theory of loose parts. *Landscape Architecture Quarterly,* 62 (1), pp. 30–34.
Seath, J. (2014) This playground: magic in the fabric of an island *Playworkings* [Internet blog]. Available from: https://playworkings.wordpress.com/2014/02/21/this-playground-magic-in-the-fabric-of-an-island/ [Accessed June 12 2015].
———. (2014/15) *RE: Various conversations about play, playwork and experiences.* Type to Guilbaud, S.

Shaply, H. (1967) *Beyond the observatory.* New York, NY: Scribner.

Spariosu, M. (1989) *Dionysus reborn: play and the aesthetic dimension in modern philosophical and scientific discourse.* New York: Cornell University Press.

———. (2013) Exile and utopia as liminal play: a cultural-theoretical approach. *Philosophy at Play. April 9–10, University of Gloucestershire.* pp.13.

Stewart, D. & Mickunas, A. (1990) *Exploring phenomenology: a guide to the field and its literature.* Athens: Ohio University Press.

Sturrock, G. & Else, P. (1998) The playground as therapeutic space playwork as healing *IPA/USA Triennial National Conference, Play in a Changing Society Research, Design, Application.* June 1998, Colorado USA.

Sutton-Smith, B. (1997) *The ambiguity of play.* London: Harvard University Press.

Thomas, L. (1979) *The medusa and the snail.* London: Penguin Books.

Tichy, M., Burnham, C., Buxbaum, R., Christov-Bakargiev, C. & Szeemann, H. (2008) *Miroslav Tichy: Dedicated to the women of Kyjov.* Koln: Walther Konig.

Webb, S. (2001) *An analysis of the effects of playwork on the development of a group of abandoned children in a Romanian paediatric hospital.* BA (Hons) Playwork thesis, Leeds Metropolitan University.

Chapter Nine

The Land

Dave Bullough, Claire Pugh, and Ben Tawil

There is a housing estate in Wales which features high on the Welsh Index of Multiple Deprivation. There is a stigma attached to this estate and the community is acknowledged as at risk or already experiencing a range of complex issues, including disabilities, domestic violence/abuse, challenging or anti-social behaviour, low levels of educational attainment, living within workless or in overcrowded households, and drug and alcohol misuse. As well as living with these issues the children can also be subject to additional complexities such as: living with a parent(s) with a disability or mental ill health problem or in households that routinely rely on food banks to avoid malnourishment. As a result, children on this housing estate can present low levels of self-esteem and self–confidence and can lack aspiration. They can also present an inspiring robustness of character, personality and resilience. By any standard definition, children growing up on this estate are deprived; they are also at risk of experiencing further inequalities and social exclusion. These children are undoubtedly poor by numerous measures, but they are wealthy in others; wealthy in terms of freedom, time, and space, all essential components for a playful, happy childhood. This is not an accident; this is as a result of playwork.

The practice of playwork aims in its simplest form to create the conditions for play to occur, to be maintained and to develop (Sturrock & Else, 1998; Hughes, 2012; Brown, 2014). The playwork practiced there for years had two objectives: to provide a service to the children of the estate that helped to meet their play needs; this had been delivered as a simple mobile project that met with children around the estate at pre-arranged destinations and times where they would be supported to be able to play out in their community, and to make playing publicly acceptable, because it generated opportunities for children to be seen playing in the public realm. As a part of that second objective adult passers-by and parents would be met, greeted and chatted to about play and children's rights, childhood memories, the value of playing, of friendship and of community.

These two simple objectives have over time, achieved two significant outcomes and one beautiful, magical output. The first outcome is that children and children's play are valued and promoted in the community. The second is that children feel their play is valued and freely play around the community. They exercise their citizenship through their playful disposition to the world in the same way that the adults exercise their citizenship through their unique dispositions. They make the same claim on the public realm as do adults and are recognised as having the right to do so.

As a result a demand arose from children and many adult community members to create a space that children could call their own, a space in which the children would be able to extend their play to levels which a public environment would be unable to foster. A space where children could develop their play over long periods of time, knowing they could return to where they had left off in a previous session perhaps. A place that was not shared or multi-use, but a place created to specifically meet the unique needs of play and playing. That place became known as "The Land."

The Land is an adventure playground, a site surrounded by a fenced boundary and staffed by playworkers. It is operated on the premise that children will need considerable time and space in their lives free from the developed and accepted norms of adult society so that they can experiment, challenge themselves and others, fail, struggle, subvert, destroy, create and re-create, vary and adapt, find some respite, some joy and some friendship—a place where as far as is practicable children are left to control the content and intent of their own play (Hughes, 2001a), in their own lives.

The area is surrounded by an 8ft high wooden fence—which is constructed in such a way as to ensure the children's privacy—and protects just under an acre of what was once neglected wasteland. Unless you walk through one of the two gates you would never know what lay behind the fence. This is important and purposeful. The fence is a significant component of The Land. It has effectively claimed this space for children and their play. There is a sign on the gate that reads "The Land. A space full of possibilities."

Narrative

Next to the fire pit, there is a small abandoned den made from wooden pallets. The boys are filling it with paper and cardboard, fuelling a fire which has just been started. The flames get higher and more of the pallets catch fire. The heat is now too much for them to continue with the paper so they discard it and go running for more pallets. Three girls sit on a concrete tunnel adjacent to the

> fire, hands over their faces as the heat proves to be too much. They don't move though!
>
> On top of the 8ft storage container also used as an office, there are children, some standing, some sitting, some dancing and shouting, some pretending to push others off, simultaneously jostling for position to take their turn to leap off onto the mattresses and crash mats below. To the right on the slope leading from the lower reaches of "The Land" children clamber up before taking off on a homemade rope swing. For an instant they are airborne, just their hands holding them. Moments before they reach the watercourse that meanders through "The Land" they expertly adjust themselves so they are sitting on the plastic disc that serves as a seat. Some children sit, those more adept or who just prefer it, stand on the swing as it traverses the stream to the other end of the playground. Even they comment on the heat of the fire.
>
> One of the playworkers has just filled an extra bucket of water and is standing back, close enough to rescue but far enough away not to ruin things. Across the way another playworker rips a piece of carpet off a nearby pallet, just in case the children choose this one to throw on their fire—affecting a "perceived indifferent" disposition (Hughes 2002), when in actuality they are engaged in an intricate and complex dynamic assessment of the play behaviours of the children, the ambiance of the space and their desired influence on it. There's an atmosphere, it's exciting, children are smiling, children are immersed (Hughes 2001a) and there's an implicit sense of permission (Hughes 2001b) and ownership.

The Land was funded through a WREN (Waste Recycling Environmental Limited) grant, which awarded the local community £125k to redevelop a fixed play area and "develop" an adventure playground. The fixed playground took less than 6 months to develop, including consultation with the children and the community. Fixed playgrounds are a socially acceptable play facility. They indicate that children are valued and welcomed, and also inform children where they should play and in some cases how they should play. Despite the narrow and somewhat directive nature of the fixed equipment playground, the process was positive and the community were thrilled to have new equipment, and it still is the most popular fixed equipment playground for miles.

The development of the adventure playground wasn't quite as problem free. Despite overwhelming support there were still trials and tribulations, mostly concerning space. At one point it was feared the funding would need to be returned and the project would never come to fruition because claims and counter claims on the land in question were so vociferous. In truth, the space, which is now known fondly as "The Land," was in fact a land grab, the last attempt at claiming some space for the children it now serves. On one of the final and probably most crucial days in the acquisition, The Land had to undergo an "environmental audit." Officials with clip boards swarmed over the site, each of which had the power to stop the development. When it was identified that bats might "home" in one of the trees, it was as if the whole world was against the development, but a snap decision to re-route the perimeter fence, leaving out "said tree" was all that was required to get the "green light." The potential bat tree now sits just outside the perimeter of the fence.

Playwork—the practical approach we intended to use on The Land—has always been a Jack-of-all-trades, master of none, kind of profession. Perhaps this is as a result of historical low levels of funding, but equally likely as a result of its underpinning realisation that frequently real world problems will need to be resolved to facilitate play. That may mean having to clean up dog excrement, glass or litter before being able to deliver a play session out in a community space. Playwork also tells the children that you will do what it takes to help, that you won't give the responsibility of solving difficulties to others who can't be accessed or challenged. It is a vital part of a can-do approach which, if said collectively meant that we could actualise our needs and wants. On this occasion that meant drawing-up plans for a playground. Our attempt was terrible, so help was sought from the community. We believed that inclusion, participation and ownership by the local community were essential ingredients for the maintenance and longevity of any play project particularly this one.

Finally we were able to submit the planning application which, after an anxious evening meeting achieved full approval. A lease on the land was granted and from this point on, the project team would be architect, planner, builder, plumber, electrician and every other profession.

For several months throughout the winter of 2011/12 play opportunities continued to be provided on the prospective site of The Land and across the community as a part of the street play project, together with project managing and creating what would eventually become "The Land." In the hope that children would gain a sense of attachment to the space, different loose parts (Nicholson 1971) were taken to the wasteland every day. We knew that the strategy was working when children would refer to the space, and ask for a play scheme to run from there and would even play there independently. It was during this period that children started to refer fondly to the space as "The Land."

Due to the funding parameters of the project, the staff team were commissioned to erect the eight-foot tall perimeter fence. Although children didn't dig the first hole or put in the first fence post, they had already taken ownership and were in a constant process of creating and reshaping their play space. The building work never impacted on their play, they were never prohibited, nor were there any protective fencing or keep out signs. The children were present every step of the way.

Today The Land is grassy in places, muddy in others, with a high mound of earth that has random holes in it and dug out tunnels underneath, situated in the centre of the area. At the time of writing children are mining, using pick axes to tear away the earth, and shovels to remove it. There are slopes, child made paths and also a watercourse that runs through the space. Trees adorn the area, natural affordances (Gibson 1977) which change with the seasons. Amidst all of this naturalness there is "junk"—items such as tyres, wooden pallets, exercise bikes, a piano, a "dead" boat and the charred remains of fires. It may look terrible to many adults and it can be difficult to see beyond the perceived chaos, the untidiness and sense of disorder. It might be a bold move; a risky practice that runs contrary to that employed by many conventional adventure playgrounds but it has a striking resemblance to the "junk" playgrounds of the 1950s, 1960s, and 1970s.

The Land is a space that is conducive to playing. It is subject to constant change, evolving in response and at the request of children's subjective needs and desires. It is a space of diversity, a space of construction and destruction, a place where adults believe in children and their capabilities. It offers stimulation and excitement but in contrast it also offers tranquillity, serenity and mundanity.

The Land is furnished with "junk" for a reason; children are naturally curious and attracted to the novel (Hughes 2002, Morris 1964, Sutton-Smith 1997), and novelty seems to generate new ideas and opportunities. The Land offers children the opportunity to experience newness with this ever-changing environment.

Except for The Land itself and "Claire's office"—Claire is the project manager—there is no element of permanency—no fixed structures, no fixed equipment—or any aspect of longevity. Everything within the fenced boundary is temporary and of little if any monetary value. This is intentional. The lack of monetary value reduces adult anxieties about protecting the materials or equipment, and children are therefore freer to explore and to try new things as a consequence. Adventure playgrounds visited prior to setting up The Land seemed to be dominated by fixed structures and lacking in novelty, flexibility and adaptability as a result, as well as providing a rather biased experience.

Experiences with play schemes, street play and other short term and temporary provision demonstrated the value of keeping the loose parts element, and recognising that novelty, change, flexibility and adaptability were key to the longevity of a quality play offer. A contrasting argument might suggest children need consistency; that they need to feel safe and secure. This is true for the children at The Land too, but change is essential, and on The Land it is only undertaken sensitively and as a result of reflection; it's thought out and mindful of the playing child. The stability and familiarity children may also crave is ensured through consistent and reliable playwork practices like, opening on time, and a stable staff team, as well as from the familiarity of the ramshackle shipping container everyone, refers to as Claire's office.

LOCATION, LOCATION, LOCATION

The Land is disadvantaged in much the same way as many play spaces are in that it is situated on a space left over after planning or more accurately where building houses would be difficult. This means that the playground is situated in close proximity to housing—the nearest, a row of terraced houses is only about 10 meters away. The majority of the residents accept and support The Land, but a few did have to be won over.

During the public consultation part of the planning process, daily phone calls were made to the planning officer to ask if there had been any objections. The 28 days consultation period seemed like a lifetime, and only on the 26th day was an objection registered. A resident had decided that they didn't want the playground in their back yard. Given that reducing time scales meant losing the funding, this was crushing, and it was feared that one adult voice of disapproval might outnumber the voices of all the children, and the playground be stopped as a result. But playworkers advocate for children; that is their job, their responsibility to the children they serve; so advocacy is what had to be done.

Meeting with the resident wasn't easy, being shouted at and having to listen to unfounded fears was difficult too, but it had to happen if there was to be a chance that the objection would be lifted. The many benefits of the playground's existence were identified, the most important being that the children would have somewhere to play. Conditions and compromises were made, and the objection was lifted.

The final addition to the playground's infrastructure came with the arrival of two large shipping containers, one for storage and one to be converted into an office space. As a way of ensuring friendly co-existence with our neighbours, they were consulted on where they would like them to be placed, so that they wouldn't feel overlooked There have been a few issues since, but none that have jeopardised the children's opportunities. To promote good relations, the project works with residents, often emptying gardens of old furniture and fence panels to our mutual benefit. On one occasion a resident talked about his own den building days, demonstrating a developing link between his childhood and that of the children at the project.

To gain the lease for the land, all of the planning conditions were accepted. One of them forbade the playground to be open after "dusk," but "dusk" is subjective. Fires were lighting up The Land, the nights were getting lighter and the playground would rarely close before 8pm. However this novel situation was only temporary. Darker afternoons would eventually be a reality, and in the depths of winter, closing at dusk would mean being open for approximately half an hour a day. One of the original planning conditions also forbad any external playground lighting because of the impact it might have on neighbouring houses. The playwork "team" began work to have that original condition amended, by talking with parents and adult community members', and to drum up support for lighting, by communicating and being transparent about what any changes would mean in reality to influence any objections. The process was long and protracted, running from January and finally receiving approval for the erection of temporary winter lighting in August. Facing these challenges together as a community—staff, adults, parents and children—alike has been a rewarding experience for all concerned.

RULES

One aspect of playwork practice is the creation of opportunities that compensate children for the lack of time and space they have these days to play without always being under the watchful eye of adults (Hart, 2002). The implication being that whenever possible, children are left in control over the what, where, how and why they play. This means that rules on "The Land" are organic and co-created, i.e. there isn't a list of rules at the gate. There were no pre-determined views or ideas about children's behaviour when the project was started, and if either the team or the individuals in it had their own personal ideas they each tried to act without preconceptions in the play space—learning with the children, what was acceptable or not, and why (Hughes 1997; 1999).

Fires play a large part in the children's play on the playground, and the only rule governing fire is do not have fires without a bucket of water.

Narrative

I remember clearly one morning before the kids got there, the night before they had smashed up a lot of chairs that were donated from an old people's home. We didn't have long before The Land opened so we figured if we set fire to the chairs they'd disappear. We placed them all together, like a mini bonfire and lit a match. What happened next was pretty scary. The sky filled with thick black smoke, the fire was too big and hot to go near. There was plastic coating on the chairs that had escaped our notice, our eyes were stinging the sky was getting darker and there was nothing we could do except wait and also make a mental note about ruthlessly checking for plastic coating on things you're going to burn.

So a rule was born, don't burn plastic. Of course children challenge this, and at times playworker intervention is necessary, but always considered, play centric intervention.

On "The Land," we see it as of fundamental importance to know the context and background of the children's lives. We achieved this through our interactions with them, through careful scrutiny of what they do and how they do it, and of what they say and how they say it, and also through opportune meetings with their parents and other associated adults and professionals. This ensures that any interventions made will be considered and individualised. A playworker should offer the children they serve unconditional acceptance, always being able to forgive and forget. It is not the playworker's job to teach children, rather, it is to support them, to be there to pick up the pieces and to be a stable, reliable trustworthy adult influence in their lives. Needless to say, if a child was at risk of harm, a playworker would always intervene, highlighting that amidst the seemingly chaotic ambiance of "The Land" lies a sense of order created by the children and the playworkers together.

Narrative

> Fraser is a new kid, he doesn't come often but the first thing he asks for is a lighter. He hasn't quite mastered how to make a fire, but loves to watch paper and cardboard boxes burn, he seems to really enjoy that moment when a big box goes up in flames! On this night there was already a fire when he arrived. He wasn't put off, he made it his own. He came to me with a long piece of foam and asked if he could put it on the fire. He couldn't but I didn't want to just dismiss his curiosity by saying no. I thought for a moment, he's new, he's not seen foam or plastic burn and the effects it has. Maybe he needs to. So after I'd tried explaining why we can't burn foam, I encouraged him to place a piece on the fire and we watched as the smoke turned black. He carried on burning wood and cardboard.

Children know you're there for them if needed, so there is no need for a continual interaction with them. On this occasion, it was nearing the end of the day and the fire, which had been pretty big was being put out, but this was taking some time. Ben who was an infrequent visitor to The Land and someone the project team hadn't got to know particularly well, was playing a short distance away on the periphery of both the team's sight and vision.

Narrative

> Ben was close by, muttering. The words "you fucking prick" were pretty prominent as I attuned my senses in an attempt to figure out what was going on. This continued, offensive words were used; they seemed to get louder as he became

more confident that the adults weren't challenging him. The first choice of intervention had been to ignore the language and the challenge. It is quite normal for new kids, or kids that have learned to distrust adults, to regularly challenge you and what they think the rules are, to see if you are trustworthy, to see if the reality matches the rhetoric.

Ben was bent down collecting nails. As he stood he started to throw the nails at us shouting "nail the bastards." Of course an intervention was made, it was necessary and appropriate. It wasn't a complex intervention just a very assertive shout, "Oy, don't do that," I didn't threaten him with exclusion or banning but the intervention was enough to make him leave anyway. When all the children had left, we spoke about Ben, about things that had happened throughout the day, in an attempt to figure out what was going on for him. Nothing stood out, nothing out the ordinary had happened, so we began to explore the context and background of his life. This enabled us to develop a greater understanding and also a pre-determined strategy for supporting him.

Although Ben had no experience of playworkers, he had had some difficult and unsuccessful relationships with other adults. He needed time to adapt, to trust the team and to understand that the team had no expectations or agendas. Ben was offered the permission and freedom to fail, he wasn't judged nor would grudges be held and he certainly wouldn't be banned. Since then our relationship with Ben hasn't been easy. There have been times when Ben has left the playground angry, times when he has smashed things up on the way out, times when direct interventions have had to be made. Over many months, and as a result of these interventions a playworker/child relationship based on a starting point of mutual respect is evolving with Ben.

ZIP LINES

Many of today's playgrounds offer some sort of large swing or zip line. We had often discussed having a zip line prior to The Land opening and wondered if the words adventure playgrounds might build up an expectation of large fixed equipment? However, it was decided to stick to our philosophy of simple responsiveness, flexibility, change and adaptability, and resist the temptation; fixed equipment had never been included as a part of the initial design and build of "The Land."

In time however, the children did ask for a zip line, and some of the older boys made one. It went from the top of the playground to the bottom, and no accidents occurred. The smaller children didn't want to try this "grown-up" version, so a smaller scale one was made in the corner of the playground. It was still exciting and covered quite a distance including over the stream. The line was made from wire, and the handle (for getting out of bed) was donated by the local hospital. Every so often it would get stuck and you'd hear a child shouting for help as they hung precariously over the stream (a terrifying drop of 80 cm).

When the children stopped using them they were removed. They didn't cost anything, they were an experiment, they didn't have rules, and they didn't need protecting and they had no permanency. This meant that those parts of "The Land" they had temporarily occupied were able to be utilised to meet other play needs. This kind of "environmental modification" is key to ensuring the neophilic requirements of the children (Hughes, 1996, 2002). Modification means change and enhancement. When playworkers assess that the children's interest is waning, when they've exhausted the potential of the environment as it is, things need to change. Modification only happens very gently to ensure the children aren't overwhelmed or feel that change is out of their control. The playground should be responsive, and only evolve and develop as the children's interests and agendas change.

Sometimes adult interventions have the effect of short-cutting what the child is doing, assuming that what the child is attempting to do is obvious. For example, butting-in to show a child how to use a hammer or a paint brush. This is how you hammer and this is how you use a paint brush.

The problem is that this kind of intervention cuts-short the child's imaginative exploration of the hammer or the paint brush, and makes it difficult for them to find out things and develop themselves. By failing to recognise the different mechanisms of the play process, adults risk walking rough shod over what these mechanisms are for, and how they serve the evolutionary process (Bruner 1972), demonstrating how little they value children and their ideas and intentions.

However, sometimes, the possibility for invasive intervention needs to be prepared for. One time Mike, one of the more dominant kids on the playground was on top of the shipping container, positioned ready to back flip off it, on to a pile of mattresses. Mike had gathered quite a crowd of spectators; the space around the shipping container had taken on the feel of an arena with a mix of excitement and fear:

Narrative

> Mike is 14, dominant, but still needy for status from his peers, sometimes without regard for his own safety. This was at the forefront of my mind. He was about to do a move on the very edge of what I knew to be his capabilities. I position myself close enough to take action if necessary but keep a low profile; Mike needs to be in charge of his own choices. He screamed obscenities at the kids who were watching, encouraging him. "Shut the fuck up everyone or I'll twat ya," being cautious to exclude his best mate and the only other kid

> on the playground that was definitely tougher than him, from that statement! I can't be certain this was intended to stimulate a response, but Mike's best mate shouted from the audience "Mike it's not worth it mate, what if you break your neck we'll not be able to work in the Café again." Moments later Mike turned 180 degrees faced forwards and jumped down from the container in a normal fashion. The Café was a make shift affair which had sprung up out of nowhere, but was incredibly popular for a time. In this case it seemed like it provided the face saving device Mike had needed to extricate himself from a sticky situation.

No invasive action needed to be taken on this occasion, and neither does it in most cases. In this instance Mike, his friends and spectators were all a part of a shared experience with many ramifications. Although their processing and resolution is complex, children need to engage in them, and our non-invasive intervention enabled that.

One of the most common adult misconceptions of children is that if they are enabled to do something in one setting /environment they will replicate it in others. The misconception is borne out of a failure to recognise children as competent discerning decision makers. In reality the opposite is more commonly true. Children are attracted to the new and novel, but every time they see it or do it, it becomes less new and novel. Letting them do a thing once or twice in a considered context has a much more positive and beneficial effect on their ability to manage, than out and out prohibition. Children will respect you for having blurred edges, undefined boundaries, that mean you are often different from the other adults they come across. Strict rule setting is much more representative of adult life, and children are subject to it and they recognise it as such. All too often, adults say one thing and then do another. We believe that children value and recognise the honesty of the approach at "The Land." Broadly speaking it is equitable, and that's what it aims to be.

For example, for some children, the easiest way to get them not to throw foam or other combustibles in the fire, is to let them throw them in a controlled way. This takes the lure of the "forbidden fruit" phenomenon out of the equation. When the kids are refusing to leave the playground at closing the best way to get them off is to give them ten more minutes, the best way to get them out of the van is to give them 5 more minutes in the van. Often this is because they are enjoying themselves so much, but equally, it's because they are testing your resolve. You may have created a power hierarchy by the way your requests have been made, and that is contrary to what they understand "the Land" is about. You now have to be patient, and start again from the child.

Ascertaining the risks of most of the situations the team are presented with is relatively easy, because one way or another, the team has probably experienced them in part or in whole, in one context or another. Most "dangerous" things can be made safe for experimental reasons, and that's what the team endeavours to do. Finding opportunities for children to try things out in a controlled environment so they don't go experimenting in less safe environments, putting themselves and others at risk, is a part of playwork. Playwork is responsive. It's the response to a moment that may never have happened before and may never happen again for any particular individual child or group. That sort of approach cannot exist on rule boards. Children are much more on your side when they know you're part of this moment too, that you're undecided if things are okay or not, and they know that your view can even be swayed by them. They sense it when you relinquish power to them, they respect you more for it and in a roundabout way they will listen to you more when you need to reclaim and exert that same power over them, you're being honest with them, working in parallel with them. You have to good effect shed off the adult power they give you, or perceive you to hold and they readily recognise it. It's a very powerful phenomenon.

So any approach to intervention must have a fluid outline, not based on a set of rules. It's a whole host of momentary considerations based on principles of practice rather than arbitrary homogenous regulations. The subject of dens has perhaps been the most challenging and talked about topic for intervention since opening. The den culture is a vibrant and emotional one, balancing precariously between the twin poles of creation and destruction. As a playworker, you know this culture can't exist in perfect harmony, and you know the importance of the disharmony. This example captures the disharmony, its importance, and the playworker intervention.

Stuart and Marc, were a double act from the top of the estate, thick as thieves, both unpredictable, destructive, and aggressive, normally characterised as den destroyers rather than builders, so it was refreshing to see them have a go at den building. As a result of their usual behaviour, our playwork approach was one of the distanced observer (Hughes 2002)—sometimes maintaining a watchful eye, and at other's creating opportunities and facilitating their experience, but not as yet the familial "all in this together" relationship the project strives for.

Narrative

The boys had already chosen a location for the den when they asked me to help. "Top of the bank, in the middle of the path, although with Stuart and Marc involved, I doubted if this den would last! But I put that to the back of my head and worked as requested in the pursuance of the fulfilment of their wishes."

With these two arguing, then falling out, it was an emotional roller coaster. One of them would try to kick the new den down, and then the other would

> follow suit, then they'd make up and carry on. I remained silent and neutral throughout. Their relationship is intricate, and long standing, and they understand it far better than I ever will. One way or another their den was established, as were the grounds of their relationship.

The following day was a whirlwind, loads of children, but interestingly, no Stuart and Marc. During the course of the day, their den was knocked down, and then changed into a completely new den by a new girl called Wendy and a few of her siblings. Wendy was from a family new to the estate. She had seemed shy around the playworkers but also seemed to have garnered a certain respect from many of the other regular kids. In a perfect world somebody would have tried to preserve the boys' den and encouraged Wendy to build somewhere else. The Land doesn't represent a perfect world though.

Twenty minutes or so into the next session, Stuart appeared at the end of the path. There was all of 15 seconds before he would discover the new situation. These are the kinds of the thoughts that flashed through my mind in that instant,

- Stuart's going to be gutted! Surely he'll kick it down?
- I'll feel quite sorry for him
- His den was in a vulnerable position though!
- And he has knocked down loads of other kid's dens, maybe good for him to feel it?
- Maybe he'll make this his new den?
- No, he'll definitely smash it up, and the therapy of that may be important to him, to assert his dominance, vent his anger . . . maybe?
- Will he be angry with me for "letting" it happen? Will he lose faith in the staff? The Land?
- He's an emotional guy! But he's a thinker; his conscience is almost visible at times.
- Will Wendy be gutted? Will she even come again? She didn't seem that into it but I don't know her that well.
- Will her siblings kick off; Stuart doesn't know they're her siblings . . . .
- I'm kidding myself if I think anything I'd say would change Stuart's actions anyway, He's a force of nature at times and I'm certainly not his favourite member of staff. He'd flip out if I tried to explain any of it to him.
- I'm not going to say anything
- What about Marc, Marc's not here so whatever happens now is going to happen all over again when he gets here
- I need a hammer; I may need to do some de-nailing. (Making safe the timbers discarded in the potential ensuing destruction)

As it turned out, Stuart looked, froze, and then kicked the den down (getting his revenge). Wendy's siblings said (relatively calmly) "that was our sisters'." Stuart said "Oh sorry, I didn't know," and they all just carried on with their day. Later Wendy came up the path to a chorus of, "Stuart's smashed your den down!" to which she replied "I don't care, it was just something to do."

Taking the decision not to pacify Stuart, to let his reaction unfold naturally was a risk. But if playworkers hope to create a space in which children can fully express themselves, then that space is inevitably going to be fuelled with strong emotions, ranging from joy and despair. Playwork practices need to accommodate these emotions. There are times when one may have to step in, but one should not actively strive for a harmonious, predictable, adult pleasing environment, that will stifle the children's play behaviours and their development, because of that. To experience discord, even negativity is useful. A life of harmony alone is a mirage, and an idealised one prepares you for nothing.

Bob was a tiny little chap with a big reputation. Playing with him was mostly about aggression and hurting people. He had a tough older brother, as well as his hard-case Dad, but with Bob it always seemed like he merited his status in his own right. Sometimes we would distract Bob by engaging him in whacking tennis balls with a racket, he liked that. He'd whack them, ball after ball, focusing intently on the activity, while the playworker throwing the ball, fell into an almost trance-like state, having to go as fast as possible, picking up balls quicker and quicker to keep Bob engaged, whilst the other kids played without feeling any immediate threat.

Intervening in Bob's play was the most effective way of saving him from himself and certainly the only way to save the other kids from him. Becoming Bob's play mate is a "complex intervention" (Else & Sturrock, 1998, Else, Sturrock& Russell, 2004), of trying to model functional play skills and behaviours through our play with him. Without this level of intervention Bob would hurt or upset someone as a result of the dysfunctional nature of his play. Bob loved fighting, martial arts, and films about fighting, but got rough and tumble very wrong. Becoming his rough and tumble partner was therefore an essential role for the playworkers. For although physically powerful, his mood, his movement and demeanour were very playful, even if being on the receiving end didn't feel like it, this was play to him. Although it may not have looked like play to the untrained eye, he was engaged, the playground felt safe, and during these frequent play episodes between Bob and the team, more functional play behaviours were being modelled, via facial expressions and exaggerated body movements when he went in too hard, but lighter touches were reciprocated.

Bob had the potential to be one of the most difficult and aggressive children on the playground when he was in certain moods or company. He often mixed with young people older than him, "notorious," young people with reputations. Which of those he was with at any given moment often affected which Bob arrived at the playground.

At one extreme he was the child who stopped you at the gate of his house eager for you to see his most recently born kitten, while at the other he could terrorise the playground and all the children in it within minutes. One thing was for sure though and evidenced by the fact he wanted to show us something he loved, like the kittens, the playground, and the relationship the playworkers had with him was important to him. He thrived off it, and valued it, even though some of his regular gang cared much less for us or what we offered. The Land was often an emotional roller coaster in the early days. Bob and his friends would go through phases of making our lives very difficult, intimidating other children, setting fire to everything, fighting, stealing from the office and so on. None of these boys were lost causes, they all had moments of fun and engagement, and times where we all enjoyed each other's company and the sense of community The Land produced, they were just "the challenging boys." Saturday was the day they were most likely to congregate and that became the day we all dreaded as a result:

Narrative

We'd have maybe 2 or 3 plucky younger kids who'd come on Saturday, but would soon be frightened off by the gang. Their most common "activities" were attempting to burn car tyres and smoking in dens. This Saturday was no different. The boys were in their latest den, trying their best to have crafty ciggies, while 2 younger children played by the office. Sitting with them, the only way to see if they were smoking or not, talking to them, and pointing out to one of them, John (arguably the most difficult child on the estate), why there were no other kids coming to the playground. Bob was with John, and this often made for the most difficult version of Bob.

Ten minutes later I saw Bob and John dash behind the office, where the two younger children were playing. First they tried soaking them with water, but were put off when I started filling a bucket of my own. They darted off, I walked away, and then they darted back. This time when I rounded the corner, both had cigarette lighters, and were flicking them in one of the terrified children's face. I got myself between them and what followed—I cannot remember exactly—was the most assertive and eloquent verbal torrent of disgust and threat that has ever left my mouth. I know I clearly told the boys how disgusted I was with their behaviour, and how incomprehensible I found it for such behaviour to be meted out on other human beings for no good reason at all and that although many things might be ok at the playground, spiteful acts of violence and persecution

> were not. I do know that I ended by saying that if it continued I would be left with no option but to call the police and that I would do that every single time I saw their faces again from that day on. I never actually intended to follow through with that last threat, I never intended to ban these young people, they weren't irredeemable, and they weren't beyond benefitting from the playground. But this was the only way I could show them how bad things were. Although on the brink, these relationships were worth this intervention as opposed to phone calls to higher authorities. The boys left immediately although they weren't asked. They'd never seen this side of a member of staff before, it's an extremely rare occurrence, which may be why it worked so well. When I say it worked so well, I don't mean because they left, I mean because they did come back. It was a last resort unloading onto Bob like this, we'd shared so many moments, made fires together, play fought, just generally shared space over a long period of time. John valued playwork less, but still found benefit in it, occasionally, with his friends, at the playground.

Banning those two would not have benefitted them or the project. Instead it would have undermined all that the project aimed to do in flattening the hierarchy and shaking off the "adult power." As playworkers we expect to give relentless forgiveness and second chances. Playworkers are not push-overs, but they do their best to forgive and forget and to move on, giving a "Hi," a smile, or a biscuit to break the ice if kids come back the next day. Slowly but surely, this approach blows their minds. Perhaps it's the respect, the patience and forgiveness, perhaps it's the love they've never had before, or perhaps the project simply provides a place where even the darkest corners of their personalities are somewhat understood, or if not understood, at least accommodated.

Often when things are kicking off, when children are fighting, or one child has hurt another, or ruined what they're doing, adults can easily over-react to the emotive nature of the incident, or, of the story told. Playworkers try to avoid that over-reaction, the children need to be at the playground, not banned or excluded, or stood by a gate. Rather they need to be made aware of the look on the other children's faces, how the other children feel as a result of their thoughtless actions. Children's challenges, fallouts and incidents are most commonly resolved or over quickly. Things change and it is possible to ride out these powerful storms and once they're over, the air is clearer. Sending a child to the gate is simply bottling up the storm for later. Not only that, but by taking that course of action you put yourself at the top of a hierarchy and in so doing make yourself a target for the kid's aggression. Although Invasive Intervention is a must, holding the power to enforce punitive measures is a step we have chosen to avoid. Removing the means by which one might hurt another, removing children from each other, arguing till you're blue in the face, each tactic is part of the job, but always on as equal terms as possible.

Narrative

> 2 days later Bob was spotted walking past The Land with his brother as we were closing. "Alright Bob" understated but friendly, "Alright" Bob replied similarly. Although not the warmest exchange, it let him know the door was still open, and grudges were not being held.

Slowly, Bob started coming back, eventually very regularly. Since that day there has never been the same level of problems with those boys and the playground thrives with lots of children, young and old. Perhaps it was the fact we showed them that we were human, that we had feelings too and they weren't the only important people in the universe, and that we weren't pushovers and would stand up for right and wrong in extremis. Somehow this period and this instance affected our whole context for each other and many others that witnessed or heard on the grape vine about the incident. Bob, remains at the top of the hierarchy, he's learnt to do back-flips here, he cooks for other children, he cares for the playground pets, he brings presents for the staff regularly, he refers to me as his "second dad," and the little girl he flicked his lighter at? He calls her by her nickname, "chicken," and says hi to her whenever she arrives.

MODIFICATIONS

The first couple of months of The Land were just like a play scheme that was never packed away. It was great not to have to pack away, and the kids loved returning to their stuff. "The Land" operates on the premise that loose parts (Nicholson, 1971) and a stimulating environment support children's play. Those loose parts are often re-used and re-appropriated by children from one play episode to another. They also become broken beyond repair or usefulness, dangerous, and useless. At that point they become distracting clutter that detracts from the potential affordances (Gibson 1977) the playground can offer. Similarly, other aspects of the environment become stale, outlive their novelty, become worn and in need of care. Adventure playgrounds, junk playgrounds as they used to be called, must be continually monitored, to ensure they continue to offer the flexible, adaptable and variable experiences (Hughes, 2001b) and are inviting to children. Continuous modification (Hughes, 2001b) is necessary, a) to preserve some play opportunities for children, b) to create that element of surprise that sparks or initiates play in the first place, and c) to make safe the kind of hazards children may not consider before leaping in to commence playing. But modification, whether by the children or the workers, should never be about stagnation.

With dens for example, some children build, some watch, some inhabit, some never set foot in the door, some steal, some share, some store trinkets, some make rolled up cigarettes, some destroy dens, some burn them down, some make dens for themselves, some make dens for everyone, and most children do all of the above at some point in time. There are children who are termites, there are cuckoos, there are beavers, and magpies and there are birds of paradise. Most noticeable however is how fleeting dens are, how momentary, and how vital it is that children are not only supported to build, to discover, and destroy, but also to realise that play is not about permanence, but about the moment. Failing to grasp this could involve the child in an unproductive and repetitive cycle rather than in a playful forward trajectory (Hughes 2016).

For over three years the playground space has been modified in countless ways; dens, bridges and shanty towns have been built, lily pads and garlic planted, holes dug, red carpets laid out, gems planted in the brook, treasure buried, bonfires prepared and even a cafe built. The playground has to satisfy the child's continual need for exploration, it needs to be changeable, and ever changing. A playground should never get built, but always be under construction.

Certain playground spaces provide for different play opportunities, and even different feelings. Children associate with different groups, moving on and returning to people and places as and when it or they meet their interest. The playground should not be the only place children play. It has not evolved to compensate them for play opportunities they can find elsewhere. Rather, it exists to compensate them for opportunities they may have difficulty accessing and experiences they seek to extend and develop their play without fear of interruption or cessation. For these reasons the playground must be a constantly changing place not a stagnant representation of children's play outputs.

We buried a treasure chest once, deep underground, we intended that it should be found but had no idea when that would be or who by, that was left to fate:

Narrative

When he found the buried treasure chest, he had been busy digging in the soil to find worms for a fishing adventure planned for the next day. He dug up the chest, looked a little confused, then slightly enchanted opened it to reveal jewellery. He went through each item, tossing them away, each with their own evaluation, "gay, girl stuff, gay, girl stuff" before finding a pair of earrings at the bottom he thought his mum might like, and shoving them in his pocket, before going back to digging worms. A much younger child, waiting patiently in the wings, then moved in picking up the box. Her face, her whole body language full of awe and enchantment having watched the events unfold. She put all the jewellery in the box, and scurried off to one of the dens.

Discovery brings so much magic and enchantment to a play space and it is that discovery that modifications can offer. Quirkiness, trinkets and wild ideas are embraced at The Land every day. It's a continuous process of generated ideas, some of which are enacted, whilst some drifting off on the wind. This ebb and flow of continuous change is represented in the following passage:

Narrative

One day the children found a slow worm and brought it to the playground. They insisted they were keeping it at "The Land" and that an enclosure was needed. A make-shift snake cage was created the following day. The children and playworkers co—created the "snake's" habitat, making changes to the design, and making it bigger, then the slow worm was moved in. He was "the playground" for some of the children for a few days. They Googled slow worms at home, they drew him in school, they put him in their pockets, and they even jumped off the container with him.

However, after about a week he disappeared, it remains a mystery where to. The day after, sitting on some new steel chairs recently donated to the playground, while one of the boys was making toasties for everyone, the snake was mentioned, but they weren't too devastated at his disappearance. The boy making the toasties remarked how the new furniture looked café-esque and suggested we make a cafe. The group all smiled and agreed, but no instant action was initiated. Sometimes things develop, sometimes they don't.

A chance donation of kitchen units resulted from a visit to a local supermarket of all things. The units arrived the next day, and a café was built, five feet from where the snake enclosure had been just two days before. When the café was completed we painted "Bob's Café" on the front.

For the next 3 days, the children completely ran their own cafe, cooking toasties, making tea, cleaning the surfaces, washing their hands, taking phone orders, writing menus, all completely independent of playworkers. The snake was all but forgotten and only 4 days after its opening even interest in the cafe was beginning to wane. Play moves on, and playgrounds have to move too.

Everyone agrees that playgrounds should change, this doesn't mean knocking down all the structures every ten years and building big new ones though. The Land does change continually, but on a physically smaller scale, over weeks, days and hours because that reflects the pace at which the children change. In the last 15 days we have been bonfire makers, snake enclosure builders, cafe builders, parkour/shanty town designers and much more. And in the next fifteen?

Over the years the project's playworkers have got better and better, becoming increasingly perceptive of the children, and their play. They have become more attuned to understanding what needs changing and when, and what needs to remain. The children's challenging behaviour towards staff has dwindled, perhaps as a result of our improved performance. It's hard to get angry when you keep seeing things that make you happy.

REFERENCES

Brown, F. (ed) (2003) *Playwork: Theory and practice.* Buckingham, Open University Press.

Bruner, J. S. (1972) The nature and uses of immaturity. *American Psychologist,* 27 (8).

Gibson, J. (1977) The theory of affordances. In: R. Shaw and J. Bransford (eds) *Perceiving, acting, and knowing: Toward an ecological psychology.* Abingdon: Routledge.

Hart, R. (2002) *Children's participation.* New York, NY: UNICEF.

Hughes, B. (1996) *A playworkers taxonomy of play types.* Ely: PlayEducation.

———. (1997) Playwork in extremis. In: *Proceedings of the World of Play, The Changing Nature of Children's Play and Playwork*, San Antonio, TX: University of the Incarnate Word.

———. (2001a) *Evolutionary playwork and reflective analytic practice*. London: Routledge.

———. (2001b) *The first claim: A framework for playwork quality assessment*. Cardiff: Play Wales.

———. (2002) *The first claim—desirable processes: A framework for advanced quality assessment*. Cardiff: Play Wales.

———. (2012) *Evolutionary playwork.* London: Routledge.

———. (2016) Personal Communication.

Morris, D. (1964) The response of animals to a restricted environment. *Symposium of the Zoological Society of London*, 13, 99.

Nicholson, S. (1971) How not to cheat children. the theory of loose parts. In: *Landscape Architecture Quarterly.* Vol.62, No.1, October 1971, pp 30–34.

Sturrock, G. and Else, P. (1998) The playground as therapeutic space: playwork as healing. In: *Proceedings of the IPA/USA Triennial National Conference, Play in a Changing Society: Research, Design, Application*. June 1998, Colorado. USA.

Sturrock, G., Russell, W. and Else, P. (2004) *Towards ludogogy parts I, II and III: The art of being and becoming through* play (The Birmingham Paper), Sheffield: Ludemos Associates.

Sutton-Smith, B. (1997) *The ambiguity of play.* Cambridge, MA: Harvard University Press.

Chapter Ten

The Playground as Palimpsest

Joel Seath

These particular ribbons of words are written, first and now, in a notebook on a frosty late morning in January, though *you* may be reading them one hot afternoon in July. I'm sitting on a wet wooden bench, which is slowly thawing, at the hill that overlooks the city where I live. I have found myself here, on occasion, for over thirty years. This is where I came with possible partners, where I sit just to ponder, where we released balloons to mark the anniversary of my father's passing, where the children of my family have come to play in the autumn leaves. Down below is the city that has both changed and not changed. Here there is the fizz of time.

So it is with the playground. There is time and there are times. The seasons change, the play folds and unfolds and evolves and shifts, the children and the things they play with come and go: yet, it is all a whole. Every playground is, or could be, perceived this way. The inquiry to hand is in the manner of capturing a ghost glimmer, in the poetic analogy, of this.

There is a need for some definitional acuity at this point, crossing a threshold: a doorway into the grammar of a piece of writing, just as the playground has a descriptive grammar of its own. By *playground*, here, I refer specifically to the adventure playground in west London which is the base of my considerations, in their presentness, and also generally and potentially to every place where adults' awarenesses are open to the possibility of play. This awareness-open stance embraces perception, which communicates with its in-the-moment sensory and its intuited facets: what is written here of *this* playground should be translated to fit the perception of any other given place by the reader. Regarding perception, and drawing on Edie's (1964) analysis of Merleau-Ponty's "primacy of perception" thesis, we are "immersed in the world" of the sensible, but there are "various levels of experience" too.

I will write about the playground as a palimpsest arrangement and this should be read in terms of, but not limited to: a layering of time and times; the folding and unfolding and evolutions of narratives of play; the play that has happened here in its play marks, leftoverness, "residue" (Guilbaud 2011), and the play that is happening, paused or in continuance, or that will happen here; the amalgam of times, the embeddedness of time, which I shall refer to as places, as opposed to spaces, within the overall place of the playground; objects, as opposed to elements (due to the potential for ambiguity), being the physical phenomena implanted into or laid upon or above the notional flat of the playground (perhaps a tree, structures, a hill), can be translated as best fits the particular geography, geology, or topography of any other place; magic, consciousness change, floods and trickles through it all. The playground is perceived as animate, of myth, of story, that which can be connected with, spoken and listened to. It is of the interchange of the ordinary and the extraordinary in its threshold in-betweens and inter-woven path traversings, its places and its temporal strings.

The playground as palimpsest is *this* playworker's way of seeing. It is intended that the play-minded reader might, in time and times, also receive such perspectives by the place of play that presents itself to his or her awareness. What might transpire in further appreciation of where the play-minded is? What "might" transpires (Guilbaud 2011).

How is it that our ways of seeing make themselves apparent? Intuition comes to us by ways we cannot immediately explain: within it there may be traces of previous experiences and observations, derived from the sensible world (that which may be sensed), traces initially unrecognised, in our anticipations of what will soon be. Some years back, when the playground was outwardly different, I stood with a colleague in the centre of it all as we observed, a hundred yards or so away, a child carrying a container of water towards the hammock swing where another child stood with an umbrella up. "Is that water going over or under?" I asked. Something of *some* experience told me it would go over the umbrella, and soon after it did. Our intuition though may also be in the feel or the texture of the place around us, in the moment, and in our engagement with the reception and creation of this. Abram (1997, p.52) writes of the reciprocal nature of our relation to the world. He draws reference to Merleau-Ponty's (1968) notion of "the collective flesh," "both *our* flesh and the 'flesh' of the world," i.e., flesh as "presented . . . as an element, much as air or water are elements" (Bernasconi 1995, p.555), in which the things of the world are treated as animate: in the interpretation, we observe something and *something* observes us. "Perception . . . is precisely this reciprocity, the ongoing interchange between my body and the entities that surround it" (Abram 1997, p.52, after Merleau-Ponty).

Something told me of the texture of the place one smoke-hazy day in February, and later that year *something* told me of the nature of this playground as the children's domain, in which we adults tread carefully, one unusually warm late October day when, after coming back from a trip into the mass of the city, I saw the calm and enormous beauty of that playground as I stepped through the gates. *Something* spoke, and we communicated. There is something old, something ancient, in this. Huizinga writes of times prior to the formation of us-shaped gods,

> when the powers and forces by which primitive man felt surrounded had not yet assumed human shape . . . when seized upon by the mysterious and tremendous menacing forces of life and nature [the mind evokes] . . . the sensation of shadowy beings. (Huizinga 1955, p.138)

Something spoke.

Something invited a feel of its texture: it is a feeling. Damasio (2004) writes that "feelings are perceptions" (p.85) where "a feeling is the perception of a certain state of the body along with the perception of a certain mode of thinking" (p.86). The *sight* of the sea, he suggests, results in a certain body state, and it is this body state that is then feeling-perceived, directly or via the brain's "body maps" (Damasio 2004, p.91–112). As I read this, and briefly supposing ourselves here outside the magic of the world, there must then be an internal-external feedback loop: our homeostatic balance or imbalance affects our connection to the external world.

Whether, in regarding our intuitions, we're in consideration of our previous experiences of the world or, after Merleau-Ponty's "flesh," we think of the texture that we are a part of and that is a part of us and that which we can't fully explain, or if we give thought to the body mapping of body states that Damasio terms "the immediate *substrates* of feelings" (2004, p.87), we start perhaps—preconceptually—from that which is sensed.

Of the world external to the body, Abram cites Merleau-Ponty in exposition of "the profound intimacy of the body's preconceptual relation to the sensible things or powers that surround it" (1997, pp.54–55):

> I give ear, or look, in the expectation of a sensation, and suddenly the sensible takes possession of my ear or my gaze, and I surrender a part of my body, even my whole body, to this particular manner of vibrating. (Merlau-Ponty 1962)

The world must be engaged with, suggests Abram, in reciprocal fashion, via the senses.

> Things disclose themselves to our immediate perception as . . . styles of unfolding—not as finished chunks of matter given once and for all, but as dynamic

> ways of engaging the senses and modulating the body . . . in a world that speaks. (Abram 1997, p.81)

Certainly the world can speak to us in this way. One early December day, picking up the plastic straws cut and left a few months back by family children in the garden at home (straws grown through, sucked down by grass and moss), I had the sudden rooted feeling of time beyond all this modern life, out in the raw cold, with the mud and the wet grass on my fingers: a genetic flashback, if you will, to ancestral times, surviving in the land, being a part of the land. It was of my sight and touch, and *something* speaking. It shifted abruptly, but an after-image lingers, still. Whilst Damasio writes, in neurobiological terms, that "mental images of the objects and events outside the brain are creations of the brain . . . rather than passive mirror images reflecting that reality" (Damasio 2004, p.199), this dryness misses what Bachelard terms (in this case, regarding a dwelling-place) as retention of "the treasures of former days" Bachelard 1994, p.5). The world that speaks is a poetic one.

According to Abram, within "the activity of perception" (1997, p.61) in the world that speaks, there is an interconnectedness of senses:

> A raven soaring in the distance is not, for me, a mere visual image; as I follow it with my eyes, I inevitably feel the stretch and flex of its wings with my own muscles. (p.61)

In the context of the playground, there may be the empathy-tension of muscles in the sight of the flex of wood in the softer branches that the children climb, or in the creak of the dry ones that they use to get up that far; there is the patina and depth infusion of wandering wood-smoke from the fire, which infiltrates the mesh of hair and the fabric of clothing, and the activity or inactivity of movement; there is the expectation of the feel of rough dry wooden pallets, stacked in piles in the spring sun, or lined on end, fingers to trail along the possibility of splinterings, or there is the anticipation of the give or slightest spring, beneath the boots, of pallets laid across the winter mud. The interconnectedness of senses within the individual wooden objects of the playground (the tree, the fuel of the fire, the pallets) is also a further interconnectedness in awareness of all that is wood on site. The world of the wood on the playground speaks in multiple languages.

The playground speaks, is perceived, by direct sense input from the external world, and by intuited texture given to us, and by our reciprocity: a resonance in the flex of it all. Bachelard writes of his reaction to certain features of his environment, with reference to what he terms "topoanalysis" or "the systematic psychological study of the sites of our intimate lives" (1994, p.8): "And what dynamic, handsome object is a path! How precise the familiar hill paths remain for our muscular consciousness!" He refers, in passing, to the poetic "cadence of roads," (p.11) as suggested in the writing of Jean Caubère (1994, p.11). The playground also has its cadence, its inflections of various fallings of speech: within the tonal arrangements of light-brown woodchips sheltered under the slide and sodden dark versions out in the open is the crisp of the dry and the give of mud, and the in-between of these, in navigating routes; the frost of mid-winter, lying across the sand pit in the late morning shade, makes hard little hillocks that once were soft and thudding; there is the slip of the wooden platforms in the deluge of rain and yet, nevertheless, still there is the running play, carefully held. Stevens (2007, p.210) cites Lynch (1960) regarding kinaesthesia and how it "can aid memorability, for example when people move along a curved or sloping path." The playground speaks directly to the muscles.

All this that we can feel of the playground's texture, but which we can't fully and absolutely transmit in words, necessarily becomes relayed in stories, which transmute into myth. This playground is as myth. It is a way of making sense of the not fully explicable, the intangible, the invisible, or the intuitively felt. Huizinga (1955, pp.4–5) writes that "In myth, primitive man seeks to account for the world of phenomena by grounding it in the Divine." In this sense, and of the playground, we are "primitives" in the poetic positive: we try to catch a glimmer, the edge of a feather, the trace of a dreamed interaction, perhaps, of some texture, this way.

How is it that I may perceive the playground of invisible but intuited texture? I create a construct I call the palimpsest, in myth and divinity, which has its own language and grammar, which in my connection to it and vice versa, as animate entities, speaks of its experiences as I do of mine. The playground is scattered with its physical play marks, leftoverness and residue, replete in its tracings of all that has happened here, as originally sense-perceived, but now lingering.

Inwood (1995, p.383) writes of Edmund Husserl's inquiry into some form of a lingering, as I read it, of how to "experience a temporally extended object *as such*" (Husserl 1905). That is, for example, in listening to a tune, if a listener hears only the note given to him at that time, having no awareness of any other notes, then at no time is he "conscious of a temporally extended tune, but only of the note that is occurring *now*" (Inwood 1995, p.383). All of the notes, it is claimed, cannot be heard simultaneously because of the jumbled mess (think here of the playground). Husserl's solution, writes Inwood, was in the notion of the present note forming a "primal impression," whereas the notes before this are retained (the expected notes to come will be "protained"). "Thus . . . retain[ing] not only the individual notes of the tune but the order in which they occurred" (p.383). Something of this ordering nature can be seen to occur on the playground, in its songs and rhymes, or in the play in one place over times, for instance, to both of which I shall return. Inwood adds that "Husserl does not . . . regard time as atomized into a series of discrete instants, or periods: our time-consciousness is a *continuous flux*" (p.383). In attempting to remember an earlier phase of the playground (or, in the analogy, Husserl's attempts to remember an earlier phase of a tune), there is impairment of full appreciation of its present phase; retention of earlier phases is essential, though, to my appreciation of the present phase. One boy, one day, filled the surface of the pool table with water from the hose, with sand and with paint. He was angry at his play being stopped. He climbed up onto the roof. The next day, he attacked a pallet by throwing the sledgehammer at it and by bouncing two hammers off its planks. These are only some of the phases retained in this particular tune of play, discordant as it is. The broken pallet was left lingering at the wood store.

The palimpsest embraces time and is, in short, a depth story, formation of myth, in attempting to capture a glimmer, edge of a feather, trace of a dreamed interaction, perhaps, of some texture, of something given, something felt which cannot be fully written or said. The palimpsest is a construct of baroque quality, multi-layered and inter-woven, embracing that which is of the "marvelous real" (Carpentier 1975). In his lecture entitled *The Baroque and the Marvelous Real*, and with reference to art, Carpentier highlights what he calls the "baroque spirit" (p.90). Rather than being an era of time in artistic endeavours, the baroque is defined as "a constant of the human spirit . . . art in motion" (p.93). It is, writes Carpentier, of Shakespeare's "disordered theater" (p.96), of Proust's "sentences within sentences" (p.97), of Rabelais' word inventions (p.91); it is, architecturally, of a lack of central axis (p.94) (we can compare this with the asymmetries of the playground); it is, sculpturally, in how light seems to make figures move (pp.93–94). In the baroque spirit, there are layers and inter-weavings, in art and in society. To this all, he then adds what he terms "the marvelous real." That is to say, linking to that which is "extraordinary," or "not necessarily lovely or beautiful" (p.101), the marvellous real can be seen as infused in the baroque net: it is the strangeness of details of stories, real though they have happened, and the extraordinary oddness which is, actually, the common-place. The baroque and the marvellous real converge, as I think of the playground, into a palimpsest arrangement, where the extraordinary is ordinary and the ordinary is extraordinary.

Here, the children buried a bird because it was dead; over here, a volcano rose up; there, the children floated on the breeze with open umbrellas; this is the route of the funeral procession following the death of a cardboard box; this is the murder scene of a teddy-bear, spiked through and through and bleeding red; this is the slide where, once, there was an incidence of surfing on paint, amongst other once-nesses of experiment; here is where the computer, the radio, the barbeque, the CD player spilt their entrails onto the paving slabs; this is where the box in which a boy gave birth was; this is where the children lay, one summer day, and turned the playground into treacle with the magic of their lilting songs; this is the site of the dig, where untold treasures of stones were found; here is where a boy secured his friend, at the edge of the drop, sat on the plastic chair, wrapped around and round with masking tape. These all, and more, of the marvellous real, are places and developing places within the palimpsest.

There is a difference between "place" and "space" in the grammar of this inter-woven exposition. Within the palimpsest arrangement, there are places that the children come back to time and again. That is, the "place-ness" is given to this perceiver, by the playground, in the accumulation of the children's returns. Kozlovsky (2013, p.237) discusses Dutch architect Aldo van Eyck's "notion of place making [as opposed to] 'space' associated with modernity," with reference to his post-war Amsterdam playgrounds. Hertzberger (2001, p.193) refers more specifically to van Eyck's thinking, in quoting: "Whatever space and time mean, place and occasion mean more. For space in the image of man is place, and time in the image of man is occasion" (Van Eyck 1962). Bachelard (1994, p.8) writes: "In its countless alveoli [little cavities] space contains compressed time. That is what space is for." It is, in the interpretation, van Eyck's human connection to the object of the playground, or to the whole of it, that renders it with embeddedness. Bachelard's conceptualisation of space-time begins to impress place-ness into what become playground significances. These are the centres of children's returns, in all their scattered states, and they need not be just the monolithic structures and expanses that are all too evident: there is place-ness, as observed, on *this* playground, in the "tree house" and the "fire corner," or the "fire pit," and on "the pitches," but also in the area between and around what were the "tyre swings" and "the tyre wall," where all manner of fantastical arrangements get played out but which can't always be fully read; there is place-ness in the wooden strip between the old fire pit and the ex-vegetable patch where the turnip club was found, a strip which was a railway line, and which is now a path; there is place-ness in the hammocks, and the sometimes swings, and in the two- or three- or four-sided dens that flux and flow beneath the tyre wall. Here, all, there is time compressed. Space, however, in the grammar of this construct, is not infused with times: it is the air that's bounded, the strips and blocks that are to the sides of the path traversings, those "drawings that have been lived" (p.12), that which is even to the edge of the threshold in-betweens.

Of "in-betweens," Hertzberger writes: "The threshold provides the key to the transition and connection between areas with divergent territorial claims and, [it is] a place in its own right" (Hertzberger 2001, p.32). Stevens (2007) clarifies the threshold, in the context of urban environments, as "a point on the boundary between inside and outside that can be opened" (p.152). There are forms of thresholds fizzing throughout the playground, bounded by physical objects and surfaces and areas, and by the virtual as-played edges and edifices that are invisible-but-there; bounded by psychological frames of play and by the play of times. Stevens writes that the threshold is "a passage, a transitional place where people spend time" (p.152), which is a simple statement but one that inspires a deeper reflection on the nature of time. There are playground thresholds along the narrow stretch of wood that marks the edge of safety in chase-tap play, on the edges of the shifting kingdom of Arendelle or around the being in/being out of "the restaurant," and there are thresholds temporally threaded between the chunks of time that accumulate within and around the fire pit and in the qualitative shifts perceived between these times. The retaining, the primal impression, and the protaining of play, and the temporal thresholds that are bounded by these phases, is a dimension of the palimpsest, which has a certain density. Space, within the grammar of this piece, is not time-space: space is to the edge of places, and to the edge of threshold in-betweens, in waiting.

Whether we have strayed into place or space, we cannot always be sure. We must trust in perception reciprocity: as Abram writes, "speak *to* the world, not about it" (Abram 1997, p.71). We must ask the playground about its play marks, its leftoverness, its residue, the drawings that have been lived, but also about that which is given to us in other ways: the marks left on us of songs and songlines (after Chatwin 2003) and other stories. What we'll be told, if we listen, is that there is a "played-with-ness" (Guilbaud 2011) to the places and to the place as a whole. Guilbaud writes: "[Played-with-ness] indicates the need to be sensitive to the environment of children's play, to the life of the things and spaces, to the detailed creation of the space by intersecting layers of play" Slight disparities in definitions of "space" notwithstanding, it is this reverence, this understanding of treading carefully, that we will hear in our voices if we speak to the world of the playground, the texture of it all, that which we are a part of and that is a part of us and that which we can't fully explain.

We give places names in the speaking to because, I consider and suppose, as Bachelard (1994, p.9) writes: "The more securely [memories] are fixed in space, the sounder they are." It is curious that *this* playground is a peculiarity quite unique: in part, studded through and through with the grit and glitter of names that children, and others, have sometimes sewn and sown into it. Huizinga (1955, p4) asserts that language is infused with play and that the naming of things raises them "into the domain of the spirits . . . in giving expression to life man creates a second, poetic world alongside the world of nature." The poem of the palimpsest sits alongside and within the nature of it. Chatwin (2003, p.267) writes that "man 'makes' his territory by naming the 'things' in it" and he tells a tale of touring Aboriginal "Dreaming" sites in Australia (p.95):

> Not far to the right, we passed an outcrop of weathered sandstone, with free-standing pinnacles about twenty feet high . . .
>
> I nudged Big Tom in the ribs.
>
> "Who's that one?" I asked.
>
> "Him a small one . . ."
>
> "Witchetty?"
>
> He shook his head strenuously and, with the gesture of feeding a grub into his mouth, said, "Smaller one."
>
> "Caterpillar?"

This playground has no places named like "witchetty" or "caterpillar" but, at this point of writing, it does have a place some children call what, for now, I won't disclose the full name of—not because I'm squeamish of response but because this name I feel as in need of some small protection—including the designation "sex" as it does, once quietly written on its wall; also, as quietly emerged in playworker conversation of observations of play, there has come to light the presence of the place named, in passing, after genitalia (whose name I also preserve for similar reasons), being an uprooted post, sunk in discarded concrete, left by the main gate where "one-touch" football got played before the mound of earth was deposited there. There's "homey," when the prosaics of names like "sand pit" aren't in play. This playground has "the pitches," despite the pitches' singular not plural nature, the bland but everyday of "the structures," and "the tree house," despite this being entirely unsurrounded by the presence of tree. There are also blends of adult-child formations, whose origins are more lost in time ("where the mad-house was," or "the new mad-house") and more time-specific fragments which have the potential for narrative re-emergence in "this is where the weaponry or the maze was," "the Peaceful Epiphany," being the child-given name of a wooden block boat, painted on its side in fading letters, later re-christened as "the Painful Epiphany," and the at-one-time coined "fire corner" (where children discussed whether the fire pit could be called "a corner" at all, given its generally circular disposition). There are also all the transitory dungeons, dens and jails, castles and kingdoms that emerge and re-emerge, that glisten on for days, then peter out and fold into other strata of the whole. This playground is, like others, unique with its sometimes names: studded fixed or drifting by with the change of children, days or seasons, and with us. In namings, in the singing of the land into existence, Chatwin writes of Aboriginal songlines, of how "an unsung land is a dead land" (p.52) and how the songlines' "endless accumulation of detail . . . structures of kinship reach out to all living men, to all his fellow creatures, and to the rivers, the rocks and the trees" (p.70). On the playground, its stories keep it alive and, as can be interpreted via Battram (2007), there is the hint of songlines in the heritage of play.

We can trace the evolution of actual songs and rhymes across the playground too: they can be read, in the noticing (Guilbaud 2011), within the palimpsest if we recognise how to follow them. The songs and rhymes leave their play marks just as physical objects do, but they leave invisible, ethereal though indelible marks. For a couple of months, a colleague made occasional reference to the "Bloody Mary" play, which started in the toilets, apparently, and which I missed and couldn't fathom in the re-tellings anyway. I continued not to catch it anywhere on the playground. Then, one day, I was at what were the tyre swings and I heard it right in front of me. The singing girl had earlier brandished ladles whilst at the fire pit where the children cooked soup. There was a debate over whether "fricking" was a swear word or not and the girl with ladles sang about being a "fricking sexy chef." At the tyre swings, now with camera pressed into another child's face, she sang: "Bloody Mary, sexy fairy, I'm a sexy chef." The individual clauses of the rhyme now, for me, have their loci of recounted and directly observed genesis indelibly marked at the toilets, the fire pit, and what were the tyre swings. The rhyme will move on more, and may have done so already, even as I write.

The names and songs and songlines are of spells: incantations of consciousness change. So too is the magic circle that we may draw around the place, in reverence, in order to receive the playground's myths and stories and other leftoverness that marks, its path traversings, drawings that have been lived, its threshold in-betweens and all the marvellous real in the baroque net of the palimpsest. Time and times are embedded in the whole, which is a depth story. What we might see, in our in-the-moment sensory and intuited perception, is a glimmer, edge of a feather, trace of a dreamed interaction, perhaps, of some texture, something given: animate us, playground and the play-minded.

How might we be in disposition? Scott (1974, p.5) asserts that there are three separate humanities: these being those who live within five senses, those who *suspect* but who remain, nevertheless, with "an unease in the blood," and "those who *know* . . . as experience." His writing is, admittedly, related here out of its original context (it being in reference to the former Dr. Richard Alpert, later known as Baba Ram Dass), but it serves *this* writing in preparation for conclusion. That is, in similar vein and towards disposition, as Scott (p.11) has it: " . . . how could a man who had seen a rose as a coalescence of pure energy be expected to take his mortgage seriously?"

The playground as palimpsest gives itself. Here there is the fizz of time.

REFERENCES

Abram, D. (1997) *The spell of the sensuous: perception and language in a more-than-human world*. New York: Vintage Books.

Bachelard, G. (1994) *The poetics of space*. Boston: Beacon Press.

Battram, A. (2007) Cited in Palmer, M., Wilson, P., Battram, A. (2007) *The playing that runs through us all: Illustrating the playwork principles with stories of play*. In: Russell, W., Hanscomb, B., Fitzpatrick, J. (eds) (2007, pp. 130–131) *Playwork voices: In celebration of Bob Hughes and Gordon Sturrock*. London: The London Centre for Playwork Education and Training.

Bernasconi, R. L. (1995) *Merleau-Ponty, Maurice* in Honderich, T. (ed) (1995) *The Oxford companion to philosophy*. Oxford: Oxford University Press.

Carpentier, A. (1975) *The baroque and the marvelous real*. In: Zamora, L. P. and Faris, W. B. (eds) (1995, pp. 91–101) *Magical realism: theory, history, community*. Durham, NC: Duke University Press.

Chatwin, B. (2003) *The songlines*. London: Vintage.

Damasio, A. (2004) *Looking for Spinoza: joy, sorrow and the feeling brain*. London: Vintage.

Edie, J. M. (1964) *Introduction*. In: Merleau-Ponty, M. (1964), *The primacy of perception*. Evanston, Illinois: Northwestern University Press.

Eyck, A. van. (1962) Unreferenced quotation. Cited in Hertzberger, H. (2001) *Lessons for students in architecture*, 4th revised edition. Rotterdam: 010 Publishers.

Guilbaud, S. (2011) *A phenomenological inquiry into the possibility of played-withness in experiences with things* [Online]. Available from: www.playful.org.uk [Accessed February 3, 2015].

Hertzberger, H. (2001) *Lessons for students in architecture*, 4th revised edition. Rotterdam: 010 Publishers.

Huizinga, J. (1955) *Homo ludens: a study of the play element in culture*. Boston, MA: Beacon Press.

Husserl, E. (1905) *Lectures on the phenomenology of internal time-consciousness*. Cited in Inwood, M. J. (1995, p. 383) *Husserl, Edmund*. In: Honderich, T. (ed) (1995), *The Oxford companion to philosophy*. Oxford: Oxford University Press.

Inwood, M. J. (1995) *Husserl, Edmund*. In: Honderich, T. (ed) (1995), *The Oxford companion to philosophy*. Oxford: Oxford University Press.

Kozlovsky, R. (2013) *The architectures of childhood: children, modern architecture and reconstruction in postwar England*. Farnham: Ashgate Publishing Limited.

Lynch, K. (1960) *The image of the city*. Cited in Stevens, Q. (2007, p. 210) *The ludic city: exploring the potential of public places*. Abingdon: Routledge.

Merleau-Ponty, M. (1962) *Phenomenology of perception.* London: Routledge & Kegan Paul. Cited in Abram, D. (1997, p. 55) *The spell of the sensuous: perception and language in a more-than-human world.* New York: Vintage Books.

Merleau-Ponty, M. (1968) *The visible and the invisible.* Evanston, Illinois: Northwestern University Press. Cited in Abram, D. (1997, p. 66) *The spell of the sensuous: perception and language in a more-than-human world.* New York: Vintage Books.

Scott, E. (1974) The Start. In: Ram Dass, B. (1974) *Doing your own being.* London: Neville Spearman Limited.

Stevens, Q. (2007) *The ludic city: exploring the potential of public places.* Abingdon: Routledge.

Chapter Eleven

Adventure Playgrounds

A Brief History

Tony Chilton

INTRODUCTION

I was prompted to write about the early developments of Adventure Playgrounds by a range of factors, particularly those referred to in the latter parts of this paper. Further to this however, I, along with many others connected to this area of work, became increasingly concerned that the fundamental philosophy underpinning the operational practices initiated by the pioneers of Adventure Playgrounds, was being somewhat misunderstood, forgotten and even disregarded. In addition, I am aware that many Playwork training programmes do not appear to emphasise the importance of the original concept. In determining this, I rely on my direct experience of being an Adventure Playground Worker over a long period of time and a trainer involved in writing and delivering basic introductory courses through to degree and post-graduate levels of training.

When I expressed my intention, to a number of respected and appropriate people, to write about the history of Adventure Playgrounds, I was particularly encouraged by the support of my very dear friend and past work colleague, Professor Fraser Brown. Fraser was himself a lone Adventure Playground Worker operating on an isolated site on a large social housing estate in the north west of England when I first met him many years ago. In preparing and writing this paper he has been tremendously helpful in offering his professional assistance in providing constructive assessment and human support for which I thank him unreservedly.

THE BEGINNING

The concept of what we now refer to as Adventure Playgrounds had its beginnings in the early 1940s and perhaps even before. As early as 1939 there were clear examples of a more enlightened approach to the provision of play areas, as indicated by a playground in Bolton, Lancashire, UK. Here, instead of the traditional metal swings, slides and roundabouts, there was an abundance of unconventional wooden structures of a wide and stimulating variety. Elsewhere, a number of play sites throughout the UK witnessed the introduction of "unusual" play items such as old loco engines, disused lifeboats, old buses and unwanted railway carriages. The latter two items were later often adapted to accommodate equipment storage and indoor play on emerging Adventure Playgrounds.

The prospect for a more imaginative and exciting approach to play opportunities was being explored by a wide range of organisations including some forward thinking local authorities. This was as a consequence of and a realisation that there was a need for more child oriented, clearly defined and dedicated spaces for children's play—places where children could express themselves in a free and unrestricted manner in response to their instinctive urge to explore, experiment, invent and extend their various and multi-faceted patterns of play behaviour.

This was demonstrated by children (and I was one of them) who during and after World War II were often to be seen playing on bomb sites, lighting fires, building a variety of structures, mainly dens and the like, using the materials readily available there. If and where trees were to be found, children invariably made swings, tree houses and such. In place of trees, the cast iron arms of the street lampposts would be used for swings! Such improvisation of course, reflected the imagination and play instincts of children since time immemorial.

There was a gallant effort to accommodate such play behaviour as highlighted by a project in Morden, Surrey and reported in the Evening News, November, 1947 when a "Junk Playground" was created on waste ground with "a grown-up who can help, but won't boss—and the rest is up to children." The newspaper went on to refer to similar developments elsewhere, for instance an "Under-Fourteens Council suggested the scheme for our big cities." They stated that, "Stepney and Shoreditch Councils have already reserved pieces of land for the scheme. Westminster has just bought two sites intending to use them as ordinary playgrounds. This seems to be a chance to try out the idea in another area where it is badly needed."

Coincidently (and perhaps ironically), Morden was not only the possible birth place of the Adventure Playground concept in the UK, but also the birth place of Fraser Brown, an Adventure Playground Worker in the mid-1970s and the first Professor in Playwork in the U.K.! How curious is that!

When the "junk playground" concept began to gather momentum, it was clearly recognised by the early pioneers that provision needed to be a totally child centred environment where supervision was not so strictly applied. This was so that children and young people could be free of unnecessary constraints and simply be themselves. They needed to be places which would be without adult imposed controls and intervention, as profoundly stated in the newspaper article referred to above; places where *"a grown up . . . won't boss—and the rest is up to children."* A clear enough statement of intent; it was to be an environment where there were no meaningless rules, regulations and play-restrictive controls.

Development of such a concept was originally determined by Professor Carl Sorenson (1931), a landscape architect by profession. He arrived at a considered view of children's play needs as a consequence of witnessing children persistently accessing construction sites, bomb sites and landscape development areas in order to use loose materials for play experiences within such locations. Sorenson recognised the need for a place where children could express their individual and collective imagination and creativity; a specific space available to children when they most needed it—when not in school i.e., evenings, weekends and all school holidays.

Sorenson's "Junk Playground" as it was referred to, was established in 1943 in a small urban area, Emdrup just outside Copenhagen. It was provision which reflected Sorenson's idea that "children could create and shape, dream and imagine;" an understanding long since recognised as essential elements of primary play behaviour. The latter two are very often overlooked aspects of play, yet so much of this takes place in the child's mind. Children are frequently imagining, fantasising, creating, exploring and determining their play in their minds, much of which absorbs them for long periods of time. Of his concept, Sorenson (1951:314) stated "of all the things I have helped to realise, the Junk Playground is the ugliest; yet for me it is the best and most beautiful of my works."

Carl Sorenson also stressed that children ought to be free of external controls in their play by determining for themselves how, when and where they played, thereby maximising the opportunities to establish their own play parameters to the greatest possible extent. With regard to this, it was suggested that adults ought to be exceedingly careful when seeking to intervene in the play lives, events and behaviour of children. Such an approach was later reinforced by visionaries such as Drummond Abernethy and Lady Marjorie Allen (refer to sections 2 and 6).

The appointment of a "supervisor" in the Emdrup situation, as was also the case in Morden, later to be referred to as a *Play Leader,* was considered to be required to ensure that "dangerous" and potentially harmful activities on the site were noted and children offered assistance when asked for or needed. It was generally agreed however, that children had to consider their own capacity for confronting and dealing with risks.

John Bertelson, the first Play Leader in Emdrup, also had responsibility for identifying potential sources for the regular supply of tools and materials. These were items such as timber, old tyres, ropes, nets and other resources provided so as to enable children to have constant access to creative play opportunities. All such re-usable materials added to and helped develop their play experiences through imaginative and creative uses. Bertelson emphasised that: "The purpose of the leader was not to govern children from outside and direct their building activity to a useful goal, but rather to act from within, by allowing them to pursue their own projects" (Kozlovsky 2007: 8). He also strongly advocated that initiative must come from children themselves and went on to say; "I cannot and indeed will not, teach the children anything" (Bertelsen 1972: 20).

The Play Leader was seen, by the children as someone who, among other things, was able to protect their play environment and prevent outside intrusion and interference, perhaps through the introduction of various control mechanisms such as fences and gates (see Taylor 2008).

EARLY DEVELOPMENTS IN THE UK

As a direct result of a visit to Emdrup in the mid-1940s, Lady Allen of Hurtwood reinforced the concept of "Junk Playgrounds" in Britain. Marjorie Allen as she preferred to be known was herself a landscape architect and no great lover of bureaucracy or stringent planning control mechanisms. She stressed the need to keep such provision "out of the hands of officials and professionals." (This was emphatically expressed to me during a conversation I had with her prior to the extension of Blacon Adventure Playground undertaken in 1969/70 to accommodate more disabled children)

It was in late 1948 and clearly after the Morden project and other similar initiatives, that a more defined approach to "Junk Playgrounds" was established and the first Adventure Playgrounds, as they became known in Britain, opened: Lollard Street and Clydesdale Road, both in London and another in Rathbone Street, China Town, Liverpool. These Adventure Playgrounds were at the forefront of a more substantial movement, and further organised voluntary provision followed in urban areas such as Grimsby, London, Liverpool, Bristol, Manchester, Birmingham and other areas in the Midlands, Sheffield, Newcastle, Cardiff and Edinburgh. The early new towns emerging in post-war Britain also provided Adventure Playgrounds; Crawley and Stevenage for example integrated Adventure Playground provision into their high density housing developments. Such an initiative was later incorporated into additional new town areas which were created in the 1960s/1970s, e.g., Telford, Runcorn and Peterborough.

MANAGEMENT STRUCTURES AND OPERATIONAL PRACTICES

Historically, most Adventure Playgrounds were established in urban areas in response to decreasing space for children to play imaginatively and creatively. Large, densely built and heavily populated residential areas were springing up all over post-war Britain.

In the early days of their development, Adventure Playgrounds were often initiated and managed by local groups and subsequently seen as an essential, lively and vibrant component of the communities in which they were located. Most were established on land that was economically of little value, or indeed, in the case of some of the larger towns and cities, on bomb sites. Large numbers of children throughout the U.K. at this time played on derelict sites (as indicated earlier), using debris to be found there and supplemented by unwanted/discarded household material. Imaginative constructive &/or deconstructive play such as den-building with regular re-building, or making camp-fires, was a frequently witnessed event. Marjorie Allen, writing for the World Organisation for Early Childhood Education described Adventure Playgrounds as follows:

> They are decidedly messy occupations and they make the planners who are mainly tidy minded, unhappy. Nevertheless they must never forget children enjoy dirty and untidy, adults abhor it and we have to decide whether we are to make playgrounds for children or playgrounds that please the planners.

The physical content, shape and layout of Adventure Playgrounds were determined by the availability of material resources, the imagination and inventiveness of the children and staff and seasonal factors. Initially very few had purpose-built indoor play accommodation, often relying simply on self-built "play hut" type constructions in order to store tools and equipment and to house a phone perhaps. Further to this, one of the first structures to be built on the playground was quite often a shelter where Playworkers and kids could sit around a fire chatting, singing or baking potatoes and other such delicacies! This informal gathering place helped to establish mutual trust, often resulting in children revealing considerable information about their fears, expectations and so on. It was frequently the starting point for the unique relationships that developed between the Playworker and children.

With regard to the absence of other indoor provision, Playworkers often relied on local residents when wishing to access facilities for their "personal needs," there being no utilities linked to the sites! Obviously this reinforced the fact that the Playworker was indeed accepted as part of the community.

In spite of having little by way of indoor facilities, quite a number of Adventure Playgrounds kept animals on their sites. Rabbits, goats, donkeys, gerbils and chickens (many mysteriously disappearing at Christmas times!) and even sheep, were often looked after by the children and staff. Many animals arrived due to their owners not being able to give sufficient time to their care. The Blacon Adventure Playground in Chester, one of the longest established in the UK, (and still attracting overwhelming numbers of children) to this day has quite a large variety of animals as part of its urban farm, which is an integral feature of the site. The animals require considerable husbandry which is undertaken by kids and staff. The introduction of animals is a valuable asset to an Adventure Playground as it is another element of play education that too few children experience in their lives.

Adventure Playgrounds as indicated earlier, were invariably fully supported by children and the communities in which they were located and most were subsequently managed by neighbourhood groups. In many instances officers and elected members of the local authority also became actively involved and supportive. Other voluntary organisations, the local church and sometimes even local businesses took an active interest and joined management bodies. With regard to the cost of establishing and maintaining Adventure Playgrounds in the early days of their existence, most were funded by temporary government funding initiatives such as the Urban-Aid Programme and/or directly through finance from local authorities. Such funding systems were frequently supported by the use of other government initiatives of the day such as the Job Creation Programme (JCP) and the Special Temporary Employment Project (STEP). However most, if not all Adventure Playgrounds, had to organise creative fund raising activities for additional running costs or for new and further development of the site.

Few Adventure Playgrounds were established in rural areas because of the general misconception that children living in such areas had free and easy access to more adventurous play opportunities. This is a fallacy that persists even today. It has to be stressed that *all* children have a human drive to play whatever their culture, age or social and economic circumstances, and regardless of their physical, emotional and intellectual capacities (Chilton 1989). All children are special and so are their needs, which are varied and diverse, therefore, provision surely must reflect this. Children need to have access to free, unadulterated, creative, stimulating and developmental play experiences on a regular basis no matter where they live and irrespective of their individual or collective status.

INDOOR FACILITIES AND SOCIAL PROVISION

Although most Adventure Playgrounds focussed on outdoor play in the early part of their history (indeed in most instances there was no other option!), with the introduction of additional grant-aid from various sources and the need to extend the activities throughout the whole year and in all weathers, indoor play provision was given a greater focus. Many sites established such provision in a comprehensive manner. Toilets for all abilities, offices, first-aid facilities, kitchens, arts and craft rooms, storage, quiet rooms, etc. were provided in many instances. There were still many sites however where steel containers, old railway carriages and double/single deck buses were used as the only indoor facility.

The introduction of purpose-built indoor provision created opportunities for extending the range of play activity in addition to promoting and reinforcing the obvious, which is that children do play all-year round. Indoor space was also used for a variety of other social needs, such as parent and toddler groups, community meetings, probation services, the accommodating of long-term truants and children with school phobias. There were cases where the facilities were used for "home tuition" where a child had been excluded from all schools and where the child's own home environment was not conducive to such a process. These "extra-curricular activities" had to be fully understood and agreed by the children in the first instance. All such developments enabled the Playworkers to become associated with a wide variety of services for children with particular requirements. The Playworker was seen by other professions as someone with a wide and sympathetic knowledge of local children and their families and was therefore regularly involved in case discussions.

Of considerable importance in all these developments, was that at the very centre, there existed a strong, unique, trusting and binding relationship between the Playworker and the child. The Playworker ensured that the child's needs were paramount.

STAFFING MATTERS

Wherever they were located, most Adventure Playgrounds opened at times when children and young people of all ages (i.e., 3/4 years upward), needed them most—for example, after school, generally until late in the evening (often until 10 pm in summer months for older children), at weekends and during school holidays, 7 days a week—thus demonstrating that the prime concern was for the needs of children, rather than the image or requirements of the organisation providing the facility. However, staffing issues were particularly problematic because of the absence of job security such as employment contracts, adequate policies on pay and conditions and future career prospects and structure, all of which, including poor funding mechanisms, contrived to create very low, staffing levels, in terms of numbers,.

Many sites were staffed by one full-time Playworker, a good number of who were sometimes unsure of receiving their salaries because of the uncertainty and frailty of the grant-aid system which was often the manner in which provision was funded. Due to the exacting and demanding workloads, physically, emotionally and socially, there was a relatively high turnover of staff. It was not until much later that staffing levels and pay and conditions were recognised as being in need of serious consideration. The recommendation that there be at least two full time members on site with additional support during peak school holiday periods was eventually accepted after many years of discussion. It has since been established through many discussions and debates organised by Playwork organisations and other bodies, over recent years, that in order to be able to respond to the out-of-school play needs of children (and also the out-of-work needs of young people aged from 15 years upward using the facilities), the employment of three full-time Playworkers be the accepted basic staffing level, supplemented by additional sessional workers during busy holiday periods.

It is worth recording that the term *Play Leader* was changed in the 1970s to *Playworker* because of the need to emphasise that the leaders in play were indeed the children; the Playworker being seen as the facilitator or enabler rather than someone who initiated play behaviour. This change evolved from discussions within the APWA (see Section 6), which led in turn to the first published use of the term in Bob Hughes's *Notes for Adventure Playworkers* (1975). Playworkers undertook to operate alongside children, working with them, for them and on their behalf, but rarely if ever taking the lead, even though on certain occasions they would initiate or generate interest in a particular event. Knowing when to intervene and when to withdraw was critical in the unique relationship between the child and the Playworker.

Volunteers from the local community were heavily and frequently relied upon to give support to the paid Playworker. Further to this, some Adventure Playground projects also used volunteers from abroad organised through the International Voluntary Service Council (IVS). During the long school holiday periods some projects even used local police cadets as volunteers as well as college and university students. It is worth emphasising that voluntary support, included young people who had used the sites for many years, and in a number of situations later became paid Playworkers themselves or went into other related fields of work as a result of their experiences of working on Adventure Playgrounds.

SUPPORT AGENCIES

In the late 1950s and early 1960s a number of movements were established with the intention of developing underpinning values and operational principles, philosophical, political and practical foundations for creating and sustaining Adventure Playgrounds. Initial organisations for furthering the new concept of adventure play were:

The *Adventure Playgrounds Workers' Association* (APWA) among other activities aimed to create a more enlightened understanding of the role of Adventure Playground Workers and produced the first "Pay & Conditions for Playworkers Document" in addition to initiating discussion around the Politics and Philosophy of Play. The APWA was also instrumental in helping to establish the Joint National Committee for Training in Play Leadership, playing a very prominent role at the inaugural meeting held in a pub in Chester in 1973. It is worth noting that all the members of APWA attended meetings in various locations throughout the UK and did so without their expenses being re-claimed. I stress this in a clumsy attempt to highlight the sheer commitment of those involved in Adventure Playgrounds at a time when they received little support other than from each other. Such collective support together with very determined and united operational aims and gallant attempts to improve working conditions, was in my view, as near to a union of Playworkers as we have ever achieved. I would strongly suggest that such a united approach is in considerable contrast to what is perhaps seen in today's disparate Playwork movement.

The London Adventure Playground Association (LAPA) now named Playlink, as a major body in the Adventure Playground movement, was also an organisation which was responsible for overseeing a wide range of administrative matters including working conditions in liaison with the Inner London Education Authority (ILEA). In addition to other organisational responsibilities, it oversaw operational practices, training for management committees and staff. LAPA also determined terms of references for Adventure Playground workers in the London area.

The Fair Play for Children Campaign was launched in 1973 as a direct result of the Bishop of Stepney expressing deep concern in a letter to The Times about the deaths of two children who were playing in the Regents Canal. He linked this tragic incident to the lack of appropriate recreational spaces and places where children could express their developing personalities through play. The Fair Play for Children Campaign, supported by the NPFA, through its Regional Officer structure, initiated the concept of regional play associations/play councils which were subsequently established throughout Britain. Most of them provided direct support and assistance to the Adventure Playground movement in their individual region.

The National Playing Fields Association (NPFA) from its inception and early development campaigned vigorously for greater consideration to be given in protecting and developing spaces for recreation and children's play. The NPFA had considerable influence with regard to establishing the Adventure Playground movement throughout the country. It provided starter grants to many, which were often supplemented by the County Playing Fields Associations operating in most areas of the UK. Such grants were used to promote/provoke financial support from local authorities.

Drummond Abernethy (1977) of the NPFA, along with Lady Marjorie Allen, was energetic, vocal and tireless in stressing the importance of free and developmental play as pursued by children using Adventure Playgrounds. Through its Regional Officer structure, the NPFA offered constant support to the creation and ongoing management mechanisms needed for the enhancement and protection of provision (many of the Regional Officer staff were experienced Adventure Playground Workers). Further to this and in addition to the London APA, many local voluntary support structures emerged such as the Manchester Adventure Playgrounds Association (MAPA), Liverpool Adventure Playground Association in conjunction with and supported by Merseyside Play Action Council (MPAC), Bristol APA, and other such Associations throughout the country.

ADVENTURE PLAYGROUNDS AND INTEGRATED PLAY OPPORTUNITIES

All those involved in Adventure Playground provision from the very beginning, supported the concept of play environments for *all* children as referred to in section 3 above. With limited resources, they endeavoured to accommodate the different levels of developmental needs of children of all abilities in their everyday work. However, such an approach required a much more determined focus if provision for disabled children was to be seen as relatively equal. The Handicapped Adventure Playgrounds Association (HAPA) (1970s terminology), fully supported by Lady Marjorie Allen, was created to promote and develop the work and this resulted in the creation of the first Adventure Playground for disabled children in Chelsea, London, followed by another four in other areas such as Wandsworth, Hackney, Islington and Stockwell. A little later Calder Kids Adventure Playground was established in Calderstones Park, Liverpool, managed by Gerry Kinsella and Jim Stanton respectively, to provide opportunities distinctly for children with disabilities. I recall being involved in helping to make arrangements for a long-distance charity wheelchair push undertaken by Gerry, himself a wheelchair user. The route of the "push" and it was a real physical push because the technology of wheelchairs in those days had not developed to the extent that they are today, was from Liverpool to Hamburg and back. Gerry and Jim raised a considerable amount of money for the Adventure Playground at Calderstones.

The first fully integrated Adventure Playground outside of London was created in Blacon, Chester in the early 1970s when it extended its existing site, which involved staff and kids working alongside each other, in order to provide additional space for the introduction of extra activity areas.

Organisations such as Kids Active, now KIDS (as HAPA became) have been more than vociferous and energetic in their aim to establish the rights of *all* children to be able to access the joys and other benefits of adventure play. All Adventure Playgrounds now aim to pursue a concept of *play for all*, and indeed all Playwork training programmes should, as many do, emphasise the same philosophy.

DEVELOPMENTS ELSEWHERE IN EUROPE

Elsewhere in continental Europe during the 1960s and early 1970s, the Adventure Playground movement gathered momentum with provision being reinforced and further established in Scandinavia, Germany, Holland and many other countries. With such interest there became a desire to create an exchange of information, views, philosophies, and skills. Subsequently a loose collection of interested Adventure Playground workers and supporters formed an informal European alliance. This resulted in a number of conferences and seminars in various locations in addition to an exchange system where children and Playworkers visited and stayed in other countries whilst experiencing respective play opportunities in the different Adventure Playgrounds.

ON THE DECLINE?

Adventure Playgrounds, with 150 or more in London, began to flourish in the late 1960s and early 1970s. In the mid-1970s, a survey I conducted accounted for over 500 Adventure Playgrounds throughout the UK. However the late eighties saw a decline in their numbers due to a wide variety of factors, such as the changing social attitudes of post-war Britain. The country was becoming a society obsessed with consumerism, and social attitudes began to change, shifting gradually but perceptibly, from a nation where street and community life was based on cooperation, the sharing of resources and values and strong neighbourhood support mechanisms, perhaps to one of competition, individualism, prejudice, insularity, territorialism and social independence. The physical profiles and operational practices of Adventure Playgrounds were being perceived as eyesores and a stark contradiction to the "sophisticated" designer play provisions now being marketed. They were seen by many to be ill-disciplined, messy and noisy ghettoes. With their large, unorthodox often imposing and ramshackle timber structures built from reconstituted and recycled materials, they did not reflect the emerging and more sophisticated aspirations, attitudes and developing affluence of Britain. In addition, many officers and indeed elected members of a number of Local Authorities, considered Playworkers to be anarchists, hippies and/or aggressive and combative and ill-disciplined individuals! In my opinion they had to be all of these and much more if they were to survive and make a difference to children's lives, which most of them did (see Hughes 2012; Cranwell 2003; 2007; etc).

By far however, the greatest threat with regard to the future security of Adventure Playgrounds at this time was the Health and Safety at Work Act 1974 which began to be universally applied across the country on all work based activities and more. It was not because of what the Act actually said but because of the way people sought to misapply or misinterpret it, indeed as many still do today. A number of local authorities used the Act as an excuse for withdrawing support for Adventure Playgrounds, because of so-called safety issues. This was particularly the case in Manchester in the late 1970s when the local authority decided to close *all* the Adventure Playgrounds in the City because of its perception of safety factors relating to such provision. The Officers and Councillors chose to close the sites the week before the long school summer holidays were due to begin, demonstrating how ill-considered their decision was. Fortunately at the last hour the Council was "persuaded" at a specially convened meeting, to reverse its decision through a sensible and obvious argument suggesting that children were more likely to come to harm if left to wander the streets in search of adventurous experiences, rather than by being on the staffed sites. It is a pity that they failed to take note of the fact that Adventure Playgrounds were places where children were given opportunity to encounter risks, confront them and develop techniques to manage them. As Marjorie Allen (1968) said, "It is a rewarding experience for children to take and overcome risks, to learn to use tools with safety" She also stated later, "Better a broken bone than a broken spirit."

When considering risk in play, we need to be reminded and recognise that risk management for children, is not entirely about physical risks. Clearly many Playworkers have long understood that there is considerable social and emotional risk attached to play behaviour, but greater thought needs to be given to this aspect of play.

Further negative effects on the status of Adventure Playgrounds were, in my professional view, created by the introduction of the Children Act 1989. The misinterpretation of the Act in many cases again gave the opponents of free unadulterated play provision, ammunition to close them by cutting off funding—aided and abetted by the Government of the time. There was considerable confusion, misconception and a misapplication of the child registration process of the Act which many used to restrict and control the numbers using Adventure Playgrounds.

Further to this, the operational requirements for "childcare" environments and child/staff ratios required under the Act were wrongly applied to the informal settings of Adventure Playgrounds and other play provision that is characterized by children's free choice.

Then along came the introduction of the Out of School Child Care Initiative which directed millions of pounds to after-school child-care provision, but little if any specific funding for Adventure Playgrounds.

No-one in the Playwork profession demonstrated any hardened grievances with regard to the need for quality childcare provision at the time, quite the opposite. It was mainly supported and we all wished to see improved quality and increased provision for child care. Indeed, Play Wales for example in 1989, helped to campaign for greater child-care funding for Wales, because at that time, for every single child care place there were over 300 Welsh children in need of it. However what was of some concern was that out-of-school childcare was seen to be more weighted in favour of an economic agenda than children's play or care needs. In fact its primary stated objective was to create opportunities for young mothers to gain access to work opportunities.

Rather curiously, the creation of out-of-school child care provision was seen to be a major focus by central and local government and the only type of provision worthy of, and in need of, financial and political support. It was considered by many directly involved in Playwork, to be focussed on giving out-of-school child-care a high priority at the expense of all other out of school play facilities particularly Adventure Playgrounds. This it was felt, would mean children's access to comprehensive play opportunities would be considerably compromised.

MANUFACTURED ADVENTURE PLAYGROUNDS

It is fairly widespread practice now and has been for some time, for play equipment manufacturing companies to promote the sale of "adventure playgrounds" as they perceive them. Such a description is applied to a variety of manufactured timber structures and other items, many of which are based on items originally designed and constructed by children using traditional Adventure Playgrounds over many years. Here are a few examples:

- *Cantilever swing,* initially constructed by kids using old telegraph poles a third of which was buried at an angle in the ground and with a knotted rope passed through a hole at the top of the pole or attached to a very large eye bolt—was usually referred to as the *single pole swing.*
- A*erial runway* (or *Death Slide* as the kids called them!) was created by using telegraph poles to provide a launch platform and landing area. A snatch pulley that could be removed in the evening was the sliding mechanism from which hung a rope and/or tyre.
- S*pace nets*, on Adventure Playgrounds were originally made from a central pole and large cargo nets resourced from the dockland areas.
- *Timber forts* built on a progressive basis, added to throughout the year and every year then finally knocked down so kids could start again, all made from discarded timbers.
- Low-level *Linked play systems* that utilised old tyres, planks, logs and poles etc. to create opportunities for continuity in play, now called *trim trails* by the manufacturers.
- *Timber play huts and dens* now called play houses
- *Clatter bridges* now referred to as suspension bridges, and so it goes on.

There are so many examples of how the manufacturers have imitated the ideas which originally sprang from children's initiatives, too many to list. One of the most vital aspects that they cannot copy however, with regard to physical structures, is the process of play development. This involves a whole range of intellectual, imaginative, creative, emotional and physical activity, most of which occurs in the child's mind. There is a high level and direction of concentration and other thought processes that focus on the planning, consideration of the siting and actual construction of the structures, for instance. Then there is the use of tools and materials that means so much to children. In addition there is the sheer intensity of focus that binds and holds children together for such long periods, coupled with the realisation that they had the opportunity to determine what and how things were built and most importantly, how long they lasted! The intellectual, social and emotional process is so vitally important in play, much more so than the actual and resultant material product. This is particularly so when children engage themselves in other forms of play which are not essentially physical (see Brown 2003).

The term "adventure playgrounds" is also used all too frequently to describe play settings in commercial provision such as theme parks, holiday centres etc. All such claims are erroneous to say the least in that they harm the original concept of Adventure Playgrounds as referred to in this paper and elsewhere.

Adventure Playgrounds are places for children to pursue a comprehensive range of play experiences determined by their individual and collective play behaviour and decision making processes. Essentially they are places in which children can determine and change the content as and when they themselves decide. Much of child's play behaviour is focussed on social, imaginative and creative play. In addition, children play *with* rather than simply *on* the equipment that they create. Further to this, there are many occasions when children simply determine to *do nothing*; times when they choose to reflect, or discuss things with each other and maybe with the Playworker, the latter being a key element in the Adventure Playground setting. Very often the Playworker will be seen by the children as someone they can trust and confide in about a wide range of issues they are concerned with and which are impacting on their lives at a given time, in addition of course to being of assistance with the supply of resources for on-going play.

Frequently children will indulge in play behaviour that provides them with an opportunity to express a variety of emotions prompted by events in their individual lives. This was particularly emphasised when I assisted in creating a temporary Adventure Playground as a consequence of many people losing their homes through floods in North Wales some years back. A large number of families had to be housed in temporary accommodation. Children using the play area close to where they were temporarily accommodated, were often to be found "re-living," through play, a variety of dramatic and traumatic events that impacted on their lives during the time of the floods. Freud (1974) calls this "reconciliation"—a process that involves children using play to come to terms with traumatic events in their lives.

Manufactured adventure play areas clearly have some value and indeed are required as part of a comprehensive and wide approach to neighbourhood play provision in many localities (see Chilton 1989). However they represent a presumption that all play is based on physical activity when of course, as highlighted earlier, this is far from being the case. In over-emphasising the physical aspect of play, we are creating the same image in the eyes of the public and indeed in the perception of potential funding agencies including governments and other funding sources such as the National Lottery. It is not within the scope of this paper to describe the comprehensive differences between the original concept of Adventure Playgrounds and that of the manufacturers' catalogue (see NPFA n.d.; Chilton 1989; Chilton 2003; Brown &

Taylor 2008), but I should hope that the readers of this chapter will readily recognise the clear and obvious distinction. The process relating to the creation of a play environment and its content, is by far, more important than the finished product.

OTHER SO-CALLED INITIATIVES

There is an increasing awareness within the Playwork profession that finance from various sources of funding, including national governments and the National Lottery, is being directed to projects that purport to be Adventure Playgrounds when clearly they fall some way short of satisfying the traditional concept that has been referred to in this paper. It is of concern to learn that facilities consisting of minimal play opportunities are being claimed to be comprehensive Adventure Playground provision. This is particularly worrying when it is described as such to local communities, including children, local authorities and funding agencies. The worry is that all these bodies might well believe that such provision is fulfilling the comprehensive play needs of children of all ages. This is a misrepresentation of the original and well-grounded philosophy and spirit of the hard-working pioneers of the movement who dedicated, in exceedingly demanding circumstances, so much time and emotional, intellectual and physical energy in order to provide and protect an essentially child centred environment such as that provided by the traditional Adventure Playground.

It is unacceptable practice in my view to be promoting, as an Adventure Playground, a facility that perhaps does offer outdoor play opportunities including such things as den building, fire lighting and the like, but only does so for four hours a week and limited periods of the year. I am aware that many of those involved in promoting and delivering such provision do so entirely with the needs of children in mind and perhaps in the hope that the scheme will develop into something more substantial in the long term. Maybe it could also be the case that a little is better than none. However to insist on calling such provision a fully-fledged Adventure Playground, is a compromise too far and is doing considerable harm to the concept. More importantly it is misleading and selling children short. Although such facilities are well-meaning and do indeed offer a valuable service to children even if only on a limited basis, they should be used to emphasise the fact that children deserve decidedly much more than this. Although a full-time Adventure Playground is not cheap to operate, it is not expensive in the long term when it saves so much by way of children's lives and contributes so much to their all-round growth and development. Furthermore there are so many real short and long term benefits to the local and wider community. We surely must campaign for and stress the fact children deserve and need comprehensive all-year round play opportunities which are staffed by well-trained and properly resourced Playworkers and local management bodies.

DOES THE SPIRIT OF ADVENTURE PLAYGROUNDS STILL SURVIVE?

A few years ago, in response to the distinct absence of a comprehensive understanding of the real value of traditional Adventure Playgrounds in many areas of the UK, Play Wales determined that there was a need to regenerate interest in sustaining and promoting the ethos underpinning a well-established and proven concept. Play Wales subsequently organised a Seminar in North Wales with the title, "The Spirit of Adventure Playgrounds." The Seminar attracted considerable interest from across the UK and has proved to be a well-supported, impressively attended annual event and has been held in Cardiff ever since.

Sadly, in my personal view, Play Wales decided to remove Adventure Playgrounds from the title and so the Seminar is now called the *Spirit of Play* or simply *The Spirit.*

So, does the spirit of Adventure Playgrounds still persist? Do the original operational practices still exist, particularly with regard to the need for the sites and their content to be constantly changing so that children can develop new ideas and ways of approaching the use and development of various play features? Is it still the case that Adventure Playgrounds are creating a feeling among children that there is always something new going on! Or is the physical content of Adventure Playgrounds left in a state of semi-permanency because the Playworkers have been too much involved in the building and "ownership" of the main structures? In this context I am mindful of the observation of Bernard McGovern in his book *Playleadership* (1973), he suggested that:

> Many of these playgrounds now consist of mammoth man-made constructions such as forts, towers, giant slides, tunnels, and tree houses, buildings with all modern conveniences and in some cases as many as four or five play leaders now on the staff. . . . We have now reached the stage where the Adventure Playground equipment is being commercially manufactured with the accent on safety. Designs are changing and the Adventure Playground is in danger of becoming new look conventional playgrounds, with little to stimulate the imagination of children who frequent them.

I have to express some support for McGovern's concerns, having visited so many sites myself over the years. There appears to be little enthusiasm from some Playworkers to follow the traditional maxim that Adventure Playgrounds should be constantly changing by reflecting children's need to regularly try out new ideas and extend their creativity and their imaginations.

They are/were places where there was/is always something new and different happening. If Playworkers take too much control in developing the content of the play environment, then the rich pattern of play behaviour changes and is replaced with repetitive, perhaps static play, through being focussed on the same permanent items. It is distinctly possible that if the Playworker becomes over-protective of existing features which he or she has had a prominent role in creating, regular change to layout and content of the site would not be encouraged. As a consequence there would be little scope for children to exercise their own initiatives. Spontaneity, a very vital part of play, continuity and creative play, together with collaborative behaviour would perhaps fail to emerge or be considerably stunted. Further to this, the desire for learning and developing new skills would also be given little opportunity for expression.

PLAYWORK FOUNDATIONS

The Playwork profession has its roots undeniably embedded and firmly attached to the intrinsic nature of play and is unique in its approach to working with children in that it is decidedly focused on, among other principles, the following:

- Establishing a child centred focus on the creation of a free-play environment
- Developing a variety of outlets and opportunities for children to pursue their own play choices in their own time, in their own way and at their own pace.
- Enhancing and enriching the play environment by the creation, and through the promotion of opportunities for a wide and varied range of experiences relating to exploration, invention, creativity, experimentation, social interaction, improvisation, and a strong sense of self- realisation.
- Establishing appropriate practices for addressing the negative and destructive forces of play deprivation.
- Promoting a process of communication and other human response mechanisms which recognise the individuality and developing personalities of individual children.

- Providing and protecting a flexible, adaptable physical and social play environment able to accommodate a child's individual and changing needs.
- Adopting a style of intervention that is responsive rather than reactive, to the expressed needs of children.

When considering the understanding of the *spirit of adventure play* in the context of staffed provision, I am reminded of all those who were directly involved in the very early days of the creation of Adventure Playgrounds. Those who established and were wholly committed to the concept and who worked so hard to develop them by making them, in my considered view, one of the most comprehensive and successful means of providing for all types of play for all types, sizes, ages, abilities and backgrounds of children.

I take this opportunity not only to acknowledge the commitment and efforts of those I have had the distinct pleasure of working alongside and being in the company of in many years gone by, but to thank them unreservedly for highlighting the importance of children's play in human terms. These are people who worked without any sense of job security, outdoors in all weathers throughout the year (some even opened on Christmas Day because of the express needs of the kids!) and who worked with no indoor accommodation or welfare facilities for themselves and with little or no support and understanding of how valuable their work was and indeed is:

- Those who were faced with difficult operational conditions in some of the most socially neglected, hostile and challenging communities in the UK.
- Those who confronted the local authorities and indeed central government with arguments and demands to improve the quality of play provision in local areas.
- Those who made the effort to knock on every door in the communities where they worked in order to generate involvement and create awareness of the importance of children's out of school play needs.
- Those who chose to live in the communities where they worked so they could develop a more enlightened view of local social problems and establish an empathy with the rest of those living there.
- Those who worked in very isolated districts and were very much unsupported but carried on because of their commitment to and belief in the play needs of local kids.
- Those who laid the foundations for so many successive developments in Playwork generally, for I believe the precursor to so much that has been established in the profession today in the UK, stems from the Adventure Playground movement of earlier times.

- Those who set the scene for adequate and appropriate working conditions, support mechanisms, training, and an understanding of the philosophical and psychological approach to play development.
- Those who chose to determine that Playwork was an independent profession in its own right and one not to be dovetailed into or attached to other areas of work and in doing so have its importance considerably undermined and diluted.

In highlighting the professional and unselfish commitment of those involved in the early development of Adventure Playgrounds, I hope I have raised an awareness of the importance of the need for our on-going support. If we are not only to protect the child's right to play but to also ensure that the concept is given due political support and financial consideration, then we need to do so much more. Currently we appear to accept provision on the criteria of funding systems and politically determined requirements rather than on actual and real need.

If a minimum of staffed play provision is seen to be acceptable then we would be demonstrating a serious disservice to all those who dedicated so much of their working lives in the interest of children and young people and the undeniable importance of play in human development. I refer to those who have gone before us and those currently among us in this profession, who believed and still believe passionately in the value of play as an essential and integral part of a child's life. In particular the early pioneers contributed enormously to the creation of the concept of Adventure Playgrounds, rightly seeing them as a significant contribution to the human and developmental play needs of *all* children and young people. It is therefore vital that we all ensure that we do not compromise on the level of provision or undersell play by accepting unrelated, externally determined criteria and restrictive funding mechanisms that fall short of what is required. We have to stress that provision should not be seen as a cheap and undervalued means of simply "keeping kids off the street" or as an anti-crime device, it is so much more essential and vital than this. Play has to be recognised as an integral and natural part of the child's right to healthy and total development. So above all else, we have a responsibility not to compromise to the child's detriment by accepting poor quality responses to what is needed. Should we not prioritise now in relation to the provision of quality play experiences for current and future requirements, or do we pay later with expensive intervention methods when all too frequently, it is far too late?

Finally, I am of the firm belief that if we intend to stand by a commitment to the promotion of the vital importance of play in the all-round human development of children, then we need to take more than a cursory glance back at the history of the Adventure Playground movement. We surely must give serious thought and undertake vigorous and determined action to sustain the unselfish commitment of those, who in the past gave so much for the future. In this regard I am reminded, of the words of Maya Angelou:

No man can know where he is going unless he knows exactly where he has been and exactly how he arrived at his present place (*New York Times*, April 16, 1972).

REFERENCES

Abernethy, D.W. (1977) *Notes and papers: a general survey on children's play provision.* London: National Playing Fields Association.

Allen of Hurtwood, Lady (1968) *Planning for play.* London: Thames and Hudson.

Bertelsen, J. (1972) Early Experience from Emdrup. In: Bengtsson, A. (ed) *Adventure playgrounds*. London: Crosby Lockwood.

Brown, F. (2003) *Playwork theory and practice*. Buckingham: Open University Press.

Brown, F. & Taylor, C. (2008) *Foundations of playwork.* Maidenhead: Open University Press.

Chilton, T. (1989) *Where can children play?* Rhyl Community Agency.

———. (2003) Adventure playgrounds in the 21st century. In: Brown, F. (ed.) *Playwork: theory and practice* Buckingham: Open University Press.

Cranwell, K. (2003) Towards a History of Adventure Playgrounds 1931–2000, in Norman, N. (2004) *An architecture of play: a survey of london's adventure playgrounds.* London: Four Corners.

Cranwell,K. (2007) Adventure Playgrounds and the Community in London (1948–70): An Appreciation of the Ideas and Actions that Shaped the Spirit of the 1960's Play Movement, in Russell, W., Handscomb, B. and Fitzpatrick, J. (eds.) *Playwork voices: in celebration of Bob Hughes and Gordon Sturrock.* London Centre for Playwork Education and Training.

Evening News (1947) "Junk Playground Keeps These Children Happy." *Evening News,* Thursday November 6.

Freud, S. (1974) *The standard edition of the complete psychological works of Sigmund Freud.* 24 volumes, translated from the German under the general editorship of James Strachey, in collaboration with Anna Freud; assisted by Alix Strachey and Alan Tyson. London: Hogarth Press, Institute of Psycho-Analysis.

Hughes, B., (1975) *Notes for adventure playworkers.* London:CYAG.

———. (2012) *Evolutionary playwork*. London: Routledge.

McGovern, B. (1973) *Playleadership.* London: Faber.

NPFA (n.d.) *What is an adventure playground?* London: National Playing Fields Association.

Pellis, S. & Pellis, V. (2009) *The playful brain: venturing to the limits of neuroscience.* London: Oneworld Publications.

Sorensen, C.Th. (1931) Open Spaces for Town and Country. Cited in Allen of Hurtwood, Lady (1968) *Planning for play.* London: Thames & Hudson.

———. (1951) Junk Playgrounds. *Danish Outlook* 4.1.

Taylor, C. (2008) Some Reflections on the History of Playwork in the Adventure Playground Tradition. In: Brown, F. & Taylor, C. (2008) *Foundations of playwork.* Maidenhead: Open University Press.

Chapter Twelve

Hysterical about Playwork

Maxine Delorme

INTRODUCTION

Play should be dictated by the child; that is the content, intent and mode (Hughes 2014). Play is absolutely vital and should be accepted for what it is—a natural human behaviour, unquantifiable by science, with benefits that are complex, personal, circumstantial, and situation specific. Since I was introduced to the unique practical application of playwork and its theoretical concepts I have been hooked on exploring these and understanding how they work in practice. This exploration has developed my understanding of reflexivity (the relationship between cause and effect) and led me to question the sequential nature of the relationship between the effect that the practical application of playwork theory has on children's play, and the relevance of our professional ideology and its underlying theory in relation to the ever changing circumstances of the world we live in. Critical thought is essential to professional development and this chapter is an overview of some of my thoughts around the analysis of the playwork profession in terms of its theory's relevance to the current situation, since its beginnings in early adventure playgrounds.

In my opinion the most basic yet pertinent playwork concept is the idea that play should be fun, free and flexible (Brown, 2014). Of course there are many benefits to play such as communication, socialisation, increased confidence and self-esteem, but these are secondary. Without the three F's, play loses its identity. Its characteristics and personality are lost and all that remains is structured, prescriptive activity of some description for children to take part in. One of the key differentiators between playwork and other childcare professions is the inherent understanding of the value of play in its own right, without any adult-centric agendas. This contrasts with other situations where activities are often predetermined in order to enable certain developmental attributes to be observed, such as gross and fine motor skills in certain age groups of children. Generally speaking, playwork supports a child-centred agenda, which many other childcare professions do not. However, even within the playwork profession, practice often reflects what is thought by adults to be the "best way" simply in order to be seen to be implementing "good practice." This is an example of an *inadvertent agenda*, wherein the adult believes they are doing what is best for the child by following prescribed methods, but this preoccupation means that the child is no longer the priority. This is what I have come to know as seeking status (as a playworker) without the solidarity that comes from a sound understanding of the application of theory in practice.

Playwork is often found in after school provision, holiday clubs, hospitals, prisons and adventure playgrounds (Brown, 2014). Of the above settings, adventure playgrounds are alone in providing children's spaces, whereas playwork tends to be a secondary provision of the other examples alongside their primary functions. The original intent of adventure playgrounds was to enable children to create their own spaces during a period of devastation to infrastructure, communities and individual families during World War II (Kozlovsky, 2013). The resources used consisted of anything that was readily available at the time and children did as they pleased, often building fires and structures in order to keep warm, heat water or cook upon. The fire was a result of the circumstances and the fact that this involved a degree of risk was inherent in the activity. In the re-created children's play spaces that exist today, fire has been appropriated as a tool that affords risk. Originally, circumstances demanded that fire be an aspect of adventure playgrounds for practical reasons that are no longer present. Creating a play space to influence behaviours that adults know to be beneficial is effectively an example of what is understood to be adulteration (Sturrock and Else, 1998). Adulteration is adult interference or intrusion in children's play, which effectively removes the control, content or intent from the child. It is my view that there are two-forms of this, beyond simply "adulteration." Any obvious adult interference such as dictating, redirecting or actively constraining a child's play constitutes primary adulteration, while secondary adulteration is more complex and may arise from a range of circumstances. One of the main features of the adventure playground should be that the children design, build and create the space. There are playgrounds today that have the same structures that they did fifteen years ago, nothing has changed and the structures no longer mean anything to anyone other than the adults who once played there and possibly some nostalgic Playworkers. This is an example of secondary adulteration.

Adventure playgrounds are completely unique to the geographic location and the children who play there. There should not be a typical structure defining its function or appearance, as every one should be unique and specific to location and the people who will use it. In contrast, the *playwork aesthetic* is a term for the overall appearance of the profession based on the threads (components), which give the profession its overall appearance. Adventure playgrounds have become a key thread in the playwork aesthetic and without generalizing too much, many modern day adventure playgrounds have adopted the components of the aesthetic, but have ignored or wrongly understood the rationale and in many cases what I describe as an *inadvertent agenda* has developed. The intention to support an environment that is conducive to good practice is evident but the understanding of the theory and adaptation to circumstance has been missed. This misinterpretation of theory or misrepresentation of the ideas in practice leads to settings with diminished playwork value.

The example of the adventure playground is just one of many that depicts my frustration with the way playwork is (mis)interpreted and (mis) understood. Another example of this is the use to which Hughes's (2002) *Taxonomy of Play Types* are put. In many ways this is insightful and useful for practitioners to identify and understand the complexities of children's play. Through personal experiences in after school clubs for example, it is clear that many (not all) playworkers use this theory as a means to structure play or activities with the hope of children exhibiting a range of play types as this is seen to be good practice. But this is effectively turning the theory on its head—the play types are simply terms to describe play behaviours exhibited by children. They were never intended to be a tick list of behaviours that playworkers should strive to ensure are performed. This is yet another instance of the misinterpretation of theory and misrepresentation of playwork ideals in practice.

Play itself should be flexible but the theory that gives the compensatory, facilitatory playwork profession its structure should be absolute. The theory supports playworkers' understanding of the notion of "fun, freedom and flexibility" (Brown, 2014). Therefore, different individual interpretations are not consistent or representative of the underpinning thinking behind playwork. Cultural variations and evolutionary changes in society will always provide new meanings for the role of a Playworker, and playing will always be a flexible engagement of actions by children and playworkers based on children's individual needs. Despite these inevitable variations within the social realm, playwork seems to be regressing towards components of its past, such as fire and den building, and these are becoming threads of the new playwork aesthetic. By regressing towards the past, playwork is contradicting one of its key aspects, flexibility. Flexibility is an essential component in adapting to the child's needs and how they want to play. We live in a time where realistic digital gaming has become a popular way of playing during childhood and adolescence, and there is evidence against the view of this as a solitary, motionless activity with negative implications for children's behaviour and psyche (Olson, 2010). It seems obvious that playwork should be embracing the many different ways of playing, including those that take place virtually, in order to fully satisfy its own claims of flexibility as well as children's desire to play freely.

The role of the playworker is to captivate and accommodate play in order to preserve play's freedom, purity and fluidity and to ensure that it is uncontaminated by intrusion. In order to achieve this, playworkers and the playwork profession must understand these changes and how this affects the relevance of theory and its application in practice. Bourdieu's theory of practice sheds light on the nature of the relationship between playwork theory and practice, while Lefebvre's concept of socially constructed space provides new perspective on the analysis of influences on children's play. Towards the end of this chapter I introduce my own ideas regarding intent, agendas, and modes of play with the aim of showing that there are deeper complexities to some of the theories that are seen as absolute, and that by understanding this we as playworkers will be better equipped to properly implement theory-based practice.

A BOURDIEUSIAN ANALYSIS OF PLAYWORK

Abbott (1988) explores the ideal profession in relation to medicine and law, suggesting that the system of professions have a control of knowledge, skills and work tasks, which are the most important aspects of the profession. In relation to Playwork, if we don't have control over the knowledge, skill set and work tasks (specificity in the way we practice within the profession), we cannot hold professional status when the theory that constitutes the profession is being distorted through lack of knowledge and understanding.

Twentieth century French social philosopher Pierre Bourdieu's concern with the philosophy of the everyman led him to develop his *Theory of Practice*, which has been applied to analysis of a range of subjects *(Grenfell, 2008)*. Bourdieu used his own terminology to describe the complexities of social groups, their experiences and their typical routines. Application to the field of Playwork sheds new light on the relationship between playwork theory and playwork practice—the progressive nature of the field's influence on the individual and the subsequent impact on the field of the individual *agent*'s actions.

In Bourdieu's terms, the *field* describes the current time, location and state of a profession, but includes the current knowledge, development, past understanding and all involved including practitioners and beneficiaries. It is the network of relationships within a social space (not only of people, but of knowledge, power, wealth and all other social constructs). Everything the individual knows about the world is established through the individual's perceptions of the field, which are a combination of (1) *doxa*, the unquestioned realities that inform practice regardless of their legitimacy, and (2) *habitus*, a set of perception-, appreciation- and practice-generating dispositions. Doxic experiences inform our habitus, which in turn informs our actions. An example of this might be "working class kids tend to get working class jobs or middle class readers tend to enjoy middle-brow literature," even though there are no explicit rules that dictate this behaviour (Grenfell, 2008). Note that practice and field are not synonymous—practice is a phenomenon derived from individual agents' habituses within a contextual field.

Habitus and field present a dialectic in which practices produce and reproduce the world that is at the same time making them (Grenfell, 2008). Social practices are characterised by social regularities without explicit rules (i.e., what we understand to be "the norm"). But conforming to the prevailing doxa without thought or question can be damaging, particularly when their arbitrariness is recognised yet practiced regardless (*orthodoxy*). This may lead to the situation whereby *hysteresis* may occur—the de-synchronization of habitus and field. While habitus and field are mutually constitutive, habitus can be driven by conditions that no longer exist yet may continue to influence practice. If recognised this is a chaotic situation in which practice is no longer informed by relevant conditions and as such there is opportunity for change and progression. If unrecognised this has the potential to be detrimental to the profession in terms of limiting the scope of progression. Those well-equipped in terms of standing within the field (*capital*) are best able to exploit these opportunities, while those whose actions are aligned to past habitus are ill-positioned to capitalize on the current situation. In contrast, my research is an example of *heterodoxy*—the intent to challenge the prevailing doxa based on a recognition of it as such; in this case the recognition of the hysteresis between the intended application of theory and current playwork practice.

Although a time is not known exactly as to when and where Playwork emerged there is much to suggest that Playwork began and still acts as a compensatory profession. Playwork's compensatory attributes began based on a set of circumstances and conditions that are believed to stem from the Second World War. Those circumstances left children with almost nothing specifically to play with—it was their chance to create their own play environments based on how they felt and what they were interested in, with little or even no interruption from war-aftermath-preoccupied adults (Kozlovsky,

2013). Despite the horrific conditions at this time, this was perhaps the freest time for children truly to play for their own reasons, in their own way without any influence from adults—something that we strive for as playworkers. The conditions prompted children to use the natural environment and anything they could get hold of to create shelters, structures and fires. These examples developed into the common features of early adventure playgrounds, as at this time these were the environments that children would choose for themselves. Part of the playwork ideology is maintaining a flexible approach in practice in order to meet the needs and agenda of any child. Today it would be fair to say that Playwork is often characterised as building dens and building fires, rather than these being intrinsically motivated features of a child's own play environment. Many modern-day adventure playgrounds feature these circumstantial features derived from the conditions that children found in the immediate aftermath of the Second World War. By continuing these practices, whose conditions are arguably now irrelevant, the playwork profession is demonstrating hysteresis.

INADVERTENT AGENDAS

In playwork one of the key components of good practice relating specifically to the way in which we work and relate to children, is "agendas." I find the concept of an agenda difficult to characterize simplistically, as in one way or another everyone has one, despite conscious recognition. It is implicit that a Playworker must work with children in a way that is fully supportive and facilitative of their needs and preferences so that it is, as much as possible, child led. The idea of "leaving your problems at the door" is crucial in maintaining a child focused environment. The concept of adulteration (Sturrock and Else, 1998) (adults intruding and influencing play) is very relevant in the discussion of agendas. Adulteration can be very obvious to identify, for example, an adult interrupting a child playing because he or she believes they can show the child how to play in a "better way." This is an example of adulteration, but also it demonstrates that the adult does not possess an agenda that is indicative of the knowledge and understanding that fully supports the value of child-led play.

An *inadvertent agenda* can be defined as possessing an agenda that is unintentional or consciously unknown to the individual (Delorme, 2014). This can be because of hysteresis, as described by theory or practice, or because the individual/agent seeks the *status* of being a playworker, but lacks *solidarity* as their agenda is not child led. Due to the *hysteresis effect*, a playworker may continue to act in a manner derived from their understanding of good practice, when this understanding is conditioned by their experience (habitus and doxa) within the field, which is itself derived from conditions which no longer exist. *Inadvertent agendas* are what I believe to be a possible cause of the "misinterpretations of playwork." It seems that in order to have complete clarity of one's own agenda it is imperative to have a complete understanding of three things first: 1) the importance of play and child-led play; 2) what affects children playing in their own way for their own reasons; 3) the extent to which children's play can be adulterated. By acknowledging these provisos, the likelihood of establishing a child-led agenda is increased.

A LEFEBVRIAN ANALYSIS OF PLAY

According to the French philosopher Henri Lefebvre, time, space and social interactions make up everything. Without time we would have no concept of life or routine, without space there would be no realm for life and without social interactions there would not be any of the social structures that allow individuals to live their lives (Lefebvre, 1991). The three are interconnected—without one the other two are meaningless. Play exists within and relies upon all three of the previously mentioned components—time, space and social interactions.

Lefebvre's idea of socially constructed space lends its self well to the analysis of children's play. When we understand play as a non-physical combination of space, time and social structure, Lefebvre's terms—lived, perceived and conceived spaces—become highly applicable. Conceived space is that which is defined by dominant groups in society, such as government, urban designers and architects, through prescribed rule or regulation. It confines people within either physical or more temporal barriers, which can include anything from walls and boundaries, to law, policy and rules. Perceived space embraces the idea of social practice—the space is a product of the normative functions and everyday routines that people go through. These routines of everyday life are learnt through organisation, rationalization and commodification. Organisation and rationalization are stages that must be completed before absolute perception and commodification of the space is possible; commodification is accepting the culture of the space, without having to organize or rationalize the routines within that culture. Lived space exists outside of the rules and barriers that intervene in our ideal worlds (Lefebvre, 1991).

> Play lies outside the antithesis of wisdom and folly, and equally outside those of truth and falsehood, good and evil. Although it is a non-material activity it has no moral function. The valuations of vice and virtue do not apply here. (Huizinga, 1949: 6)

While Bourdieu's theory is applicable to playwork practice, Lefebvre's spatial triad is more appropriate for analysis of play and the influences upon it, which may include everything from political manifesto to architecture and engineering, landscaping and social construction. Lefebvre's spatial triad makes it clear how a number of small influences or changes can combine to become something significant. As this theory is based on social construction, and is not specific to play and playwork, it is useful in understanding influences from outside of the field.

SPATIAL RESIDENCE AND DUAL SPATIAL OWNERSHIP

Ideally play should be freely chosen, intrinsically motivated (Hughes 2012), fun, free and flexible (Brown 2014) therefore play should reside between a Lived Space and Perceived Space. Based on a number of influences play might be affected in a way that causes it to move to a different space, one that is not representative of a space that is freely chosen, intrinsically motivated, fun, free and flexible. As mentioned previously, playwork is a compensatory profession. It compensates for the lack of understanding of the importance of child-led play with minimal interference, and acts as an advocate. The profession's (subconscious) intention to reside in a Lived Space is morally legitimate, however due to influences from a capitalist society that has a focused agenda of capital return, commodity, success and international social hierarchy, the ability for playwork to occupy a Lived Space has inadvertently been diminished.

It is effectively impossible to facilitate play opportunities that reside entirely in a Lived Space, and indeed it is equally impossible for any aspect of life to reside entirely in one of the three spaces alone. In the same way that space, time and social interaction are interlinked, due to the realities of the world that we live in, there are always Conceived or Perceived influences on children's play. Therefore, play will reside in a combined space, and this is what I have termed Dual Spatial Ownership (see Fig.12.1).

The stance of the profession that follows the fun free and flexible approach could in itself be construed as contradictory. The implementation of theory in practice to achieve certain goals (e.g., fun, freedom, flexibility) in itself imposes constraints upon children's play. Fun, freedom and flexibility are implicit in play that is facilitated by proper implementation of theory, and are not goals to strive for. A space intended as a "play space" is by definition precluded from being solely a Lived Space. Playwork aims to support what Rasmussen (2004) describes as "Children's Places," where children control the creation of the space and the way they play in it, more in line

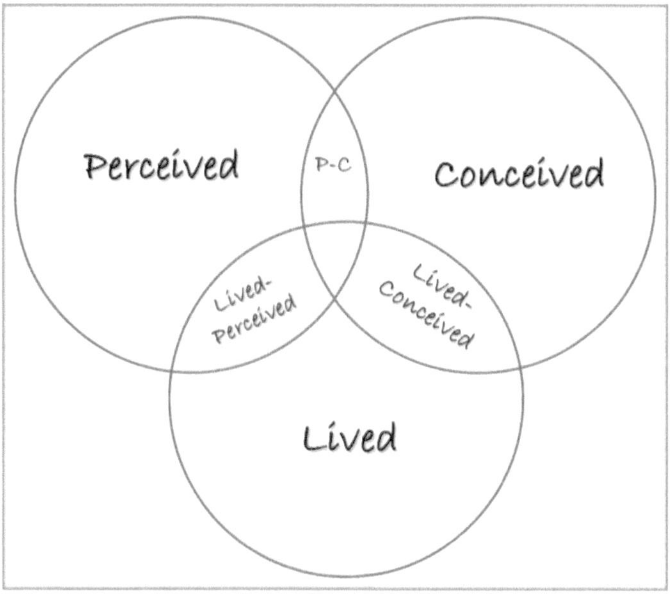

Figure 12.1. Spatial triad interaction

with Lefebvre's Lived Space. The imposition by adults of the intent for a "play space" must result in a partially Conceived Space, as these kinds of "places" or "spaces" are adult-led, designed and created with the intention of predetermining the kind of places children play in, and how they play in them, resulting in a Lived-Conceived space. Play inevitably resides partially in the Perceived Space, as by its definition this envelopes any "culture of the space." So within any play, there are elements of the perceived "norms," be they within the play itself or in the wider environment or social construct. In summary, play will always reside in a combined tri-space (the middle part of the diagram in Figure 12.1) often moving or being moved into one of the dual Lived-Perceived or Lived-Conceived spaces and the ideal completely lived space is unattainable. As playworkers we must strive to maximise play's residence in the lived space.

INTENT, INTENSIONS AND AGENDAS

Content and intent are common terms in playwork. For many of us they are learned expressions that have stuck—"children must control the content and intent of their own play, it is a biological necessity," or something similar

(Hughes, 2001). For me this became a common preface in assignment writing during my time at university. I imagine that for most playworkers, explaining what a playworker is and does becomes a monotonous activity. This is how I feel about it—I always find myself having to justify the importance of playwork, during which the topic of intent often comes up—mainly in those conversations that allow for further substantiation. It is important that the child chooses the content of their play as this is what we as playworkers aim to achieve—child-led play. Intent on the other hand is perhaps the more important aspect, as it effectively constitutes play. As Huizinga (1949) describes it, play is a step out of real life into a temporary sphere of activity with a disposition of its own (location, intent, duration, content). Without holding the intent, play cannot be play. Lack of intent results in a prescribed activity that has not been chosen by the player. That is at best a forcible imitation of play.

Commodifying or creating either capital or professional recognition is contradictory to playwork ethos as the agenda is not specifically child centric. It is sometimes what Huizinga (1949) terms "false play," having the appearance of play characteristics but being used for another purpose. Even naming the profession "playwork" is an attempt at commodifying it. Here it is important to differentiate between playwork and play itself.

Even if playworkers provide an environment with many opportunities for exploration and playfulness, sometimes other children affect the intent in such a way that less dominant children do not hold the intent for their play as they submit to that of those who are more dominant. This is one of the less obvious intent barriers children face but particularly relevant to this discussion. Despite my intentions, from time to time I find myself thinking developmentally (not in the here and now as most playworkers do) and I do not think that this is a bad thing as long as it doesn't interfere in my judgment as a playworker. Children may still benefit and find that the enjoyment of play still resides, regardless of not holding the intent to begin with. They may find that they develop intent as a result of being put in an unknown situation to begin with—for example, they might try something new in order to gain social kudos.

Playwork, from the viewpoint of its underlying theories, exists in the Macro-scale rather than the Micro-scale. Ideally, in a world of infinite opportunities the child would choose how and when to play. But even in this ideal situation a child would not have true control over the content and intent as even with all the time, space and variables in the world, social interaction would be missing, which can heavily influence both of these. The ideal is not achievable in real life as it is always constrained by something e.g., space, time, social structures. So within each situation-specific set of constraints, one or more of these may be predetermined, meaning that the child's intent is automatically diminished. Calling a space a "play space" is in itself predefining the macro intent of the space—to play. "Children's spaces" would be a more appropriate term as this gives ownership rather than definition. The macro and micro intent would be determined by the child, i.e., if, when, how and why the child plays within this space.

In terms of the way we as playworkers understand intent, there seems to be a split between the macro and micro. On the macro-scale, playworkers indiscriminately employ theory and methods that are thought to underpin good practice, such as *loose parts* play. Loose parts play is defined thus: "in any environment the level of creativity and inventiveness is directly proportional to the number of variables in it" (Nicholson, 1971). The original theory was depicting the ideal environment for children to play, with variables and resources that stimulate children. These can include the type of environment, the range of natural resources available (avoiding secondary adulteration), the weather and atmosphere. However, in many instances this theory is used to structure an activity, by providing arbitrary resources, often recycled materials, to instigate creativity and inventiveness. This is a misrepresentation of the theory which has caused conflict between theory and practical application leading to 1) secondary adulteration through structured activity in order to depict loose parts play, which also illustrates an *inadvertent agenda* 2) constrained play conditions.

So while in the ideal situation at any time and place a child might choose to play in any way, in the real world at a certain time, in a specific place children are being prescribed activities that are designed to achieve an adult determined outcome. When Loose Parts is prescribed, the macro-intent is predetermined in that the child has no control over the type of play they will engage in or when and where they will do so; but within the activity, the child will still control the micro-intent, i.e., they will engage with the variables available in whatever way they want and need.

MODES OF PLAY

One final interesting misinterpretation to consider is the understanding of play types. Many playworkers try to plan activities in order to achieve types of play e.g., "risky play." *The Taxonomy of Play Types* was developed by Hughes (2002) to describe the different ways in which children behave during play. However, this theory has sometimes been misappropriated almost as a planning tool, in order to ensure certain play behaviours are demonstrated during an activity. It is the misunderstanding of the difference between the types of play displayed such as deep, imaginative or social, and the modes

Table 12.1. Play Modes and Play Types: a small selection

Play Modes		*Play Types*
Risk		Deep
Challenge		Social
Adventure	*Play by these modes can lead*	Imaginative
Solitude	*to these play types*	Creative
Social		Locomotor
Digital/Electronic		Mastery
. . .		. . .

of play, which are the methods and activities employed by playworkers and/or the opportunities and variables within children's own play. For instance, playing digitally (which I consider to be a play mode) might lead to the demonstration of certain play types—creative, imaginative, social etc., but digital play itself is not a play type. Table 12.1 above shows a small selection of play modes and types to help highlight this difference.

FINAL REMARKS

These are a collection of my thoughts and ideas that I am accumulating throughout my research. I acknowledge that this chapter is in its own way quite critical and may stimulate discussion and potential criticism, and I welcome this whole heartedly. The purpose of this chapter and my own research is to begin to unpick the complexities of the profession, and encourage others to do so in a way that is supportive of the development and success of playwork. I hope that others will question and begin to pay greater attention to how they adhere to the theory that informs our practice. If you have read the previous pages you will know that I am not referring to the implementation of every known theory in relation to playwork practice in order to satisfy "good practice" within playwork provision. I am simply suggesting a more relaxed and realistic approach to playwork (note, the complex sociological analyses of Bourdieu and Lefebvre are a means to analyse the profession and its impact on children).

Essentially as playworkers we aspire to create opportunities for children to play because we know—aside from all of the developmental stuff—children will play wherever, whenever with whoever and whatever (paraphrasing Ward, 1979). It is absolutely a drive, a need, a compulsion and more than anything it is the best part of being a child. There aren't enough adjectives to quantify what play does for children, long or short term. If giving or taking a little criticism about our own practice means protecting what playworkers live and breathe, facilitating and supporting play, then it is certainly worth doing so. I believe it is human nature to protect ourselves or want to make justifications for our wrong doings or misjudgments so as not to appear to have done so in the first place. However, change is usually a good thing, and it is therefore essential to question the norms within the profession in order to progress, develop and continue to maintain the unique qualities of play. Further, change is essential if we as are to overcome and move beyond the hysterical set of theories that we currently base our practice upon.

REFERENCES

Abbott, A. (1998) *The system of professions: An essay on the division of expert labour.* Chicago, IL: Chicago University Press.

Brown, F. (2003) Compound flexibility: The role of playwork in child development. In: Brown, F. *Playwork theory and practice*. Maidenhead: Open University Press.

———. (2014) *Play and playwork: 101 stories of children playing*. Maidenhead: Open University Press.

Delorme, M. (2014) *Playwork in space: A Lefebvrian analysis of the evolution of the playwork profession.* Leeds Beckett University. Unpublished.

Grenfell, M., (2008) *Pierre Bourdieu—key concepts*. Durham: Acumen.

Hughes, B. (2001) *The first claim: A framework for playwork quality assessment.* Cardiff: PlayWales.

———. (2002) *A playworker's taxonomy of play types*. London. PLAYLINK.

———. (2012) *Evolutionary playwork*. London: Routledge.

Huizinga, J. (1949) *Homo ludens: A study of the play-element in culture*. Routledge and Kegan Paul. London, Boston and Henley.

Kozlovsky, R. (2013) *The architectures of childhood: Children, architecture and reconstruction in modern day England.* Surrey: Ashgate Publishing Limited.

Lefebvre, H. (1991) *The production of space*. Translated from the French by D. Nicholson-Smith. Oxford: Blackwell.

Nicholson, S. (1971) How not to cheat children: the theory of loose parts. *Landscape Architecture Quarterly.* Vol 62, No.1, October 1971, pp 30–34.

Olson, K. C. (2010) Children's motivations for video game play in the context of normal development. *American Psychological Association.* Vol, 14. No.2.

Rasmussen, K. (2004) *Places for children—children's places*. Roskilde University Centre. SAGE Publications. London.

Sturrock, G. and Else, P. (1998) The playground as therapeutic space: playwork as healing. In: *Proceedings of the IPA/USA Triennial National Conference, Play in a Changing Society: Research, Design, Application*. June 1998, Colorado. USA.

Ward, C. (1979) *The child in the city*. Harmondsworth: Penguin.

Chapter Thirteen

A Quantum Of Playwork

Playful Rhetorics Relating to Sub-Atomic Activity in Play Moments and a Playworker's Responses

Bob Hughes

> The amount of research devoted to a topic in human behaviour is inversely proportional to its importance and interest.
>
> —Murstein's Law

> All science begins in myth.
>
> —Albert Einstein

Foreword: As the reader will guess, I found the title, let alone the argument for this piece incredibly elusive—impossible to pin down. It was as if the very subject itself wanted to avoid being written about and as a consequence, it disappeared, hid, evaporated, went tiny and then huge. The subject matter was playing children's games with me; hide and seek, tag and blind man's buff, demonstrating continually that I was no match for the attempted focus of my thoughts, the tiny sub-atomic particles that fill the universe. Of course this could have been because the subject, *was* too big or complex; too big for me anyway; but it could also have been because it really didn't want to be written about! This quantum world is very strange indeed, and made more so, by the difficulty of finding language, or even mental pictures, to capture it long enough to describe one's imaginings. So what this piece represents is a preliminary attempt to capture some suppositions and surmises that I know have puzzled and intrigued me and other play people over the years.

INTRODUCTION

It is interesting that the range of metaphor applied to play has been in accord with the narrative themes of the age, from Plato to Panksepp, from democracy to evolution. The linking of play to quantum activity is simply a continuation of that tradition.

Writing this has been a fun project, but it has also been a frightening one, particularly when the literature and my imagined scenarios have together created a world I did not expect, had never even dreamed of and which destabilised my then held view; a world in which quantum and evolutionary forces collided on the anvil of the play space, forcing upon me a re-evaluation of what play is and asking how playwork may have to change in order to support it.

My Myth: That the worlds of play and quantum activity are inextricably interlinked, and that this has implications for the meaning and application of playwork.

PART 1: A BIT OF HISTORY

In the 200 years following the compilation of his *Philosophiae Naturalis Principia Mathematica* (Mathematical Principles of Natural Philosophy), first published in 1687, the thinking of Isaac Newton and his contemporaries dominated our understanding of the physical world.

Children's play, on the other hand had scant attention during the same period, being described simplistically, as a mechanism for using up surplus energy (Spencer 1873), and as a medium for an eclectic mix of children's games and past-times, which, oddly but significantly, were believed (by God) to possess at least as much significance as the activities of the children's parents (Bruegel 1650).

Eventually, the world of physics was shaken from its reliance on its classical Newtonian view, first by Planck's discovery of the quantum in 1900, and then by Einstein's presentation of his Theory of Relativity in 1905. The world would never be the same again.

The early part of the twentieth century also saw significant development in our understanding of children's play. For example, in 1904 G.S. Hall stated his interpretation of Recapitulation Theory, and in 1938, Johan Huizinga wrote Homo Ludens, which attempted among other things, to provide an analysis of the cultural significance of play.

However, although Huizinga's work in particular supported the growing idea that play was important, the scientific community still seemed reluctant to state directly that play had any major significance. Sylva (1977 p.59) asked, "What is the contribution of play to more earnest endeavour?"

The frustration felt by this cautious approach was eventually articulated—almost sarcastically—by Bruner. In 1976 (p.14) he wrote, "So while play seemed to the methodologically vexed to be an unmanageable laboratory topic, primatologists were pondering its possible centrality in evolution."

It wasn't until the late 1990s, that play's complex influences were more comprehensively articulated, when a synthesis of the neurological work of McEwan (1999) and Huttenlocher (1992), analysis by Sutton-Smith (1997), play research by the Panksepp team[1], and above all the observations of John Byers, not only linked play to "sensitive periods" but embedded it in the processes of brain growth and neural sculpting. At last play, like quantum physics, was being recognised as a formidable phenomenon. The following two statements demonstrate the power and complexity being given to it:

> The idea is that natural selection designed play to shape brain development, and most likely they [children] are directing their own brain assembly, when they play. (Byers 1999, p.4)

> the types of movements the [child] performs determines which [neural] connections will be spared and which will be cut. (p.43)

Simultaneous work by Burghardt (1998; 2005) was to give further credibility to play's role as an evolutionary force. "Play," he wrote, "was most certainly a heterogeneous category" (1998, p.6), meaning there were several different kinds of play that had evolved over evolutionary time for some reason. Then he suggested what the reason might be:

> "Different types of play may have different causal bases, functions, phylogenies and ontogenies," i.e., they might have evolved at different points in our evolutionary history, for different reasons and to do different things, perhaps to address what he called life history, ecological, physiological, and behavioural factors. (Hughes 2012, pp.80–82)

Consequently, by the twenty-first century, play and quantum activity are both clearly regarded as intriguing, if discrete and mysterious phenomena, in their own right, but might they have a closer relationship? To explore that we first need to look at the nature of matter itself.

PART 2.THE QUANTUM WORLD

What was it that so captured the imagination of the quantum physicists? A part of the answer seems to be the strange counter intuitive behaviour of *subatomic particles*, or SAP's. But what are SAP's?

Consider the following:

- Everything is matter
- Matter is made of atoms and molecules
- Atoms and molecules are made of Sub Atomic Particles (Some SAP's are made up of other smaller SAP's)
- Sub Atomic Particles are made of Energy
- There may be different forms of energy notwithstanding the nine already known to Science, which include *potential, thermal, kinetic,* and so on.
- Although energy is normally regarded as the final sub-division, it might be made up of other things. After all, it exists as a vast universal cloud of impulses, waves and reactions. So like the human brain, or an intelligence, it has been labelled by some, the Other, the Void and the Abyss, and by others, the Universal Zero Point Field.

> If thoughts equal energy and energy equals matter, then thoughts become matter. Observe your thoughts as they will manifest themselves in your life in the natural via the Zero Point Field. (Baksa, 2011)

SAP's are created when bigger particles, e.g., atoms or molecules, subdivide after collision and there are at least 80 identified or theorised SAP's currently known to science.

These include:

- Electrons
- Neutrons
- Photons
- Protons
- and others—leptons, mesons, baryons, bosons etc.,

Creating artificial collisions is one of the things the Hadron Collider at CERN is used for.

Quantum Weirdness

Sub-atomic particles have surprising qualities:

- they only exist as probabilities, because they will not allow simultaneous measurement of where they are, and how fast they are moving
- although called particles they are not solid at all, but chunks of energy
- they possess strange counter-intuitive properties that, as Al-Kalili (2012) said, "turn the world as we know it, on its head."

It may be helpful *briefly* to describe four of the best-known "counter intuitive" quantum phenomena, a) to demonstrate the weird nature of the quantum world, and b) to lay the ground for later speculation about play and playwork. They are:

1. Super-positioning, aka Many Worlds, or the Multiverse
2. Quantum Tunnelling
3. Quantum Entanglement
4. Complementarity

Superpositioning or Many World or Multiverse

> Quantum superpositioning suggests that a physical system, (say, an electron) exists partly in all its particular theoretical states simultaneously, *but when measured,* it gives a result corresponding to only one of the possible configurations. (Wikipedia 2017a)

This means that at the quantum (sub-atomic) level, before measurement, particles can be in an infinite number of places at the same time. This has led to the speculation that this may also be the case for humans. That there are parallel universes in which there are different versions of each one of us (See, for example, *5 Reasons We May Live in a Multiverse* by Clara Moskowitz, SPACE.com December 7, 2012).

Like other quantum phenomena, this is not as far-fetched to the observant playworker as it may seem to the non-play person. Imagination, narrative, immersion and the apparent adsorption of children, nature and cosmos make it plausible, perhaps possible for each individual child to lose their conscious human form and occupy many facets/levels of the Universe that we are just not aware of. Children daydreaming, swinging back and forth, watching/listening to trickling water, hurtling down a zip-wire, completely absorbed in the action of carving, staring into a fire, making colour, often accompanied by a smile as they "get it," are just a few examples of play transporting children on a cosmic escalator to another dimension. In the Beauty of Play I wrote of a child whose "invisible" den was so real that he became distressed if it was not entered through the appropriate portal. On another playground notable for the atmosphere of uncertainty it generated, I noticed a child disappearing behind a large wooden structure—after a while I began to wonder if she was still there—only to see her suddenly burst into the upper right hand frame of the camera I was using from a completely different direction from where she had originally "disappeared." The look on her face said, "Ha, that got you!" Of course I may have missed her moving, but I don't know how!

Quantum Tunnelling

Quantum tunnelling refers to the phenomenon where a particle tunnels through a barrier that it classically could not surmount (Wikipedia 2017b).

Tunnelling plays an essential role in the nuclear fusion that occurs in the sun and has important applications in some modern devices.

Quantum tunnelling is possible because of the phenomenon of complementarity (see below) where particles can exist in two (or more) forms simultaneously; for example as a wave and a particle. In this case, whilst its particle form cannot get through a barrier, its wave form can.

Quantum Entanglement

Quantum entanglement is what Einstein referred to as "spooky action at a distance." It occurs when particles interact physically (become entangled) and then become separated.

Particles which have been entangled, appear to be able to communicate with one another instantly and over great distances.

What this means is that tiny entangled particles that are far apart, can act like two dice, rolling up the same number irrespective of how far apart they remain (Wikipedia 2017c).

This suggests that in an entangled Universe everything is able to communicate with everything else instantly (see Bohm, later). Zugav (1979, p.72) elaborates:

> Evidence gathered in quantum mechanics indicates that SAP's constantly seem to be making decisions. More than that, the decisions SAP's seem to make are based on decisions made elsewhere. SAP's seem to know instantly what decisions are made. Elsewhere can be as far away as another Galaxy. How can an SAP over here, know what decisions another particle over there has made, at the same time the particle over there, makes it?

Complementarity

This refers to effects such as wave-particle duality (see Tunnelling above), where a particle can exist both as a wave and as a particle simultaneously. The complementarity principle states that some objects have properties that appear to be contradictory.

> Sometimes it is possible to switch back and forth between different views of an object to observe these properties, but in principle, it is impossible to view both at the same time, despite their simultaneous coexistence in reality. For example, we can think of an electron as either a particle or a wave, depending on the situation. An object that's both a particle and a wave would seem impossible because

> normally, such things are mutually exclusive. Nevertheless, the electron is truly both at once. (Wikipedia 2017d)

What this means is that at the quantum level, a particle can exist *in forms of matter and energy simultaneously.*

Had it not been too difficult for me to give any kind of coherent explanation, *decoherence* would have qualified as my fifth "weird" quantum category simply because it has some fascinating characteristics that place it in the very heart of the quantum phenomenon.

Also known as the "*observer effect*," decoherence is used to describe the phenomenon of observer-induced disappearance of the waves present in complementarity. It states that a wave will act like a wave until it is observed or measured and then it isn't there anymore; it decoheres. Put simply, it is the physical process that describes the transition from the quantum realm to the classical realm (Wikipedia 2017e). More on decoherence later.

These are just a few of the phenomena that are described as quantum weirdness. But do any of them occur at the "classical" everyday level, between us and our macro physical surroundings, rather than just at the sub-atomic level, invisible to the naked eye?

For years it was thought that they did not, and that in general, quantum phenomena only existed at the sub-atomic level. However, there are now good examples of quantum effects at the classical level. These include:

> the nanoscale interference behaviour of what are called "*buckyballs*," the large molecules that make up a compound known as Fullerene or Carbon 60, which are used for everything from bullet-proof vests, to HIV virus inhibitors and the development of materials that are ideal for next-generation electronics; *superconductors*, which have zero electrical resistance, and expel magnetic fields, and levitate, and *superfluids*, that act like they have zero viscosity and appear to exhibit the ability to travel in ways that defy the forces of gravity and surface tension—up hill for example. (Boysen 2017; Wikipedia 2017f & 2017g)

These effects at the classical level suggest that a visible quantum effect in children's play might at least be theoretically plausible.

Having said that, quantum activity at the micro or macro levels is notoriously difficult and complex to demonstrate, even for particle physicists, so the remainder of this chapter is more about "what if," rather than what is. Proof of quantum activity as a feature of children's play is not anticipated.

However, given the existence of quantum activity in everything, which therefore must include play, it feels hugely playful to ask how quantum phenomena might manifest themselves in the playing child, and what playwork might do to assist it.

PART 3.A QUANTUM OF PLAY—A PLAYFULLY UNSUBSTANTIATED ANALYSIS

If quantum mechanics hasn't profoundly shocked you, you haven't understood it yet.

—Niels Bohr

So, does play have quantum characteristics?

- Let us assume for a start that there has been a vast quantity of quantum activity in the Universe ever since its beginning with the Big Bang.
- Let us further assume that quantum activity has always been a significant part of the human evolutionary backdrop—and still is.
- Given that play is believed to be an intrinsic and long-term part of the human evolutionary process (Burghardt 2005; Byers 1999, etc.,) we can also assume that play may be significantly influenced by quantum activity[2] or that play and quantum activity are just different manifestations of the same thing, like light colours, musical chords, steam, water and ice, and different kinds of energy. If that were the case, play would show some counter-intuitive characteristics, which it does. For example, even though it can be dangerous, energy depleting, and leave the player open to predation, all children and the young of many other species still engage in it.

Though it cannot be taken up other than briefly here; it is clear that the idea of decoherence—perhaps moving from the sub-atomic to the classical and back again, as seen in the fragmented and fleeting moments of play episodes, has implications for playwork practice. I will return to this point later.

This idea of a universal joined-upness is supported by Bohm's (1980) exploration of the relationship between mind and matter, and also Bell's theorem, which states "All of the parts of the universe are connected in an intimate and immediate way" (Ehrenreich 2014, p.272).

Taken together with the discovery of the mysterious effects of movement and playing on brain and behaviour (Byers 1998), comes a realisation that perhaps "At a deep and fundamental level, the separate parts of the universe—including the quantum and classical play worlds—are connected in some way" (Zukav 1979, p.298).

Bohm asserted that at the most fundamental level was an unbroken wholeness which was, in his words, "that-which-is," and that all things including time, space, and one has to assume play, are a part of that-which-is (Zukav 1979, p.323–324).

Ehrenreich, describes what she terms the Other—but which has a striking resemblance to Bohm's that-which-is, beautifully:

> No one is saying that the Universe, as an entity, is alive, and certainly not that it has motives or desires. But the closer and more carefully we probe, the more it seethes with what looks like life—runaway processes driven by positive feedback loops, emergent patterns, violent attractions, quantum leaps, and always, as far as we can see, more surprises. There may be no invisible creaturely "beings" afoot, either symbionts, parasites or predators. But there are unaccountable algorithms at work in the physical world writhing and reaching, pulling matter and energy into their schemes acting out of what almost seems to be an unquenchable playfulness. Sometimes, out of this static and confusion the Other assembles itself and takes form before our very eyes. (Ehrenreich 2014, p.236)

Bell's theorem also applies this idea of joined-upness to the quantum notion of entanglement.

> That an influence is allowed to pass between two systems or particles instantaneously, exceeding the limit set by the speed of light so that a cause at one place can produce an immediate effect at some distant location. (Kumar 2009, p.380)

This again suggests a continuous joined-up nature of the Universe where quantum phenomena and play assimilate and perhaps communicate in a constant interplay.

If this is true, then play and the Universe, or whatever name you prefer, i.e., the Other, the Abyss, the Void are inextricably linked. That the phenomenon of play is at some level a demonstration, a manifestation of a universal SAP influence, and that as well as having many other qualities, the Universe also has playful characteristics. And it is the playful symbiosis between the child and the Universe, between children's SAP equivalent behaviour of unpredictability, contradiction, surprise, counter-intuitiveness, imagination, comedy and confusion, and Bohm's that-which-is, that manifests itself wherever and whenever children play.

As I write, I feel unsure where the path I am treading is leading. Whether it is unavoidably towards the question, is play a combined SAP/Evolution phenomenon, where SAP's are integrated into the minds and bodies of human children and those of other species during the processes of ontogeny or phylogeny; or is play the result of a bonding between playing species and certain characteristics in the universe via SAP's; or does the contemporary consensus hold, that what we currently believe, i.e., play has evolved over millions of years, and has not, as far as we know been affected by SAP activity, is most convincing?

Could it be that play comes from somewhere external to us, i.e., the Other, the Abyss etc., and because of the joined-upness and attraction suggested by Bohm, finds itself integrated into a feature of the human form, brain, consciousness or elsewhere—suggesting that much, if not all of what play is, is present throughout the Universe in general; perhaps individually or collectively contained in different SAPs or energy states? That the different types of play we see children manifesting are the result of a bonding preference, a predisposition, a specific attraction between human children, or the young of other playing species, and a specific playful SAP (see later), or any number of different SAPs, or different aspects of the Universe as suggested by Ehrenreich; what are essentially different algorithms.

From a playwork perspective this merging with the Other—a seemingly commonplace occurrence when working long-term with playing children—might derive from the "that-which-is" a focus for SAP activity of powerful ludic potential. The resulting "that-which-is," SAP, child and playworker interface, offering a powerful paradigm for playwork.

Oddly, even as I am writing these terms, predisposition, bonding preference and specific attraction, I am conscious that I am not recalling or remembering them, but capturing them as they flash past me—like the flying fish in Hemingway's *The Old Man and the Sea*—"netting" them as I have alluded previously, by utilising a cerebral sub-operating system, SOS (Hughes 2000).

What I am suggesting is that perhaps a predisposed Universe/child-bond works as a conduit specifically for play, allowing play to flow through the Universe and the Child. What this suggests is that play is much more than a human, social, recreational, educational, or commercial phenomenon; it, in all its beauty and diversity is a vivid demonstration of the nature of an interac-

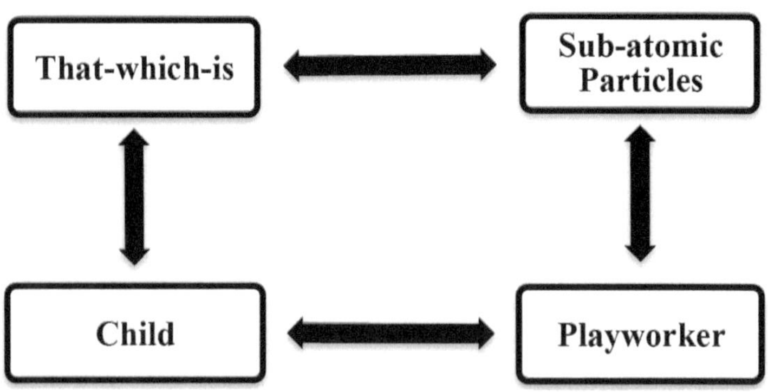

Figure 13.1. The that-which-is, sub-atomic particles, child, playworker paradigm

tive Universal relationship available to children, if they are able, or enabled to engage with it.

Might Play Be Quantised?

> They say when you stare into the abyss, the abyss stares back. I think they're wrong, I think it only winks. James Sallis, Salt River (2010, pp. 19–20)

What exercises me is how that flow might be actualised, and for that, I need to go back to quantum basics? If it were light passing through the network of connections that join everything to everything else, then that light would be "quantised," i.e., it would not travel in a continuous joined-up flow, but would travel in tiny individual pulses or chunks of light energy, each chunk a quantum in size; dashes rather than a continuous line, each dash known as a photon.

Perhaps that is also how play travels in my imaginings? Imagine, for example, one of those Department Stores that have a vacuum system for sending money and receiving change. You give the sales person money for a transaction, he places the money in a sealed tube, and places the tube in the vacuum system and sends it whizzing to the Finance Department. There, they take the money you have parted with, and give a receipt with change if you are due it, put it all into the tube, and send it whizzing back to the sales person's position. He then gives you any change and a receipt.

A rather long-winded route to suggesting that perhaps play is delivered in much the same way; is quantised into quantum sized packets, each packet I will call a ludon©.

Given the Department Store analogy, we can see that the ludon© could, like the sealed tube in the vacuum system, carry huge amounts of coded information that would influence the recipient with the playful mechanisms it contained. Bohm's basic assumption agrees, "elementary particles are actually systems of extremely complicated internal structure, acting essentially as amplifiers of 'information' contained in a quantum wave" (Bohm 1980).

The suggestion that play may be quantised, means that like quantised light, play, as well as having a heterogeneous identity (Burghardt 2005) carried within the ludon©, may also show a whole range of counter-intuitive (weird) manifestations, and like buckyballs and superconductors, may manifest some of its quantum activity at the classical level, For example:

1. Play will have a multiverse component
2. Play will be able to exist as a simultaneous duality
3. Play will be able to manifest some form of entanglement

4. Play may manifest an observer effect
5. Play will be able to manifest some form of tunnelling.

Although uncorroborated, here are just a few examples of what I mean.

Play Has a Multiverse Component

> McFadden (2000) provides us with an example, referring to an improvised play.
> At the start of each performance the improvised play can be said to be "indeterminate." . . . The play has certain potentialities dependent on the set of characters present, but no *pre*-defined plot. With no audience present we could imagine a quantum play in which all possible plots were acted out as a quantum superposition. However, in a real performance the interaction between the actors and their audience draws out the course of action, the plot for that night's performance. Just as the audience of an improvised play draws out from the infinity of possible plots a single reality for each live performance, so measurement of a quantum system draws out from the quantum superposition of all possible states, a single reality for the physical (classical) world. (p.186)

Perhaps a more relevant example for this indeterminate state, is what exists in the imaginations of children waiting to access an adventure playground. Like McFadden's play, the playground has certain potentialities—what Wilson, in this publication, quoting Massey (2005) calls "different trajectories" or stories-so-far,—AND no pre-determined activity; but as the gates open and the children scan the site, so choices are made, and from an infinity of possibilities, individual narratives emerge as interaction between SAP's and "that-which-is," occurs.

Play Will Be Able to Exist as a Simultaneous Duality

Play can be both a physical narrative and an imagined scenario simultaneously. On one playground, a rope bridge had been constructed, and many of the children used it in their off-ground tag and adventure games. Simultaneously, they were creating in their minds crossing boiling lava, being threatened by ferocious alligators and pursued by marauding pirates. This much was transmitted in vocalised form. But quite clearly what the children imagined and experienced emotionally was much more than the physical act of crossing the rope bridge.

On another playground a group of older boys discovered the sand pit for the very first time. Their initial reaction was to throw sand about, but soon, they became engrossed in digging and pouring water into the sand. Eventually, it became like a beach activity, where fantasy play was also engaged, and although the dialogue between the boys related mainly to their prowess at digging and moving the sand, they also became immersed and created sand and water structures, much the same as children would at the sea-side. Like the previous children, these boys were engaging in a physical narrative which was primarily tactile, whilst at the same time being immersed into fantasy play.

Thus play can have a physical (particle) function AND a cognitive (wave) function both individually AND simultaneously.

Play Will Be Able to Manifest Some Form of Entanglement

Relationships, particularly over long distances, are perhaps the best example of entangled behaviour in children, although they do not have the instantaneous quality the entangled SAP's have. Jung's concept of synchronicity, which holds that events are "meaningful coincidences" if they occur with no apparent causal relationship (Wikipedia 2017h) may be another—although I have no examples of it—and children will always be seen playing time-travelling and teleportation, both linked to entanglement. One idea (Hyland 2004) goes so far as to suggest that at the cellular level, particles act as material carriers of consciousness, which may explain how and why play is such a "whole" body experience, having both material and immaterial characteristics.

Play Will Have an Observer Effect

Did you see that? What? I'm not sure, but something happened between those children. These "hairs on the back of your neck moments" are quite common in playwork, as playworkers watch the children playing. Often they never work out what it is they think they've seen, because simply saying "Did you see," makes what you think you've seen, decohere. It appears that in some circumstances the very act of just mentioning a play "moment" when it's happening, is enough to change or destroy it.

Play Will Be Able to Manifest an Equivalent to Tunnelling

Although the probability of a human object actually tunnelling through a barrier as predicted by the Schrodinger equation is tiny, the cognitive (wave) aspect of play, still enables children to engage in many experiences which otherwise would be regarded as impossible. As a child I remember struggling to fly, to get off the ground, to fly through the air and finally to glide through a tree's canopy and alight on a branch. This experience was not about the physical (particle) act of flying, which I knew even then was impossible, but about the imaginative (wave) act, which I knew to be possible. I knew because I had dreamt of doing it.

On other occasions I remember willing myself to be invisible, which meant that I could stand out in the open and still remain unseen by passers-by.

Several of the different play types lend themselves to a tunnelling type function, where physical reality is transformed into a non-physical "impossible" experience—imaginative, fantasy and exploratory play for example.

Note. As the reader will have noticed, some examples are stronger than others, although I suspect that there will be those who can instantly recall much better instances—an interesting exercise in a training session for example.

PART 4. A QUANTUM OF PLAYWORK—IMPLICATIONS FOR PRACTICE

So what does the process of passing play through the "what if" quantum prism say about how we might apply our playwork practice to this new perspective? Notwithstanding my somewhat unsophisticated analysis, there is much to ponder here.

Basically until now, playwork has been about two things: the physical creation of play enabling spaces (particle?) and the more cognitive practice of enabling the qualities which make playing in such a space possible (wave?).

So what does this albeit *in embryo* quantum analysis bring to the applied playwork table? My hunch is that we're doing much of what needs to/can be done already, but paraphrasing Samuel Beckett we must, "fail, fail again, but fail better." For however "normal" play may seem, it is still obviously a very mysterious and complex phenomenon—the role Byers suggested for playful movement, is a good example.

One thing that feels urgent is that we stop categorising playwork and play provision as fringe municipal services, which seem more about containing children AND their play within an adult social construct, and, instead, see play in the same light as say astronomy or astrophysics, as vital yet mysterious, and playwork as exploring and facilitating that vital mystery.

For example, where play deprivation or play bias are evident, might it be that by not acknowledging an interface of "that-which-is" and the potentials of ludons© in play, that we "unwittingly offer a negative empathy to the complexity and shifting powers of imagination and creativity alive in the playspace" (Gray 2011), and become blinded to play's beauty and its power.

What this means in practice is that although we would still be able to use our practical armoury , the play cycle, play frames and returns, the playwork curriculum, IMEE, play types, modification [(16)] and so on, it would only provide a very rough qualitative guide. The main thrust of our practice would instead concentrate on ensuring each child is free to connect with what they perceived as the joyful and ecstatically diverse Universe around them. This is not something we as humans, adults, children's workers, playworkers have been good at. Rather we seem to have a predisposition for interference—another powerful quantum term—that has sometimes had the effect of replacing free, diverse, semi-feral counter-intuitive playfulness with something more neurotic or damaging. Repressed social behaviour is a good example.

The consequent disintegration of what every child anticipates, encapsulated in play—what in the past I have termed *evolutionary* anticipation (Hughes 2005) but given the focus of this piece perhaps quantum anticipation would be a more fitting description—is I feel, at the root of play deprivation and the destruction it wreaks. It is important that our practice, however we couch it in terms of intervention, acknowledges play's beauty and power, and its fragility and sensitivity, *and our* potential to damage it, and only sanctions intervention accordingly.

For it would appear from its outcomes that *interfering* (this is not the same as intervening) inhibits something or stops it happening altogether. What might that something be? It could be that quantised play activates specific biological processes, as explored by MacFadden (2000, p.115), and that interference inhibits what might be vital biochemical, genetic or information transfer processes.

This suggests an accompanying powerful interference, decoherence, intervention paradigm for our playwork application, to that outlined on page 11.

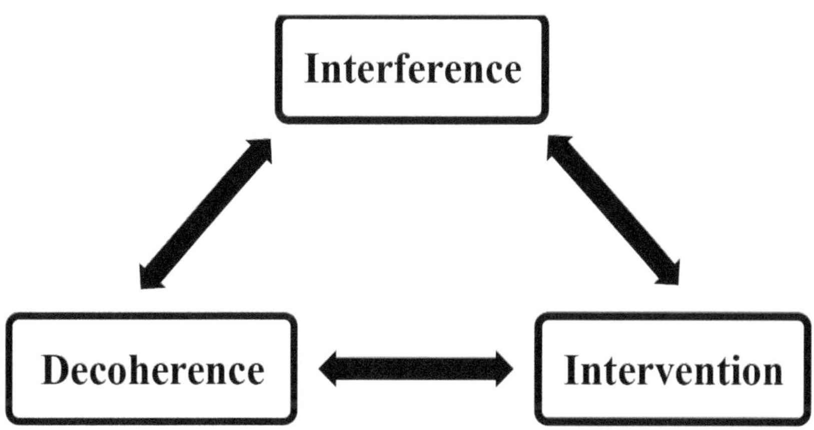

Figure 13.2. The interference, intervention and decoherence paradigm

What does feel right is that artificial play environments are able to reflect the child's world as articulated and manifested by children as they play—playful values and behaviours—rather than institutionally imposed worlds of social constraints and approved behaviours, as is all too often the current case.

For if play does have a significant quantum component, and I remain tentative from my own analysis that it does, then it is not only the phenomenon of universal beauty that so many acknowledge, it is also the two-way conduit both to the stars AND to the core of our humanity.

Play and Evolution

Finally, Stephen Jay Gould (1998) said:

> Suppose that the simplest kind of cellular life arises as a predictable result of organic chemistry and the physics of self-organising systems wherever planets exist with the right constituents and conditions—undoubtedly a common occurrence in our vast universe. But suppose, in addition, that no predictable directions exist for life's later development from their basic beginnings. (pp.359–351)

Evolution progresses in random fashion through many mutations and selections that enable organisms to adapt to ever changing factors. These factors are rarely entirely physical and are more likely to be holistic. What if evolution's thrust was not just cellular or behaviourally specific, but included parallel many worlds adaptations at the quantum level too—as alluded to by McFadden (2000) and perhaps even specifically at the playful ludon© level as alluded to earlier in this text?

For if the combination of "that-which-is" and SAP's in space, provide the equivalent of a localised quantum "primordial-soup" from which other (SAP) mutations could emerge and evolve, what is known as evolvability (Gopnik 2016, p.27), and where the uncertainty implicit in the randomness of evolution came not just from an adaptive focus but from a parallel quantum/quantized ludon© focus (many worlds) too; then the very uncertainty generated by that encounter might provide further and more complex conditions for the most novel quantum mutations, best evolved to further survive natural selection with play at the very core of this primal nano-lego, and all acted out in a theatre in which quantum and evolutionary forces are colliding on the anvil of the play space?—what Sturrock (2015) has coined "the ludic Big Bang."

My thanks to Joel Seath, Sylwyn Guilbaud and Gordon Sturrock who at different times and in their very different ways, helped me out of a hole when I couldn't stop digging!

NOTES

1. See for example, Nakia S. Gordon, Sharon Burke, Huda Akil, Stanley J. Watson, Jaak Panksepp (2003) Socially-induced brain "fertilization": play promotes brain derived neurotrophic factor transcription in the amygdala and dorsolateral frontal cortex in juvenile rats. *Neuroscience Letters* 341, (2003) 17–20.

2. A major reason for assuming this is the apparent effect of the quantum phenomenon of decoherence. In the quantum world, and it is believed increasingly in the classical everyday world, everything has an effect on everything else, suggesting that play is not only discrete behaviour or a particular mind-set, but a mix of place, space and time and crucially quantum activity too. What decoherence adds is that what we actually observe when children play is a moment by moment amalgamation, both visible and invisible, of these changing influences, snapshots of change if you like, which look to us like repeating and recognisable patterns.

REFERENCES

Al-Khalili, J. (2012) *Quantum: A guide for the perplexed.* London: Weidenfeld and Nicolson.

Baksa, P. (2011) *The zero point field: How thoughts become matter*. Huffington Post 3 October 2011.

Bohm, D. (1980) *Wholeness and the implicate order*. London: Routledge. Also [Online] Available from: www.bizint.com/stoa_del_sol/plenum/plenum_3.html [Accessed 17 July 2017].

Boysen, E. (2017) Buckyballs: Uses and applications. [Online] Available from: http://www.understandingnano.com/buckyballs-fullerenes.html [Accessed: 17 July 2017].

Bruegel, P. (1650) *Children's games* [Online] Available from: https://en.wikipedia.org/wiki/Children's_Games_(Bruegel) [Accessed 17 July 2017].

Bruner, J. (1976) Introduction. In: Bruner, J., Jolly, A., and Sylva, K. (eds) (1976) *Play: Its role in development and evolution.* NewYork: Penguin.

Burghardt, G. (1998) The evolutionary origins of play revisited: lessons from turtles. In: Bekoff, M., and Byers, J. (eds) (1998) *Animal play: evolutionary, comparative, and ecological perspectives.* Cambridge: Cambridge University Press.

———. (2005) *The genesis of animal play*. Cambridge : The MIT Press.

Byers, J. (1999) Play's the thing. *Natural History* 108 (6): pp.40–45.

Ehrenreich, B. (2014) *Living with a wild god.* London: Granta Books.

Einstein, A. (1905) Does the inertia of a body depend upon its energy content? *Annalen der Physik(ser. 4)*, 18, pp.639–641.

Gopnik, A. (2016) *The gardener and the carpenter: What the new science of child developments tells us about the relationship between parents and children.* London: The Bodley Head.

Gould, S. (1998) *Leonardo's mountain of clams and the diet of worms*. New York, NY: Harmony.

Gray, P. (2011) The decline of play and the rise of psychopathology in children and adolescents. *American Journal of Play*, Vol.3, Number 4.

Hall, G.S. (1904) *Adolescence: Its psychology and its relations to physiology, anthropology, sociology, sex, crime, religion and education*. Vol.1. New York: Appleton.

Hughes, B. (2000) *A dark and evil cul-de-sac: Has children's play in urban Belfast been adulterated by the Troubles*? Unpublished MA dissertation, Cambridge: Anglia Polytechnic University.

———. (2005) *The consequences of play deprivation*. Paper delivered at AGM, Play-Board NI.

———. (2012) *Evolutionary playwork*. London: Routledge.

Huizinga, J. (1938) *Homo ludens (1949 Edition)*. London: Routledge & Kegan Paul Ltd.

Huttenlocher, P. (1992) Neural plasticity. In: Asbury, A., McKhann, G. and McDonald, W. (eds), *Diseases of the Nervous System*, 1, pp.63–71.

Hyland, K. (2004) *Social interactions in academic writing*. London: Longman.

Kumar, M. (2009) *Quantum: Einstein, Bohr, and the great debate about the nature of reality*. London: Icon.

McEwan, B.S. (1999) Stress and hippocampal plasticity. *Annual Review of the Neurosciences*, 22, 105–22.

McFadden, J. (2000) Quantum Evolution. London: Harper Collins.

Newton, I. (1687) *Philosophiae naturalis principia mathematica*. [Online] Available from: https://en.wikipedia.org/wiki/Principia_Mathematica [Accessed 17 July 2017].

Sallis, J. (2010) *Salt River*. Harpenden: No Exit Press.

Spencer, H. (1873) Principles of psychology. New York, Appleton, as cited in Hayes, N. (1994) *Foundations of Psychology*. London, Routledge.

Sturrock, G. (2015) Personal Communication.

Sutton-Smith, B. (1997) *The Ambiguity of Play*. Cambridge, MA: Harvard University Press.

Sylva, K. (1977) Play and Learning. In: Tizard, B. and Harvey, D. (eds), *Biology of Play*. London: Heinemann.

Wikipedia (2017a) *Quantum superposition*. [Online] Available from: https://en.wikipedia.org/wiki/Quantum_superposition [Accessed 17 July 2017].

Wikipedia (2017b) *Quantum tunnelling*. [Online] Available from: https://en.wikipedia.org/wiki/Quantum_tunnelling [Accessed 17 July 2017].

Wikipedia (2017c) *Quantum entaglement*. [Online] Available from: https://en.wikipedia.org/wiki/Quantum_entaglement [Accessed 17 July 2017].

Wikipedia (2017d) *Complementarity*. [Online] Available from: https://en.wikipedia.org/wiki/Complementarity [Accessed 17 July 2017].

Wikipedia (2017e) *Quantum decoherence*. [Online] Available from: https://en.wikipedia.org/wiki/Quantum_decoherence [Accessed 17 July 2017].

Wikipedia (2017f) *Superfluidity*. [Online] Available from: https://en.wikipedia.org/wiki/Superfluidity [Accessed 17 July 2017].

Wikipedia (2017g) *Superconductivity*. [Online] Available from: https://en.wikipedia.org/wiki/Superconductivity [Accessed 17 July 2017].
Wikipedia (2017h) *Syncronicity*. [Online] Available from: https://en.wikipedia.org/wiki/Sincronicity [Accessed 17 July 2017].
Zukav, G. (1979) *The Dancing Wu Li Masters*. London: Fontana.

Index

About the Contributors

Fraser Brown is the first Professor of Playwork in the UK, and teaches on the Playwork degree at Leeds Beckett University. He is the specialist link tutor for APAC's postgraduate play therapy courses. He has presented at conferences across the UK and around the world, and has produced several key texts in the field of play and playwork. His publications include *Play and Playwork: 101 Stories of Children Playing.*

Bob Hughes—Although Bob has been a playworker since 1970 and has run three adventure playgrounds and worked on many other setting, he tends to work more as a theorist these days. His work is internationally acknowledged and he has lectured in numerous countries including Japan, the USA, Argentina, Hong Kong, Australia and across Europe. He is the author of the classic text, *Evolutionary Playwork.*

Dave Bullough is a Playworker, who started his playwork journey in 2009 as a sessional Playworker in Wrexham, Wales. In 2011 Dave came to work in Plas Madoc and is now Deputy Manger at The Land. He graduated from Bangor University with a degree in Sport, Health and Physical Education and has a Level 5 in Play and Playwork. David has a keen interest in Risk Management, and has written many risk benefit assessments and co-wrote the behaviour based Risk Benefit Analysis for Play Wales.

Tony Chilton has been involved in children's play development throughout the UK for over 50 years. He has occupied a variety of roles, from being a pioneer adventure playground worker through to that of Principal Officer for Play Development. He has initiated and developed training courses from introductory level through to Degree and Post Grad. He is one of the most experienced practitioners in the field of children's play development.

Alex Cote is the playworker at Riverdale Country School in the Bronx where she ramps up their loose parts recess and deepens their teachers' understanding of play. Previously, she was a playworker at the Hands-on-Nature Anarchy Zone at Ithaca Children's Garden since its beginning in 2013. Alex found playwork through an initial interest in playground design, but has since been captivated by playwork's focus on the deeper issues of children's rights.

Maxine Delorme has a 1st Class Honours degree in Playwork from Leeds Beckett University, where her thesis focused on the link between Playwork and lived experience, exploring the misconceptions of Playwork in society and the influence of a range of factors on the ability to play freely. She was involved in the Welsh Play Sufficiency Assessment in Wrexham, and has since worked at The Venture Adventure Playground in the same town.

Stuart Lester worked for many years on adventure playgrounds and community play projects in north west England. He was senior lecturer on the postgraduate 'Professional Studies in Children's Play' programme at the University of Gloucestershire and an independent researcher and consultant. His recent work with adventure playgrounds, schools, museums, playwork settings and public spaces, explored children's playful production of time/space through everyday encounters.

Claire Pugh is a Playworker, working with, and on behalf of children in Plas Madoc and Wrexham County since 2005. Claire graduated from Glyndwr University in 2011 with a 1st class Hons degree in Play and Playwork. She manages The Land, a junk playground in Plas Madoc, which after 8 years of playwork formally opened in 2012. Claire is keenly interested in the work of Bob Hughes and Evolutionary Play/Playwork.

Sylwyn Guilbaud is an independent researcher, artist and home educating mother of three. She qualified as a Playworker in 1997 and returned to Leeds Beckett University to complete one of the first PhDs in the sector in 2011. Sylwyn lives by the sea, where she loves to wander and wonder.

Rusty Keeler is a natural playscape designer who has been spending the last ten years spreading the word about adventure playgrounds. He proposed the idea to Ithaca Children's Garden and was a key member of the team that made it happen. He continues to bring the story of the Hands-on-Nature Anarchy Zone and other adventure playgrounds to wider audiences.

Suzanna Law began as a mobile playworker, or playranger, in socio-economically deprived neighborhoods in Manchester, UK. She graduated in 2012 with a First-Class Honours Degree in Playwork. At the same time, she help to found Pop-Up Adventure Play in both the U.K. and U.S., and leads on project coordination and online communications. She was lead playworker during a 2 month residency on Governors Island in New York City. She is currently working towards her PhD at Leeds Beckett University.

Morgan Leichter-Saxby is a playworker and co-founder of Pop-Up Adventure Play. While at University College London, Morgan began ethnographic research at playwork projects across the city. Since then, she has provided training and support in twelve countries around the world, and delivered papers and workshops at national and international conferences. She also blogs at www.playeverything.wordpress.com, and is working towards her PhD in Playwork at Leeds Beckett University.

Kelda Lyons is an inclusive playworker and play development worker based in London. She does independent research and writing around playwork and play in the public realm, and is currently completing a postgraduate certificate in Childhood Studies in Play at the University of Gloucestershire.

Joel Seath is a practising playworker who has been working with or for children and young people since 1991, including at adventure playgrounds, street and park play projects, after school clubs, playschemes, youth clubs, festivals, summer camps, and nurseries. As well as playworking he has presented, taught, assessed, advised, and written on play-related matters. His own play includes the writing of novels and short stories.

Wendy Russell began her playwork life on adventure playgrounds in London. She currently works at The University of Gloucestershire on the postgraduate Professional Studies in Children's Play programme. Much of her published research has been in collaboration with Stuart Lester, focusing on children's right to play and the politics of space.

Ben Tawil is part-time Lecturer at Leeds Beckett University and joint Director of Ludicology where he and Mike Barclay provide advice research and training to all those concerned with children's play. Ben's work has appeared in publications such as: *Foundations of Playwork, Playwork Theory in to Practice, Childhood: Services and Provision for Children* and the *International Journal of Playwork Practice* as well as various industry publications.

Sarah Wilson has been a playworker for nearly a decade. She is currently Senior Playworker at an adventure playground in East London. She completed a post graduate certificate in professional studies in children's play at the University of Gloucestershire in 2016. As well as being a self confessed adventure playground geek, Sarah dabbles in creative projects and particularly enjoys book binding in her spare time.

Mike Wragg is a senior lecturer at Leeds Beckett University and Chair of two charitable trusts, Eccleshill Adventure Playground and New Hall Prison Visitors' Play Facility, both of which have been subject of his recent publications in the *International Journal of Play* and *Prison Service Journal.*

www.ingramcontent.com/pod-product-compliance
Ingram Content Group UK Ltd.
Pitfield, Milton Keynes, MK11 3LW, UK
UKHW041103150926
475561UK00001BA/25